"And indeed,
a horse who bears himself
proudly is a thing of such
beauty and astonishment
that he attracts the eyes
of all beholders."

—Xenophon

Sky Bug Bingo

More *than* Color
Volume 2

By Frank Holmes

MORE THAN COLOR — VOLUME 2

Published by
WESTERN HORSEMAN
3850 North Nevada Ave.
Box 7980
Colorado Springs, Colorado 80933-7980
800-877-5278

www.westernhorseman.com

Cover Design
Max Tardy
1989 Sorrel Overo Stallion
(Dirty Sonny x Rocki Robin)
Photo By Dana Gookin-Owens

Design, Typography, and Production
Sandy Cochran Graphic Design
Fort Collins, Colorado

Printing
Branch Smith
Fort Worth, Texas

First Printing: June 2008

ISBN 0-9714998-0-2

DEDICATION

Photo by Darrel Dodds

This book is dedicated to Junior Robertson of Waurika, Oklahoma
(Shown here with Midnight Smokinbar and "Trooper.")

– One of the Paint Horse industry's first great breeders and marketers –
A true friend and mentor; and an even better father-in-law.

I N T R O D U C T I O N

By the time that *More than Color, Vol. 1* was completed in the late fall of 2002, it became apparent to all who were connected with it that there were many more Paint Horse stories to tell. Armed with that knowledge, plans for a second volume were put in place before the first book was even back from the printer.

The first edition of *More than Color* debuted under the banner of LOFT Enterprises LLC, of Abilene, Kansas. The book was well received and eventually sold out. In 2007, *Western Horseman* books acquired the rights to *More than Color* and plans were put in place to both reprint a revised and expanded edition of the original book and begin work on a second one.

More than Color, Vol. 2 represents a passing of the guard in more ways than one.

To begin with, it is now a *Western Horseman* book, and as such will be a part of the most expansive and well-recognized equine book stable in the world.

Secondly, many of the legendary Paint Horses profiled in the book form a sort of bridge between the pure foundation horses of Volume 1 and the specialized horses that might appear in a Volume 3.

To be sure, there are some pure foundation horses in Volume 2–Hy Diamond Boy, Calamity Jane and Sr. Don Juan among them. And there are some specialized horses as well, such as the great Western pleasure sires Awhe Chief and Skip's Artist.

But the bulk of *More than Color, Volume 2* is dedicated to the great all-around lines that were founded by the likes of Cupid Bar, Skippa Streak, Flying Fawago and Fawago King. These horses were true versatile equine athletes; the kind who could stand grand at halter in the morning and then come back in the afternoon and win on the rail, in the cattle classes and in the speed events.

And it is no coincidence that four of the stallions profiled in this book–Joechief Bar, Sky Bug Bingo, Snip Bar and Gallant Ghost–were APHA Supreme Champions. This award, after all, has always been the ultimate prize that the owners of the true all-around Paint Horse athlete have aspired to put on their trophy shelf.

Finally, in some sort of abstract way, *More than Color, Volume 2* represents the passing of the guard in the Paint Horse halter industry–from a time when all horses, regardless of color pattern, were judged under the same color-blind set of rules, to a time when a color-coded form of prejudice or bias seems to be in play.

During the late 1960s and early 1970s, tobiano halter horses competed on par with the overos. At the 1973 APHA National Show, for instance, there were 15 open halter classes. In them, tobianos tallied 17 national or reserve national championships, while overos accounted for 13.

Throughout the time period, representatives of such renowned tobiano lines as the Leo San Mans, Joechief Bars, Skip Hi/Skippa Streaks, Sky Bug Bingos and Tinky's Spook/Gallant Ghosts could be found taking on all comers and winning their fair share of the industry's most coveted halter awards.

This photo of Calamity Jane, the American Paint Stock Horse Association's first registered mare, arrived too late to appear in the body of the book. Alan Gold, director of publishing of the Cutting Horse Chatter, *provided it to us and we felt it was just too good a photograph not to be included. NCHA Hall of Fame horseman Bob Burton of Arlington, Texas, is aboard the diminutive cutting mare in this shot.*
Courtesy NCHA

In the late 1970s and 1980s, however, the show ring scenery began to change. As the cropout blood of the great Sonny Dee Bar and Red Sonny Dee horses made its way into the Paint Horse industry, breeders and exhibitors throughout the land began to gravitate toward it.

On the halter side of the street, the hue and cry went out that the cropouts were superior to the tobianos, and this became a self-fulfilling prophecy. Breeders began featuring the cropout lines in their halter programs to the exclusion of the great tobiano halter lines of the past, and the tobiano halter horse became very much an endangered species.

And the demise was rapid. At the 1975 National Show in Kansas City, Missouri, a short two years down the road from Denver, overos won 25 of the 30 halter classes offered. From 1994 through 1998, there were 190 world and reserve world halter championships awarded. By coat pattern, the score from the six shows was: overos 189, tobianos one.

In *More than Color, Vol. 2*, however, the tobiano halter horse remains alive and well. From the Hy Diamond Boys and Leo San Mans to the Sky Bug Bingos and Gallant Ghosts, you will find this bookoverflowing with profiles and photographs of some of the best tobiano halter horses the breed has ever known.

Change is inevitable, as the saying goes, and change is for the better. So the all-around horse gives way to the specialist, and the tobiano halter horse gives way to the cropout.

Has the change truly been for the better, and has it left the breed and the industry better off?

Why don't we just let you turn the pages and make up your own mind.

Frank Holmes

ACKNOWLEDGMENTS

As has been the case with every book project I've ever undertaken, I have been repeatedly reminded during the writing of *More than Color, Vol. 2*, that "no man is an island." Particularly this man.

In some ways, this book was harder to bring to fruition than were others, and in some ways it was easier. The hard part reared its ugly head as the hunt for photos got underway.

In the past, as I've taken my searches for historic photos to the home offices of the various horse registries and their breed journals, I've had far more luck coming up with usable images of the earlier breeding, show and race horses than I have of the more contemporary ones.

I'm sure a lot of this has to do with the fact that, back in the 1940s, 1950s and 1960s, the breed journals would accept photos from people for editorial and advertising purposes, and then routinely keep and file them.

As the horse industry has become more professional, and, dare I say it, more egocentric, photo contributors began to request that their photos be returned. Consequently, as the horses that appear in the pages of each new Legends-style book get more and more contemporary, photos of them are less likely to be found on file.

The easy part comes into play in terms of access to people. When I wrote the chapter on Painted Joe for the original *More than Color,* for instance, it was hard to find people who had any first-hand knowledge of a horse that had lived out his life 45 to 60 years earlier.

The majority of the horses that appear in this *MTC Volume 2* were around from the 1960s through the 1990s. That meant finding people like Kaye Kuhn, Cindy Gattis, Linda Jones, Marsha McGovney, Becky Maxson and Donna Brown made it easier to write about horses like Leo San Man, Sky Bug Bingo, Skippa Streak, Skip's Artist, Bear Cat and Flying Fawago.

As always, I am indebted to the folks at the American Paint Horse Association who have graciously provided me with registration records, production records and photographs. Included among them are Allyson Pennington, the managing director of APHA registration; Jessica Smith and Jessica Hein of the *Paint Horse Journal*; Linda Knowles and Joy Hardwick of the performance department; and Karen Utecht in racing.

Thanks also go out to the *Western Horseman* crew for their help in shepherding the book along. Ernie King in Fort Worth, Texas, provided excellent guidance and encouragement along the way, and Karan Miller in Colorado Springs, Colorado, did her usual bang-up job of hunting for reference material and photographs.

Special thanks (and condolences) to Dan Streeter in Hurst, Texas, and Sandy Cochran in Fort Collins, Colorado. Dan has edited all of my writing for close to a dozen years, and Sandy and I have collaborated on my last five solo book projects.

Dan and Sandy are, quite simply, the best at what they do. I am especially thankful that the folks at *Western Horseman* decided that, on this project, they would keep the three of us working together.

Finally, thanks go out to Laura Lyon of Howell, Michigan. Laura is a self-taught "photo fixer," and is possessed of rare talents along that line. She took a few of the photos that suffered from damage and/or distracting backgrounds, and made them well.

Putting a historical book like *More than Color* together is a daunting task. The help of all the people mentioned above makes it a little less so.

Frank Holmes

T A B L E   o f   C O N T E N T S

1 HY DIAMOND BOY
APQHA #2

*Foaled in South Texas, this speed-bred stallion
founded one of the breed's first great tobiano lines.*

FOR ALL PRACTICAL purposes, the American Paint Horse industry was born in the Lone Star State in the early 1960s. What's more, it was conceived and brought to life along two parallel lines.

In 1961, W. L. "Bill" Jones of Abilene, Texas, formed the American Paint Quarter Horse Association (APQHA), with its headquarters in Abilene. In 1962, Rebecca Lockhart Tyler of Gainesville, Texas, formed

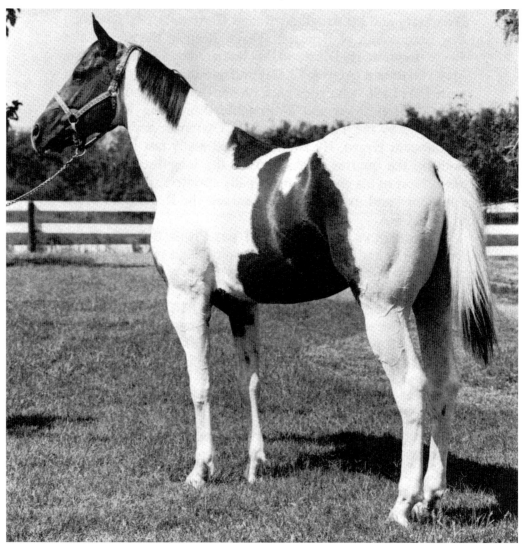

Hy Diamond Boy, the registry's first tobiano sire of note, founded a family of tall and elegant show and performance horses.
Courtesy
Paint Horse Journal

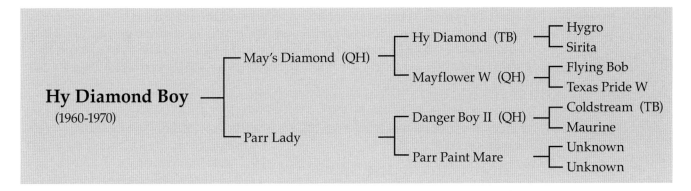

the American Paint Stock Horse Association (APSHA), with its headquarters first in Gainesville, then in Amarillo, and finally in Fort Worth.

For roughly three years, the two associations operated separately—soliciting members and horses, and striving to create new show and marketing opportunities. From the onset, APSHA proved to be the most adept at registering new animals. By mid-1965, it had enrolled 2,599 horses, while APQHA had managed to assign numbers to only 324.

As a result, APSHA began to push for a merger, and on June 3, 1965, the memberships of both organizations were presented a motion to consolidate. The measure passed and the two registries were combined to form the American Paint Horse Association (APHA).

One of the most significant gains that the new registry realized through the merger was the shepherding of Hy Diamond Boy APQHA 2 into its fold.

A Legacy of Speed

Hy Diamond Boy, a 1960 sorrel tobiano stallion sired by Mae's Diamond (QH) and out of Parr Lady, was bred by Gip Young of Poteet, Texas.

By the time the loud-colored stallion came along, the South Texas land of his birth was widely recognized as one of the true Quarter Horse "cradles of speed."

Dating back to the early 1900s, Ott Adams of Alice, Texas, had crafted a family of speedsters that included such horses as Zantanon, Joe Moore, Stella Moore and Hobo. Adams' friend and neighbor George Clegg of Alfred, was also known for the quality of his stock and added such well-known horses as Old Sorrel and Ed Echols to the mix.

To the south of Adams and Clegg, the Garcia brothers of Encino utilized the blood of Band Play to develop their own line of foundation runners; and to the north, John Dial of Goliad trained many of the King Ranch's racehorses and stood a couple of sprinting Thoroughbreds named Top Deck and Depth Charge for them.

Finally, to the west of Adams and Clegg, George B. Parr of San Diego, Texas, parleyed the blood of such horses as Danger Boy II, Slow Motion and Parr Passum into a sprinting dynasty.

Although the accomplishments of these pioneer horsemen and their famous charges have faded somewhat with the passage of time, the legacy of speed they left behind has not. Hy Diamond Boy was—part and parcel—a product of this heritage.

May's Diamond— "Diamond Boy's" sire—was a 1956 chestnut stallion sired by Hy Diamond (TB) and out of May Flower W. by Flying Bob.

Hy Diamond was the sire of 32 race Register of Merit qualifiers, including Diamond Mae, the 1954 Champion Quarter Running 2-Year-Old Filly, and Diamond Charge AAAT. May Flower W, AAA-rated and one of the toughest sprinters of the late 1940s and early 1950s, was likewise a top producer and was the dam of May's Pilgrim AAA.

Parr Lady—Diamond Boy's dam—was a tobiano Paint mare reputed to have been bred by George Parr. She was sired by Danger Boy II AA and out of a "Parr Paint Mare" of unknown breeding.

Born into an age when many of his foundation Paint counterparts were of the classic "bulldog" mold, Hy Diamond Boy stood 15-3 hands high and weighed 1,250 in good flesh. From both a genetic and conformational standpoint, his was a makeup that would prove beneficial to the breed's foundation gene pool.

A Steady Rise to the Top

The first several years of Hy Diamond Boy's life are shrouded in mystery. By varying accounts, he was either raced successfully as a 2-year-old or injured to a point that precluded any type of performance career. What is known for sure is that, by early 1963, he had been purchased by C. D. Bruce of Santa Ana, Texas. Bruce was the first man to utilize Hy Diamond Boy as a breeding animal, and it was Bruce who registered the 3-year-old with the Abilene-based APQHA on February 26, 1963.

In addition to breeding the tobiano stallion to his own mares, Bruce also stood him to outside mares. It was at this juncture that APQHA founder Jones bred two mares to Diamond Boy. The stallion's first foal crop of 10 hit the ground in 1964, and included such top performers as Hy Diamond Bailey, Hy Diamond Ring, Hy Diamond Billy and Hy Diamond Moore.

Hy Diamond Bailey, a 1964 sorrel tobiano stallion out of Shirley Spark (QH), was one of his sire's first show ring representatives.

Bred by Jones and sold as a yearling to Joe and Ernestine Owings of San Antonio, Texas, "Bailey" became APHA Champion #10, with Register of Merits (ROMs) in reining and Western pleasure.

Hy Diamond Ring, a 1964 bay tobiano mare out of Chula Judge (QH), was bred by C. D. Bruce. Sold first to L. L. Bonfoey of Richardson, Texas, and then to Dana Lee Covert of Live

Hy Diamond Bailey, a 1964 sorrel tobiano stallion by Hy Diamond Boy and out of Shirley Spark (QH), earned APHA Championship #10 for owners Joe and Ernestine Owings of San Antonio, Texas. **Courtesy Paint Horse Journal**

This ad, reprinted from the March–April, 1967 issue of the Paint Horse Journal, *documents the sale of Hy Diamond Boy by W.L. "Bill" Jones and Wyman Wilkerson of Abilene, Texas, to Dr. Mack Daugherty and Jim and Roann Cartwright of Houston.*

Courtesy *Paint Horse Journal*

Hy Diamond Girl, a 1965 sorrel tobiano mare by Hy Diamond Boy and out of Dream Girl, was the 1969 National Champion Aged Mare.

Courtesy
Paint Horse Journal

Oak, California, "Ring" earned 1967's Reserve National Champion Calf Roping Horse honors. In addition, she was APHA Champion #35, with an ROM in calf roping.

Hy Diamond Billy, a 1964 sorrel tobiano gelding out of Miss Hill Billy, was also bred by Bruce. Sold to Lester Tatum of Brenham, Texas, the talented performer was the 1968 National Champion Jr. Cutting Horse.

Hy Diamond Moore, a 1964 sorrel tobiano gelding out of Sue, was another product of the C. D. Bruce breeding program. Sold to Danny Cloud of Springfield, Missouri, he went on to be named the 1967 Reserve National Champion Jr. Gelding and APHA Champion #118.

In July of 1963, Hy Diamond Boy changed hands once more. Although the official records show that he was transferred to Bill Jones, the stallion was in reality owned by Wyman Wilkerson, who was also of Abilene.

"I had known Bill Jones for a

number of years before he started the Paint Horse registry," Wilkerson says. "He was a savvy businessman and quite a promoter. In the early 1960s, I had a commercial advertising agency and was also an active partner in a couple of ranches and farms. So, when Bill and Horace King of Cross Plains, Texas, decided to start the registry, I guess they thought I'd be a good person to bring on board.

"To begin with, I helped Bill put out a Paint Horse magazine. We only published a couple of issues before the merger, but I do believe that had a lot to do with the folks around Fort Worth sort of taking notice of us.

"Then, in the summer of 1963, Bill convinced me that I needed to buy Hy Diamond Boy. I'd always liked good horses, so the deal sounded all right to me. Bill always stood the horse down at his place near Coleman, Texas, Western Hills Ranch.

Although some accounts have maintained that Hy Diamond Boy

Hy Diamond Dandy, a 1965 brown tobiano stallion by Hy Diamond Boy and out of Miss Texas Dandy, was an ROM performance horse whose budding show career was cut short by his premature death in 1972.

Courtesy
Paint Horse Journal

had been injured as a young horse, Wilkerson cannot substantiate the claim.

"Diamond Boy was a big horse," he says. "He stood 15-3 and weighed 1,250 pounds back when a lot of the Paints were 14-1 or 14-2 and would weigh 950 to 1,000 pounds.

"Back in those days, we were running a lot of cattle on our ranches.

I utilized Diamond Boy as both as a ranch and parade horse, and I put a lot of miles on him. He was a smooth-traveling horse, and a pleasure to ride. If he had been injured, or if he walked with a limp, I simply can't recall it."

While under the control of Jones and Wilkerson, Hy Diamond Boy continued to sire champions. Included among his top performers during this stage of his life were Hy Diamond Girl and Hy Diamond Dandy.

Hy Diamond Girl, a 1965 sorrel tobiano mare out of Dream Girl, was bred by Bill Jones. Sold to Roann Cartwright of Houston, Texas, the talented two-way performer was both the 1969 National Champion Aged Mare and the Reserve National Champion Jr. Cutting Horse. In addition, she was APHA Champion #183 and earned an ROM in cutting.

Hy Diamond Dandy, a 1965 brown tobiano stallion out of Miss Texas Dandy, was also bred by Jones. Sold to J. W. Tyner of Tyler, Texas, the speed-bred stallion showed considerable promise as both a show horse and sire. That promise went unrealized when Dandy succumbed to colic on March 10, 1972, at the age of 7. Prior to his premature passing, he had achieved an ROM in Western pleasure and sired 10 registered foals.

Badger's Queen, a 1972 blue roan tobiano mare by Hy Diamond Dandy and out of Lady Uptown (QH), was an APHA Champion who earned both Versatility and Superior All-Around awards, as well as Superiors in halter, Western pleasure, heading and heeling, and ROMs in six events.

Hy Diamond Boy spent the 1969 and 1970 breeding seasons under lease to Paint Horse pioneer Jo-An Soso of Live Oak, California.

Courtesy
Paint Horse Journal

Hy Diamond Bouncer, a 1972 brown tobiano stallion by Hy Diamond Dandy and out of Bouncer's Josey (QH), was an APHA Champion who earned an ROM in Western pleasure.

In February of 1967, Hy Diamond Boy—by now one of the breed's best-known sires—sold for the fourth and final time. It was after being purchased by Dr. Mack Daugherty and his daughter Roann Cartwright, that the popular stallion made his belated entry into the show arena.

Exhibited by Roann in the Aged Stallion classes at the 1967 San Antonio and Houston Livestock Expositions, Diamond Boy placed fourth and sixth, respectively. Brought back to Houston the following year, the then 8-year-old stallion placed third in the Aged Stallion class—behind Paul Eagle and Q-Ton Eagle, and ahead of Hy Diamond Bailey, Music Maker and Squaw's Stormy Star.

It was during this stage of Hy Diamond Boy's life that he sired his top show-point earner. Dandy Diamond, a 1968 sorrel tobiano stallion out of Miss Texas Dandy, was bred by Bill Jones. Sold first to Jim Cartwright of Houston, and then to Bill Neel of Davis, California, "Dandy" became an APHA Champion and the earner of a Superior in heeling, five ROMs and 225 total points. In addition, he was the 1971 Reserve National Champion 3-Year-Old Stallion.

As a sire, Dandy contributed a number of top performers to the breed, including four APHA Champions—Diamond's Goldie, Sassie Diamond, Dandy Kat and Deanna. Diamond's Goldie, a 1974 palomino tobiano mare out of Halli Chex, was especially prolific in the show ring, earning two APHA Championships (open and youth), a youth Versatility award, three Superiors (open and youth halter, youth showmanship), eight ROMs and 433 total points.

In 1969, Roann Cartwright leased Hy Diamond Boy to Jo-An Soso of Live Oak, California. Established as a senior sire at Soso's Overo Acres, the aged stallion continued to make positive contributions to the breed.

Among his top West Coast get were

point-earners Hy Diamond Tek, Hy Diamond Bar, Diamond Coaster and Diamond Adair.

Diamond Coaster, a 1970 sorrel stallion out of Morris' Belle, was bred by Soso. Sold to Dorman Bell of Bakersfield, California, "Coaster" became an APHA Champion and leading West Coast sire.

As for Hy Diamond Boy, he was taken out of retirement in 1969 and shown to Reserve Champion Stallion honors at the Sacramento, California, show.

By this time, the 9-year-old stallion was in his siring prime. In both 1967 and 1968, he had won the get of sire class at the Houston Livestock Exposition. In 1969, he swept the same honors at the three-show California Paint Championship Circuit.

On both the West Coast and back home in Texas, his get were a two-sided threat, sweeping honors in both the halter ring and performance arena.

After being warmly received by California Paint Horse breeders during the 1969 breeding season, it was expected that the same would hold true in 1970. That expectation, however, never was realized.

At the beginning of the breeding season, Robert Soso was killed in an automobile accident. The Overo Acres horses were dispersed on June 6, 1970, and Hy Diamond Boy was returned to Houston the following fall.

In October of 1970, Diamond Boy suffered an attack of colic during the night. He was taken to the clinic at Texas A&M University in College Station, but died a few days later, on October 28, 1970.

Ironically, in the spring of 1971, APHA released its first "Leading Sires, Dams and Breeders list of Paint Horses shown from 1966 through 1970." Hy Diamond Boy was accorded a position of prominence on all five of the leading sires lists.

On both the Leading Sires of Halter Point Earners and Leading Sires of Performance Point Earners, he stood third behind Q-Ton Eagle and Mister J. Bar.

On the Leading Sires of Halter Point Earners–Most Points Won, he stood

fourth; on the Leading Sires of Register of Merit Qualifiers, he stood fifth; and on the Leading Sires of Performance Point Earners–Most Points Won, he stood sixth.

As a sire, Hy Diamond Boy accomplished in half a lifetime what many horses fall short of during a full life's span.

At the time the Paint Horse industry came into being, the "bulldog" stock horse was in the twilight years of its reign. In both the Quarter Horse and Paint Horse breeds, the bulldog was giving ground to a new, taller and more streamlined model. Hy Diamond Boy, with his beautiful head and neck, and well-balanced "running horse" conformation, was a forerunner of the Paint Horse model that was to come.

He was the right type.

Diamond Coaster, a 1970 sorrel stallion by Hy Diamond Boy and out of Morris' Bell, was an early-day West Coast show ring champion and leading sire.
Courtesy
Paint Horse Journal

2 SR. DON JUAN
#14

*A race- and ranch-bred product of the Grand Canyon State,
this colorful stallion helped establish the breed
from coast to coast.*

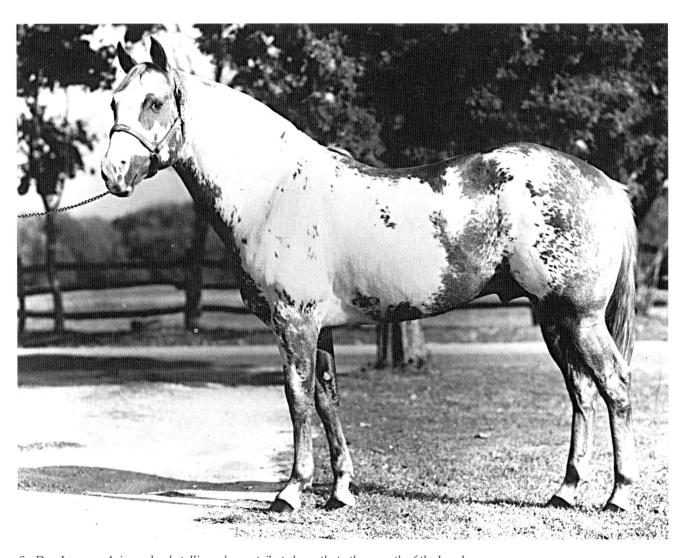

Sr. Don Juan, an Arizona-bred stallion who contributed greatly to the growth of the breed.

Courtesy APHA

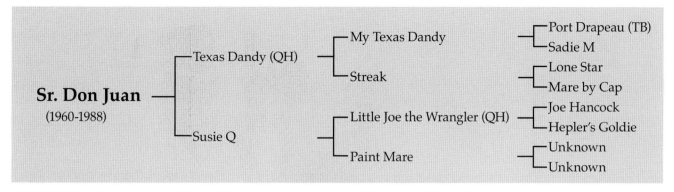

Sr. Don Juan
(1960-1988)

Texas Dandy (QH)
— My Texas Dandy
  — Port Drapeau (TB)
  — Sadie M
— Streak
  — Lone Star
  — Mare by Cap

Susie Q
— Little Joe the Wrangler (QH)
  — Joe Hancock
  — Hepler's Goldie
— Paint Mare
  — Unknown
  — Unknown

WHEN REBECCA TYLER formed the American Paint Stock Horse Association (APSHA) in 1962, she reserved the first 30 registration numbers for noteworthy stallions and mares. Numbers 1–20 were designated for stallions and numbers 21–29 were set aside for mares. And with APSHA having been founded in Texas, it was only logical that 20 of those first 29 horses would hail from the Lone Star State and its neighbor to the north, Oklahoma.

There were some notable exceptions to this rule, however, and one of these was Sr. Don Juan #14, who was born and raised in Arizona.

Well-Connected

Sr. Don Juan, a 1960 sorrel overo stallion by Texas Dandy (QH) and out of Susie Q., was bred by the Earnhardt Ranch of Chandler, Arizona, and owned at the time of registration by Debra Earnhardt.

Texas Dandy was a 1942 chestnut stallion by My Texas Dandy and out of Streak by Lone Star. A hard-knocking racehorse during the days of the Southern Arizona-based American Quarter Racing Association (AQRA), Texas Dandy became a top speed sire and a leading maternal grandsire of race ROM qualifiers.

Among his top performing get were Little Egypt, the breed's first AAA AQHA Champion, and AQHA Champions Echols Dandy and Front Row. Among his most noted maternal grandget were Doc Bar, AQHA and NCHA Hall of Fame Horse; and Dandy Bar, AAA and a leading sire of race ROM qualifiers.

"Don Juan's" dam was sired by Little Joe the Wrangler and out of a Paint

Horse mare of unnamed breeding. Little Joe the Wrangler, a 1935 bay stallion by Joe Hancock and out of Hepler's Goldie, was a top race and ranch mount in his own right, who went on to gain renown as a top broodmare sire.

While owned by Elmer Hepler of Carlsbad, New Mexico, "Wrangler" was responsible for the highly influential Panzarita Daugherty line of show and breeding horses. Then, after being acquired by Bill Coy of Torrington, Wyoming, the stallion founded a second family of champions that included the likes of Spade Ace, AQHA Champion; Viv, AQHA Champion; Sparky Joann, 1957 Rocky Mountain Quarter Horse Association Working Stakes Champion; and Coy's Bonanza, AAA-AQHA Champion and all-time leading sire.

With Texas Dandy, My Texas Dandy, Little Joe the Wrangler and Joe Hancock all appearing close up in his pedigree, Sr. Don Juan possessed the genetic potential to make a big splash in the newly formed Paint Horse registry.

And this he did—after a change of ownership and location.

A Texas State of Mind

Sr. Don Juan's first half-dozen years were spent in relative obscurity. APHA records reveal that he was registered as a late 2-year-old, on December 17, 1962.

The fact that he, a Paint stallion foaled in south-central Arizona, should find his way into APSHA's foundation gene pool might have been surprising were it not for the fact that Rebecca Tyler was the heart and soul behind the fledgling registry's early registration efforts.

San Juan, a 1968 bay overo stallion by Sr. Don Juan and out of Patsy's Hank, was the 1968 Reserve National Champion Weanling Stallion.

Photo by Dolcater

Married to George Tyler—one of the Southwest's best-connected horse traders—Rebecca was privy to the whereabouts of just about every good Paint stallion in the West. Having convinced Sr. Don Juan's owner to register him in 1962, she filed the stallion away in the back of her mind as a horse that might some day come up for sale.

Five years later, that possibility became a reality. In March of 1967, Rebecca and E. J. "Junior" Hudspeth purchased Sr. Don Juan and installed him at Hudspeth's show and breeding facility near Era, Texas.

Hudspeth was one of APSHA's charter members and owner of the popular Waggoner Ranch-bred overo stallion Pretty Badger #2. In February of 1967, Hudspeth sold Pretty Badger to Buzz and Sheryl Houston of Oxford, Kansas, and that opened the door for Sr. Don Juan to move to the head of the Hudspeth Paint Horse breeding program. The loud-colored stallion stood in north Texas for only three years, but that was more than enough

Shown here as an aged horse after winning grand champion stallion honors at the Illinois State Fair in Springfield, San Juan went on to become a top sire in his own right.

Courtesy APHA

time for him to prove to the whole country that he was a sire.

"Don Juan's" first foal crop of six colored and two solid foals hit the ground in 1968. All six of the colored foals became show-point earners, with the following four establishing the best records:

• Sassy Juan, a 1968 sorrel overo mare out of Badger's Lou—APHA Champion; ROM Western pleasure, barrel racing and reining.
• San Juan, a 1968 bay overo stallion out of Patsy's Hank—1968 APHA Reserve National Champion Weanling Stallion, 1969 APHA Reserve National Champion Yearling Stallion, APHA Champion, ROM Western pleasure.
• Juan's Cutie, a 1968 sorrel tobiano mare out of Osage Liberty Girl—APHA Champion, Superior Halter and ROM Western pleasure.
• Cutter's Dandy, a 1968 palomino overo gelding out of Cutter's Queen Bee—91 performance points.

Don Juan's second foal crop totaled nine and included six performers. Among these was San Juan Lou, the stallion's all-time leading point earner.

San Juan Lou, a 1969 sorrel overo mare out of Badger's Lou, was bred by Junior Hudspeth. In open and youth competition, she earned one National Championship, three Reserve National Championships, two Versatility awards, six APHA Championships, 17 Superior awards, 34 ROMs and 2,424 points.

San Juan Lou, a 1969 sorrel overo mare by Sr. Don Juan and out of Badger's Lou, was one of her sire's most accomplished performers.

Photo by Fred Droddy

Among the talented mare "Lou"'s many honors were a National Championship, three Reserve National Championships, two Versatility awards and six APHA Championships.

Photo by George Martin

San Juan Belle, a 1972 bay overo mare by San Juan and out of Beau Coup Bee (QH), was the 1972 National Champion Weanling Filly. The talented performer then went on to claim two additional national titles in reining.

Photo by George Martin

Miss Bimbo Juan, a 1969 sorrel tobiano mare by Sr. Don Juan and out of Firefly, was likewise the earner of multiple honors in open and youth competition.

Photo by George Martin

El Zorro, a 1969 bay overo gelding by Sr. Don Juan and out of Zorro's Deb, was the 1973 National Champion Youth Halter Horse and Reserve National Champion Youth Western Pleasure Horse.

Photo by Barbara Jean

Several other members of Sr. Don Juan's second Texas foal crop distinguished themselves, also. They were:

- Miss Rimbo Juan, a 1969 sorrel tobiano mare out of Firefly—1974 National Champion Broodmare, APHA Champion, 1972 National Champion Youth Showmanship, Superior youth showmanship, four ROMs and 186 points.
- El Zorro, a 1969 bay overo gelding out of Zorro's Deb—1973 National Champion Youth Halter, 1973 Reserve National Champion Youth Western Pleasure, eight ROMs and 190 points.
- Juan Two, a 1969 buckskin overo gelding out of an unregistered Quarter Mare—Grand Champion Gelding at the 1971 Fort Worth and San Antonio Stock Shows, first place at the Houston Stock Show.

Sr. Don Juan's third and final Texas foal crop arrived in 1970. From eight foals there were two performers and one superstar. The star was Juan's Badger, a 1970 sorrel overo stallion out of Badger's Lou, who became an APHA Champion and earned a Superior in Western pleasure, as well as four ROMs and 116 points.

In addition, at the 1970 APHA National Show, held in Amarillo, Texas, Sr. Don Juan bested such top early day stallions as Leo San Man, Skippa Streak and Yellow Mount to win the Get of Sire class. And then Firefly, owned by Charley Moore of Era, Texas, won the Produce of Dam class with two of Don Juan's get—Ring O'Fire and Miss Bimbo Juan.

Eastward Bound

In August of 1969, Tyler and Hudspeth sold Sr. Don Juan to Bernard

"Punk" Hoban of Pen Yan, New York, who owned and stood him for three years. In May of 1970, Hoban even showed the 10-year-old stallion to first place in a class of 10 aged stallions, and grand champion stallion honors at a Syracuse, New York, Paint Horse show.

During this phase of his life, Don Juan continued to broaden his reputation as a sire. Among his top performers were:

- Skipa Juan Silver, a 1971 red roan overo stallion out of Skipawa—APHA Champion.
- Juan's Mist, a 1971 sorrel overo mare out of Ouija—seven ROMs and 182 performance points.
- Dandy Don Juan, a 1971 red roan overo gelding out of Speech Teacher—Superior Western pleasure, four ROMs and 223 points.

In September of 1972, Sr. Don Juan was sold for the fourth time, going to Jan and Eve Seutter of South Seaville, New Jersey. Like Hoban, the Seutters would own and stand Don Juan through only two breeding seasons, 1973 and 1974. For them, the foundation stallion sired

such top show horses as:
- Frosted Bar Lady, a 1974 sorrel overo mare out of Mighty Lady Hank (QH)—Superior Western pleasure (open and amateur), four ROMs and 274 points.
- Cedarcreek's Holly, a 1974 sorrel overo mare out of Speech Teacher—APHA Champion, two ROMs and 48 points.
- First Edition, a 1975 sorrel overo gelding out of Coco Leo (QH)—Superior Western pleasure, two ROMs and 102 points.
- Edens Spring Rain, a 1975 sorrel overo mare out of Eden's Impy Eve—APHA Champion, Superior Halter, two ROMs and 102 points.
- Cortando Juan, a 1975 sorrel overo stallion out of Cutter Jill (QH)—APHA Champion, two ROMs and 67 points.

In the fall of 1974, the Seutters sold Edens Skipajuanita, a weanling show filly by Sr. Don Juan and out of Skipawa, to Marquerita Dallabrida, M.D. of Mt. Carmel, Pennsylvania. In December of the same year, Dr. Dallabrida purchased Don Juan and thus became his fifth and final owner.

The crowning achievement of Sr. Don Juan's Texas era was when he won the get of sire class at the 1970 National Show, Amarillo, Texas.

Photo by Dolcater

At the 1979 National Show in Oklahoma City, Oklahoma, Juan's Dandy Pants and Sonessa Shield of Saginaw, Texas, earned reserve national championship honors in Youth Showmanship at Halter.
Courtesy APHA

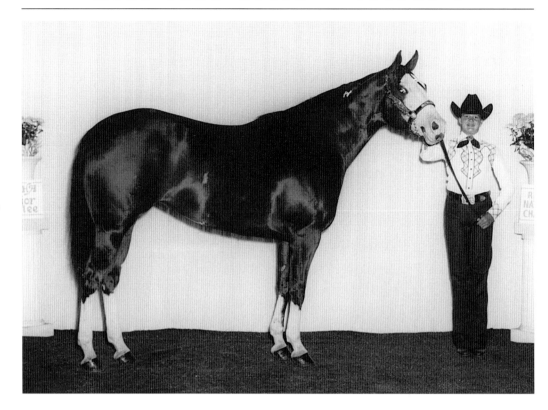

"Dandy Pants," a 1975 sorrel overo mare by Juan's Badger and out of Fancy Jo Dude (QH), was also the 1979 National Champion Trail Horse.
Courtesy APHA

The Final Years

While under Dallabrida's ownership, Don Juan added to his already considerable reputation as a top all-around sire with such top performers as:

• Juan's Apple Jack, a 1977 sorrel overo gelding out of Crème De Menthe—Open Versatility, Superior Western riding, 1982 National Champion Amateur Western Riding, 12 ROMs and 524 points.

• MD. Oh My, a 1978 bay overo gelding out of Eden's La Nina—Superior Western pleasure, eight ROMs and 311 points.

As the 1980s dawned, Sr. Don Juan began to wind down his highly successful career as a breeding horse. To be sure, he would continue on as a sire throughout the decade, but the foal crops would average just three per year.

In 1981, Dallabrida leased the then-21-year-old stallion to Richard and Christine Sullenberger of Beavers Dam, New York. And, just as he had throughout the front and middle of his life, Sr. Don Juan closed out his breeding career by siring several more top performers. Included among them were:

• Don Domingo, a 1982 sorrel overo gelding out of Two Bit Suzi Cajun—Superior trail, Youth Versatility, Superior youth trail, 11 ROMs and 388 points.

• Mr Q Ton Juan, a 1983 brown tovero gelding out of Ruby's Q Ton H—ROM Western pleasure and 42 points.

• Juans Sunny Day, a 1988 chestnut overo mare out of Have A Nice Day—Two ROMs and 48 points.

Sr. Don Juan's last foal crop numbered just two and hit the ground in 1989. As was only fitting, Richard and Christine Sullenberger—the couple who had cared for the famous stallion throughout his final years—bred both foals.

The Atonement, a 1989 solid sorrel stallion out of Two Eyed Watonga, was sold as a weanling to Scott Root of Addison, New York. Juans Grand Finale, a 1989 chestnut overo mare out of Taffys Miss 7L, was sold to Steven Fender of San Antonio, Texas.

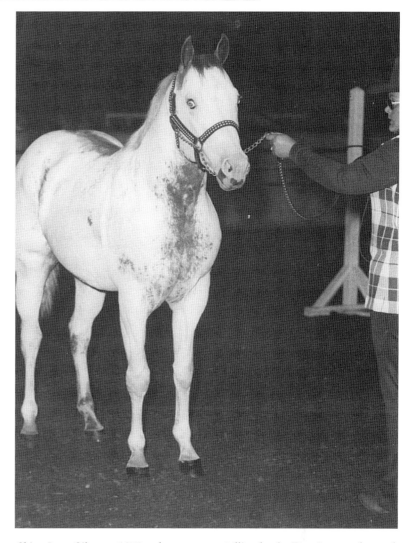

Skipa Juan Silver, a 1971 red roan overo stallion by Sr. Don Juan and out of Skipawa, was a Midwestern-based APHA Champion. **Courtesy APHA**

A Rich Legacy

As a foundation Paint Horse sire with a long and varied breeding career, Sr. Don Juan bequeathed the breed a rich legacy.

APHA records reveal that he sired a total of 22 foal crops and 190 registered foals. Of these, 47 performers have earned five National Championships, six Reserve National Championships, four Versatility awards, 30 Superior awards, 15 APHA Championships, 127 ROMs and 5,805 points in all divisions combined.

In addition to his impressive string of performers, Sr. Don Juan was also the sire of two top show and breeding sons—San Juan and Juan's Badger.

San Juan, a 1968 bay overo stallion out of Patsy's Hank, was bred by Charley Moore of Era, Texas. Shown by his breeder as a yearling, San Juan placed first at the Fort Worth and Houston stock shows, won the Texas Halter Futurity, earned grand champion stallion honors at the Tri State Fair in Amarillo, Texas, and reserve champion honors at the World Wide Paint Review in Hutchinson, Kansas, and capped the year off by being named Reserve Champion Yearling Stallion at the APHA National Show in Kansas City, Missouri.

Sold to Bill Ruggles of Three Rivers, Michigan, San Juan became one of the upper Midwest's top show and breeding stallions, and the sire of the earners of four National and World Championships, five Reserve National and World Championships, seven Versatility awards, one Superior All-Around award, 18 Superior awards, 10 APHA Championships, 57 ROMs and 3,667 points in all divisions combined.

Juan's Badger, a 1970 sorrel overo stallion out of Badger's Lou, was bred by Junior Hudspeth. He was sold first to Sam Knisley of Mt. Sterling, Ohio, and later to Daniel and Linda Griffith, also of Ohio.

While owned by Knisley, Juan's Badger became one of the youngest APHA Champions on record, qualifying for the award at the age of 24 months and 23 days.

Retired to stud, he sired the earners of one National Championship, one Reserve National Championship, one Youth Versatility award, 10 Superior awards, five APHA Championships, 24

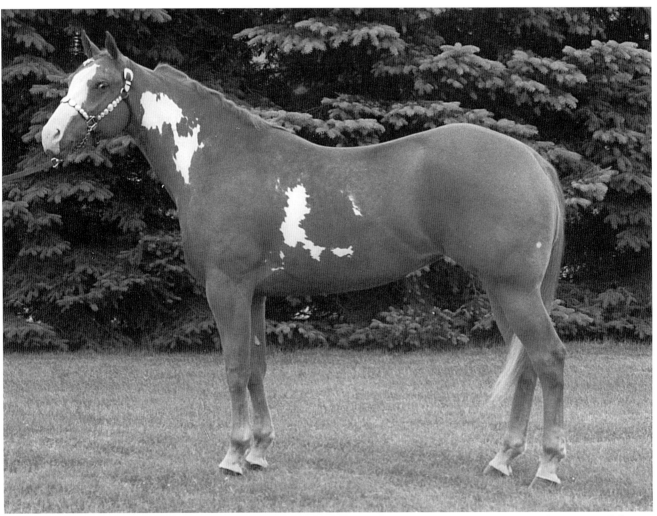

Edens Spring Rain, a 1975 sorrel overo mare by Sr. Don Juan and out of Eden's Impy Five, was an APHA Champion and the earner of a Superior halter award.   **Courtesy APHA**

Sawbucks Robin, a 1975 sorrel overo mare by C Note's Sawbuck and out of Don Juan's Robin, was the 1979 Reserve National Champion Trail Horse. In addition, the Sr. Don Juan granddaughter earned one Versatility award and two APHA Championships.
Courtesy APHA

ROMs and 1,360 points in all divisions combined.

As for the patriarch of the strain, by the fall of 1988, Sr. Don Juan's general condition had deteriorated to the point that the decision was made to have him humanely euthanized. And so, a colorful chapter in the history of the American Paint Horse came to an end.

Given the place and date of his birth, it would have been deemed improbable that Sr. Don Juan's career as a foundation Paint Horse sire would take him from the Southwest, to the Southern Plains, and then to the Midwest and Northeast.

The fact of the matter remains that it did, and the Paint Horse breed is the better for it.

3 CALAMITY JANE
#21

Although undersized and of uncertain breeding, this talented tobiano gained fame as one of the top cutting horses of her era.

Calamity Jane, NCHA Top 10 performer and the APHA's first registered mare, and Judy Burton – her teen-aged rider.
Courtesy NCHA

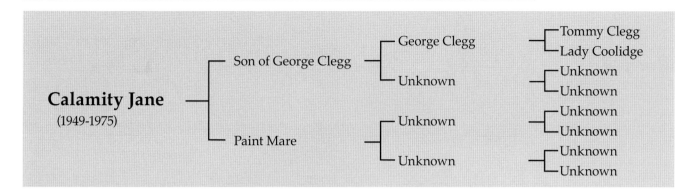

Calamity Jane
(1949-1975)

- Son of George Clegg
  - George Clegg
    - Tommy Clegg
    - Lady Coolidge
  - Unknown
    - Unknown
    - Unknown
- Paint Mare
  - Unknown
    - Unknown
    - Unknown
  - Unknown
    - Unknown
    - Unknown

AT THE TIME the American Paint Stock Horse Association (APSHA) was founded in 1962, there was a North Texas-based Paint cutting mare who was at the top of her game. She was good enough to hold her own at any level of National Cutting Horse Association (NCHA) competition, and this made her a custom-made "poster child" for the new breed registry.

In recognition of both her accomplishments and her notoriety, the cutter was honored by APSHA by being the first mare accepted for registration.

Her name was Calamity Jane #21.

A Checkered Past

Named after the notorious frontierswoman and professional scout of the late 1800s, Calamity Jane was bred by Ira Riley and foaled on his ranch near Snyder, Texas. Much of her pedigree remains uncertain.

Her original APSHA registration application, which was completed on August 27, 1963, listed her as a 1949 black tobiano mare sired by "Pal" by Joe Clegg, and out of a "Paint Mare" of unknown breeding. The sire data was later amended to read "Son of George Clegg."

Various attempts to pin down "Calamity's" sire have listed him alternately as "a son of Dempsey by George Clegg," and "a palomino stud raised by [Benny] Binion."

Ira Riley's son Doyle also later went on record as saying that Calamity's paternal granddam was a mare known around Snyder as "Sweet Pea," who was sired by a dun horse owned by Doyle's uncle.

It is the latter description that probably comes closest to pinpointing the mystery sire. It is generally acknowledged that he was a son of George Clegg, a 1939 dun stallion by Tommy Clegg and out of Lady Coolidge.

As far as the rest of the puzzle is concerned, Doyle Riley's uncle would have been Clyde Miller of Fluvanna, Texas, a prominent rancher and one-time owner of the renowned foundation sire Bartender (see *Legends 5*).

NCHA Hall of Fame inductee Bob Burton – Judy's father – is shown here with his famed cutting mare Miss Nancy Bailey.
Courtesy AQHA

The diminutive Paint mare was ridden to top placings by a variety of riders.

Photo by George Axt

"Calamity" and her trailer mate Miss Nancy Bailey gave the Burton family one of the cutting industry's best and most potent cutting tandems.
Courtesy AQHA

Miller's first Quarter Horse stallion was Texas Miller—a 1926 dun by Simms' Yellow Boy and out of an OXO mare by Dr. Mack (TB). What's more, AQHA records reveal Texas Miller to be the sire of Sweet Pea J, a 1933 bay mare out of Josephene by Ross Green (TB).

So, Calamity Jane's sire, in all probability, was an unregistered palomino son of George Clegg who was out of Sweet Pea J by Texas Miller.

But, no matter how the black tobiano mare was actually bred, one thing was soon readily apparent. She was born to be a cow horse.

A Champion in the Making

Getting back to the circumstances surrounding Calamity Jane's birth and early life, her dam was a black and white tobiano mare who Ira Riley acquired "as a fairly young mare" from a county judge.

Rumored to be originally from New Mexico and endowed with an easy-going disposition, she was used to carry the Riley kids to and from school. Included among this brood of seven children was Lanham Riley, who went on to achieve considerable success as both a professional calf roper and horse trainer.

Also utilized as a broodmare, Calamity's dam produced eight foals altogether—three fillies and five colts. All but one were colored Paints; two were kept by the Riley family and a third, known as "the Riley Paint," became a "contest" cutting horse.

In 1950, Ira Riley moved his ranching operation from Texas to South Dakota. Calamity Jane, then a yearling, was entrusted to a grandson to raise.

Several years later, Gerald Hart of Snyder acquired Calamity, and he is the man who is credited with breaking her, training her for cutting and entering her in her first NCHA contests in 1952. Her official earnings for the year amounted to $66.

Small by any measuring stick, Calamity stood a mere 13-3 hands high and weighed in at 920 pounds. Her heart, however, as was soon evidenced, was larger than normal.

It was at this point in Calamity Jane's life that she first came to the attention of Bob Burton of Arlington, Texas.

Burton was one of the better-known competitors on the NCHA cutting horse circuit, and had already trained and ridden such champions as Royal King, Hollywood George and Miss Nancy Bailey. Recognizing that Calamity Jane possessed considerable raw talent, he offered Hart $1,000 for her.

Hart turned down Burton's offer and sold the mare instead to H. R. Burden

Tommy Arhopulos, a Bryan, Texas, rancher, acquired Calamity in the early 1960s.
Courtesy APHA

3 3

of Ennis, Texas. Burden promptly secured the services of Snooks Burton—Bob's brother—as Calamity's trainer and rider. Shown by him in NCHA competition, the mare finished the 1953 calendar year with earnings of $620.20.

Bob Burton had not given up on acquiring the diminutive cutter however, and within months he was able to seal a deal to become the mare's fourth owner.

"It was sometime late in 1954," Burton said in a mid-1970s interview. " … I was buying cattle at the time when Mr. Burden told me about a little Paint mare he had that he sure would like to sell to me. I already knew the mare he was talking about, and I knew she had not been winning much.

"Since I had seen her after cattle, I figured she wasn't being worked right and took her on home with me. It didn't take long to find out how to get along with her and where everyone had been making mistakes."

After finally getting his hands on Calamity, Burton promptly turned her over to his daughter Judy. Then only 13 and 4 years old, respectively, the talented teenager and the tiny tobiano began making regular visits to the pay window. By year's end, the mare's NCHA earnings amounted to $2,181.

The following year, the duo made its first appearance on the NCHA year-end leader board. Exhibited in 15 contests, Calamity Jane earned $3,909, and that was good enough to earn her the last slot in the 1955 NCHA Top 10. The highlights of the year occurred at shows in Tucson, Arizona, and Vernon, Texas.

At the big spring AQHA extravaganza in Tucson, Calamity was exhibited by Bubba Cascio of Arlington, Texas. Competing against an arena full of world-caliber cutting horses, the little mare split third in the first go-round with King's Pistol; first in the second go-round with Little Tom W. and Miss Nancy Bailey; and third in the finals with Sugar Russom and Skeeter.

At the Santa Rosa Roundup in Vernon, with Judy Burton aboard, Calamity won the first go-round, and placed second in the second go-round and finals.

Finishing behind the winning pair were such renowned competitors as Miss Nancy Bailey and Bob Burton, Snooky and Milt Bennett, Marion's Girl and Buster Welch, and Buster Waggoner and Eldon McCloud.

Arhopulos continued to contest on Calamity Jane. Among the pair's top accomplishments was winning the first Fort Worth Stock Show Non-Pro Cutting Championship.
Courtesy APHA

Although Calamity was in her teens, she still earned honors in 1962, 1963 and 1964 as the high-point registered Paint Horse in NCHA competition.
**Photo by
Agri Photo**

From the very onset, 1957 looked to be Calamity Jane's year to shine. Exhibited by Bob Burton, Judy Burton, Snooks Burton and Bubba Cascio, the Paint mare led the nation in cutting for the first nine months.

During that time, Calamity won or placed high in NCHA-sanctioned events at Texas-based shows in San Antonio, Fort Worth and Odessa; and in Baton Rouge, Louisiana, and Tucson.

Throughout the time period, the mare also carried Judy Burton to numerous wins on the local and high school levels. Among their documented victories were first place finishes at the Dallas Kiwanis Club show, youth rodeo cuttings at Wharton and Alice, Texas, and the 1954 Texas State Championship High School Rodeo at Hallettsville.

According to Bob Burton, Calamity even won a match cutting against yet another world-caliber performer.

"Edgar Brown III, who owned Hollywood George, wanted to match them," Burton said, "and he got covered pretty quick with some good-sized bets. There are people who doubt the ability of a Paint Horse on the grounds that they are a Paint Horse.

"In my opinion, both horses were remarkable. I had ridden and trained them both. Some believed Hollywood George was the best cutting horse of his day, and, to tell the truth, he was good.

"Calamity, though, was developed to a peak of perfection. Her performance when she won the match was her best. She proved, at least in this case, that the qualities of a great performer are not affected by color. "

Calamity Jane's run at a world championship was cut short by a Burton family illness. Still, she ended the year in sixth place, with earnings of $6,730. Her finish was the highest ever by a Paint Horse in open cutting competition, and it remained as such until the legendary NCHA Hall of Fame performer Delta finished the 1973 season as the NCHA World Champion Cutting Mare and Reserve World Champion Cutting Horse.

In 1957, Calamity Jane was awarded NCHA Certificate of Achievement (COA) #237 and a bronze award for having earned more than $10,000 in approved competition. Returned to the cutting wars in 1958, she took home paychecks amounting to $2,322.

Beginning in 1958, the seasoned campaigner was sold three times— first to Allen Riley of Refugio, Texas; then to Edgar Brown III of Orange, Texas; and finally to Tommy Arhopulos of Bryan, Texas.

The transition from Brown to Arhopulos was a particularly colorful one, even by Texas standards. Big Dreams Edgar Brown III was a prototypical Texan. When he decided that his Pinehurst Stables was going into the Quarter Horse business, he went out and bought R.Q. Sutherland's entire herd of 55 halter and performance horses at private treaty. Included in the group were the legendary stallions Paul A, Beau Chance (a son of Skipper W) and Power Command.

Like-wise, when the Lone Star State millionaire decided he was going to make a big splash in the cutting horse

industry, he acquired such NCHA top ten competitors as Hollywood George, Snook, Poco Mona, Ott and Hollywood Cat. And then he hired 10 of the country's top trainers – Matlock Rose, John Carter and Bubba Cascio among them – to train and ride them.

When the cutting horse dream went up in smoke due to personnel conflicts, Brown went back to the show horse side of the street. It was at this juncture that he hired Tommy Arhopulos to manage the breeding chores, which necessitated the relocation of Paul A., Hollywood George, Beau Chance and 200 broodmares to Arhopulos' ranch near Bryan, Texas.

Once again, the deal turned sour and legal action was necessary to resolve it. At the end, Brown got all of his horses back and Tommy Arhopulos got Calamity Jane.

In between the changes in ownership, Calamity appeared in enough sanctioned cutting contests to amass an additional $8,205 in earnings. In 1960, she was accorded a silver award for having earned more than $20,000.

In 1962, while under the ownership of Arhopulos, Calamity made headlines when she was one of four cutting horses to be flown on successive days from Texas to cuttings in Washington, D.C., and San Francisco, California.

As noted earlier, Calamity was registered with APSHA in 1963, as a 14-year-old. Arhopulos, who was the mare's final owner, continued to campaign her in open cutting competition and even rode her at age 16 to win the first Fort Worth Stock Show Non-Pro Cutting Championship.

The gutsy competitor continued to perform well and added yet additional luster to her already sterling record by taking home the 1962, 1963 and 1964 NCHA affiliate trophies reserved for the high-point registered Paint Stock Horse in approved NCHA competition.

Calamity Jane saw her last action at an NCHA arena performance in 1964. That year, as a 15-year-old, she earned $343. Her total earnings, amassed over

In 1962, Calamity and Arhopulos made the news by flying from Texas to Washington, D.C. and San Francisco, California, to attend cuttings.
Courtesy APHA

the course of a 13-year cutting career, amounted to $24,591.

In 1971, at the age of 22, Calamity gave birth to her only foal. Unfortunately, it died at only 1 day of age.

As one of the top open arena performers of her era, Calamity routinely competed against the best that the cutting horse world had to offer. In the process of carving out a name for herself in a field of competition dominated by solid-colored horses, she threw open the doors for both herself and her breed. Respect, however earned, is a powerful tool. Calamity Jane, according to a host of people who knew her or saw her work, was a highly respected cutting horse. In all aspects of her personality and performance, she was truly the "little Paint who could."

4 DUAL IMAGE
#555

As one of the industry's first "triple threat" superstars, this loud-colored overo stallion was a true trendsetter.

Dual Image, one of the breed's first champion race, halter and performance horses.
Courtesy APHA

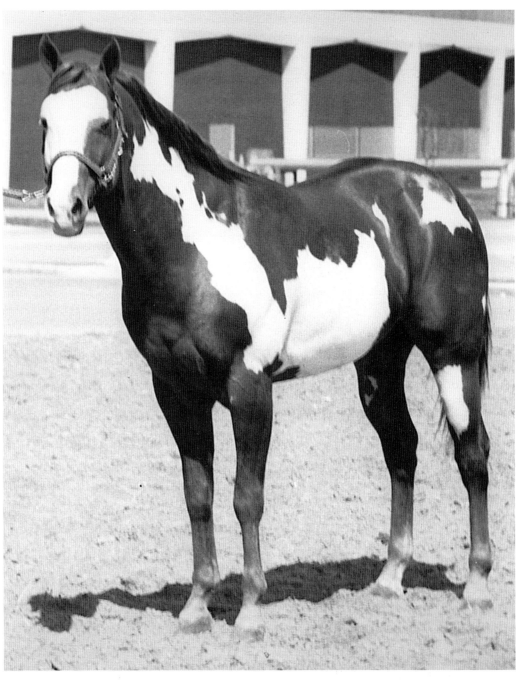

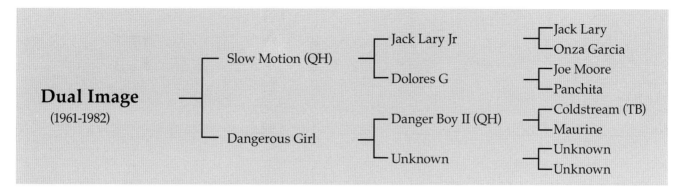

Dual Image (1961-1982)
- Slow Motion (QH)
  - Jack Lary Jr
    - Jack Lary
    - Onza Garcia
  - Dolores G
    - Joe Moore
    - Panchita
- Dangerous Girl
  - Danger Boy II (QH)
    - Coldstream (TB)
    - Maurine
  - Unknown
    - Unknown
    - Unknown

DUAL IMAGE WAS born at roughly the same time, in the same part of the country and to the same speed-bred family of horses as was Hy Diamond Boy. And, like "Diamond Boy," Dual Image found the fledgling Paint Horse industry to be fertile ground in which to carve out a name for himself.

The American Paint Horse Association identifies Dual Image as a 1961 sorrel overo stallion, sired by Slow Motion (QH) and out of Dangerous Girl. Although his breeder is still officially listed as unknown, he has, in fact, been identified as Amando Canales of Premont, Texas.

Canales passed away in the mid-1970s, but his close relative Alfonso Gonzales of Palito Blanco, Texas, was privy to the set of circumstances that wound up giving birth to a quartet of speedy full siblings.

Engineered for Speed

"My family has been in this part of the country for many years," Gonzales says. "They migrated from Spain to Mexico more than 300 years ago, and to this part of Texas 200 years ago. My great-great grandfather, Ralph Gutierrez, was the first Hispanic around here to speak English.

"My father's sister, Estephanita Canales, owned a ranch near Premont, Texas, known as La Perla, or The Pearl. I went to work for Aunt Stephanie in the mid-1950s. She had two sons—Ed and Amando Canales—and they liked racehorses.

"In the late 1950s, Amando went to a local horse sale and came home with an overo Paint mare," Gonzales continues. "She was supposed to have come into this country with a load of Thoroughbred mares from Kentucky,

but we were never able to prove this. I think he gave $50 for her."

In 1952, Amando hauled his Paint mare to San Diego, Texas, and the Los Harcones Ranch of George Parr. There, she was bred to Danger Boy. Racing under the rules and regulations of the old American Quarter Racing Association (AQRA), Danger Boy achieved a AA rating in 1945, when that was the highest rating available. In addition, he set a track record that same year at Eagle Pass, Texas, for 400 yards.

The result of this cross was a 1953 overo Paint mare, who was named Dangerous Girl.

During this same time, Amando had also purchased a top stallion named Slow Motion from George Parr. This horse had been bred by Elijio Garcia of Encino, Texas, and traced close up in his pedigree to Joe Moore, Joe Hancock, Hickory Bill and Little Joe. While owned by Parr, Slow Motion was campaigned on the tracks, achieving an official AAA rating and also earning money in NCHA competition.

In 1955, Amando Canales bred Dangerous Girl to Slow Motion. Canales Black, a 1958 solid black gelding, was the resulting foal. Despite the fact that his dam was a Paint, Canales Black was registered with AQHA. What's more, he went on to enjoy a sterling career as a straightaway sprinter.

Sent to the post 38 times, Canales Black managed 16 firsts, five seconds and four thirds. Officially rated AAAT (later converted to SI 100), he won the 1961 Shue Fly Stakes at the New Mexico State Fairgrounds in Albuquerque, and the 1962 Peter

A sprinter with officially timed AAA speed, Dual Image's straightaway exploits antedated the formation of the registry's racing division.
Courtesy APHA

McCue Stakes and Champion Stakes at Ruidoso Downs in Ruidoso, New Mexico. In 1963, he set a new track record for 350 yards at Sunland Park in El Paso, Texas.

As for the Slow Motion/Dangerous Girl cross, it was just heating up. In short order, it was responsible for three additional champions—two of which would dramatically impact the Paint Horse breed.

In 1958, Dangerous Girl produced a Paint full brother to Canales Black that was purchased by Alfonso Gonzales. Named "Texas Paint" because of an odd state of Texas-shaped white marking on his side, he went on to become a top match-racing gelding.

Bred back to Slow Motion in 1959, Dangerous Girl foaled an overo Paint filly named Crystal Eye in 1960. Also purchased by Gonzalez, she went on to stardom as both a racehorse and a producer.

Bred for a fourth and final time to Slow Motion, in 1961 Dangerous Girl produced a loud-colored sorrel overo colt who was named Dual Image and who became one of the breed's first great "triple-threat horses" —a proven winner on the race track, in the halter ring and in the performance arena.

A Triple Threat

Dual Image was born shortly before the formation of the two Paint Horse registries. This timing, together with the fact that he had a full brother who was tearing up the Quarter tracks, made the loud-colored Paint colt a highly desirable commodity.

Sometime between his birth and yearling years, Armando Canales sold the colt to Carl Vickers of Corpus Christi, Texas. Vickers registered his new acquisition with the APSHA as a 2-year-old, on May 28, 1963. Early the following year, he sold him to Jack Archer, also of Corpus Christi.

While under Archer's ownership, Dual Image was raced and shown at halter.

Exhibited by owner Jack Archer at the 1966 National Show in Baton Rouge, Louisiana, "Image" earned honors as the Reserve Champion Aged Stallion.
Courtesy APHA

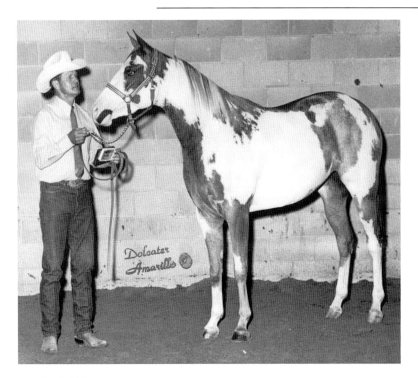

Dual's Doll II, a 1967 sorrel overo mare by Dual Image and out of Miss Hi Tex, was the 1971 National Champion 3-Year-Old Mare.
Photo by Dolcater

Having arrived on the scene before the advent of regulated Paint racing, "Image" was relegated to the role of a match racer. Although no extensive record of his track accomplishments is known to exist, it is recorded that on October 10, 1965, he won a 350-yard match race against a tobiano Paint grandson of Sugar Bars named On And On. The official track win photo reveals that Dual Image covered the distance in the solid AAA time of :18.3.

Because the race was run before any rules for Paint Horse racing were in place, however, Image's time was never recognized. And, although he was actually the first Paint Horse to run and win in AAA time under regulated conditions, he was never accorded an official APHA race rating.

The speedy stallion is also credited with being the winner of the 1965 South Texas Paint Racing Championship.

Although his race record may remain cloudy, Dual Image's halter and arena performance records are crystal clear.

Shown at halter by Archer, the race-bred stallion earned honors as the grand champion stallion at the 1966 Southwestern Exposition and Livestock Show in Fort Worth, Texas,

and won the aged stallion class at the Houston Fat Stock Show.

Exhibited the following October at the 1966 National Championship Show in Baton Rouge, Louisiana, Image was named the Reserve Champion Aged Stallion, placing behind Q Ton Eagle but ahead of Adios Amigos, Squaw's Stormy Star and Wildfire.

In early 1967, he swept the Texas stock show winter circuit by earning grand champion stallion honors at the Southwestern Exposition and Fat Stock Show, the San Antonio Livestock Show and the Houston Livestock Show.

While carving out these three prestigious wins, Image defeated such noted halter stallions as C-Note, Bear Cat, Copper Joe, Tuff Cat, Lone Wolf, Sabru Indio, Adios Amigo, Hy Diamond Boy, Hy Diamond Bailey, J Bar Flash and Balmy L Mac.

While in attendance at the San Antonio show, Dual Image came to the attention of C. E. and Larry Swain, owners and operators of the Circle Dot Ranch in San Antonio.

In February of 1967, the father and son team made Paint Horse history when they purchased Dual Image for the then-record-setting price of $15,000.

Soon after arriving at his new home, the 6-year-old stallion was put in performance training with Larry Daniels. Exhibited by both Daniels and Pam Swain, the talented stallion went on to become APHA Champion #36, with ROMs in hunter under saddle and Western pleasure.

The high point of his performance career occurred at the 1971 APHA National Championship Show in Tulsa, Oklahoma. Exhibited there by Pam Swain, he earned honors as the National Champion Sr. English Pleasure Horse.

His final APHA show record reveals that he earned a total of 89 points: 26 halter, 22 hunter under saddle and 41 Western pleasure.

Like Begets Like

Even while being raced and shown, Dual Image saw considerable duty as a breeding animal. His first foal crop, numbering four, hit the ground in 1964. From it came Snow King, the eventual earner of an ROM in calf roping.

Dual's Doll II, a 1967 sorrel overo mare by Dual Image and out of Miss Hi Tex, was the family's first legitimate superstar. Bred by Jack Archer, she was the 1971 National Champion 3-Year-Old Mare. In addition, she was a two-time APHA Champion (open and youth), a Superior halter horse and the earner of three ROMs.

Under the ownership of Circle Dot Ranch, Dual Image quickly established a name for himself as a sire of versatile halter and performance horses. Among his most accomplished get were:

• Dual Spots, a 1968 brown overo gelding out of White Specks—1978 National Champion Heeling, Versatility award winner, Superior reining and heeling, and nine ROMs.

One of the breed's first top youth horses, Dual's Doll II was shown by Chris Coffman of Miami, Florida to Youth APHA Championship #23.
Photo by George Martin

Dual Delight, a 1972 sorrel overo mare by Dual Image and out of Cody's Jazzabell was shown by Chris Coffman in youth competition at the 1976 National in Baton Rouge, Louisiana. The duo earned reserve championships in halter, showmanship at halter and western pleasure.

**Photo by
LeRoy Weathers**

- Hollywood Image, a 1970 sorrel overo mare out of Sonado Babe—1974 National Champion Aged Mare, APHA Champion, Superior halter and two ROMs.
- Ima Image, a 1972 bay tobiano mare out of Miss Ed—two Versatility awards (open and youth), two APHA Championships (open and youth), nine Superior awards, 14 ROMs and 925 total points.
- Dual Delight, a 1972 sorrel mare out of Cody's Jazzabell—one Versatility award, two APHA Championships (open and youth), four Superior awards, 11 ROMs and 466 total points.
- Spittin Image, a 1973 palomino overo gelding out of Queen Polly Bee (QH)—one Versatility award, two APHA Championships (open and youth), eight Superior awards, 14 ROMs and 783 total points.
- Sterling Lady, a 1976 black overo

mare out of Bold Negra Bar (QH)—1982 Amateur Reserve National Champion Hunter Under Saddle, 11 ROMs and 236 total points.
- Dual Reflection, a 1976 sorrel overo mare out of Leotoe Bars Doll (QH)—two APHA Championships (open and youth), six ROMs and 190 total points.

In June of 1976, Dual Image was sold for the fourth and final time to Charles Parker of Grapevine, Texas. By now, the stallion was considered to be one of the breed's top sires, and under Parker's ownership he continued to turn out a steady stream of champions.

Dual Image's first North Texas foal crop was born in 1977. From it came Corporate Image, his most prolific point earner. A 1978 sorrel tobiano gelding out of Dude's Darling, Corporate Image earned two Versatility awards, two APHA

Championships, 10 Superior awards, 20 ROMs and 1,891 total points.

Several additional Dual Image champions were born during this stage of the prolific stallion's life. Among them were:

• Blazing Image, a 1980 sorrel overo stallion out of What A Lady—Superior Western pleasure, six ROMs and 231 points.

• Barely An Image, a 1980 sorrel overo mare out of Leotoe Bars Lady (QH) —APHA Champion, Superior Western pleasure, one ROM and 101 points.

The year 1981 marked Dual Image's last significant foal crop. Numbering 22, it included such top performers as Tiger Image, Handsome Image and Dual Blue Eyes.

Tiger Image, a 1981 sorrel overo gelding out of April Moon Charger (QH), was the earner of four Superior event awards, eight ROMs and 414 points. Handsome Image, a 1981 bay tobiano stallion out of What A Lady, was the 1990 Amateur Reserve World Champion Heading Horse. In addition, he earned a Superior in Western pleasure, five ROMs and 173 points.

Dual Blue Eyes, a 1981 sorrel overo stallion out of Picotte Rose, stands out as Dual Image's last big-time performer and one of his best.

To begin with, Dual Blue Eyes was impeccably bred on the both the top and bottom sides of his pedigree. Picotte Rose, his dam, was a 1973 sorrel overo mare by Leo Bingo (QH) and out of Dandy Bar Rose (QH), tracing close up in her pedigree to such horses as Leo, Three Bars (TB), Beggar Boy (TB) and Texas Dandy. The earner of 27 halter points, she was the dam of only one foal.

As a performer, Dual Blue Eyes was an APHA Champion and a Superior Western pleasure horse. In addition, he earned ROMs in Western pleasure and trail, and amassed 121 total points: 61 Western pleasure, 21 halter, 18 trail, seven Western riding and three reining. At halter, he earned four grands and four reserves.

Bred by Charles Parker, Dual Blue Eyes was sold as a 2-year-old to Roger Tannery of McKinney, Texas. Tannery showed the good-looking stallion to his APHA Championship, then, in July of 1987, sold him to Bill Benning of Beaumont, Texas.

In January of 1988, the then-7-year-old stallion was sold to Johannes Orgeldinger of Germany. Orgeldinger finished "Blue Eyes' " ROM in trail

Blazing Image, a 1980 sorrel overo stallion by Dual Image and out of What A Lady, was the earner of a Superior Western Pleasure award and six performance ROMs.

Courtesy APHA

Dual Blue Eyes, a 1981 sorrel overo stallion by Dual Image and out of Picotte Rose, was his sire's last top performer. An APHA Champion and Superior Western Pleasure award winner, "Blue Eyes" was ultimately exported to Germany. **Photo by K.C. Montgomery**

in October of that year, before selling the seasoned campaigner to Thomas Hofacker of Germany.

Dual Blue Eyes' last recorded owner was Angela Fuerste of Ahlum, Germany. With what stood to be a promising and productive stateside breeding career severely curtailed by his exportation to Europe, the Dual Image son sired only 33 APHA registered foals and three performers.

Shilohs Spotted Star, a 1996 red roan overo gelding by Dual Blue Eyes and out of Bonnington Shiloh, stands out as one of his era's top European performers. Owned and shown by Heike Strambach of Baumenheim, Germany, in youth competition, "Shiloh" was the 2006 Gold European Champion Western Horsemanship and Hunter Under Saddle horse, and the 2006 Silver European Champion in Hunter Under Saddle and Western Pleasure, and the 2006 Bronze European Champion Aged Gelding.

In addition, he was the earner of a Versatility award, a Superior in Western horsemanship, and ROMs in Western pleasure, hunter under saddle, trail, hunt-seat equitation and showmanship at halter. In open and youth competition, he earned 257 total points.

Corporate Image, a 1978 sorrel tobiano gelding by Dual Image and out of Dude's Darling, was his sire's most prolific point earner. All told, he earned two Versatility awards, two APHA Championships, 10 Superior awards, 20 ROMs and 1,891 points.

Photo by Don Shugart

As for Dual Image, the patriarch of the strain, his last two foal crops hit the ground in 1982 and 1983. Numbering 14 and nine, respectively, they produced no performers.

Dual Image passed away in 1982, at the age of 21.

In retrospect, this stallion was one of the Paint Horse breed's first legitimate superstars. With his excellent conformation and flashy markings, he turned a lot of heads and generated a great deal of interest in the new "Sports Model" stock horse registry.

A true triple-threat individual, he displayed AAA speed on the track, champion-caliber conformation in the halter ring and versatile athletic ability in the performance arena. And while displaying his considerable talents on a regular basis, he played an important role in wooing new fans to the Paint Horse breed and its fledgling registry.

All things considered, Dual Image had much to do with projecting a positive Paint persona. He was absolutely the right horse, and he appeared on the scene at absolutely the right time.

Dual Image, shown here as an aged horse, passed away in 1982 at the age of 21.
**Photo by
Don Shugart**

5

CRYSTAL EYE
#2022

A top racehorse in her own right, this loud-colored mare went on to found one of the breed's first great speed lines.

AS NOTED IN the previous chapter, foundation sire Dual Image had two highly accomplished full siblings— Canales Black and Crystal Eye.

Canales Black, despite being out of an overo Paint mare, was registered with AQHA and became a AAA-rated, stakes-winning racehorse.

Crystal Eye found her way into the proper registry, and, as a result, carved out her name as the founding matriarch of one of the Paint Horse breed's first great racing lines.

Born of the Land

Crystal Eye, a 1960 sorrel overo mare by Slow Motion and out of Dangerous Girl, was bred by Armando Canales of Premont, Texas. At an early age, she passed into the hands of the man who

Crystal Eye, a South Texas racehorse of note and matriarch of one of the breed's top speed families.

Courtesy Alfonso Gonzalez

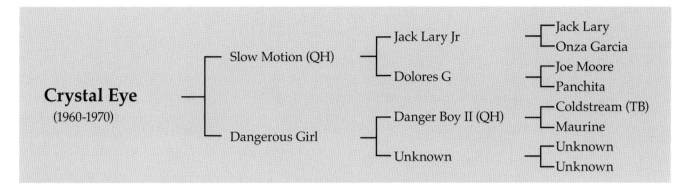

would own her for the rest of her life. Born of the same land, this man and horse were a perfect match.

Again as noted in the previous chapter, Alfonso Gonzales of Palito Blanco, Texas, was born into a family that had called South Texas home for more than two centuries.

"My ancestors were originally from Spain," he says. "They came from there to Mexico in the late 1600s and to what is now Texas in the late 1700s.

"My grandfather, Ferman Lopez, was the man who did the most to build up the family's land holdings. His ranch was known as Loma Alta, or 'High Hill,' because he built his three-story home upon the property's highest point. From it, he could see all of his land."

Alfonso, Ferman Lopez's great-grandson and a fifth-generation Texan, was born in 1932, in Premont. Like most of his forebears, he was raised to appreciate good horseflesh.

"Grandfather Lopez did all of his farming and ranching with horses," Gonzales says, "and he owned many fine riding horses and racehorses.

"J. M. Canales, another of my relatives, also had good horses. He owned a son of Ott Adams' Little Joe that wasn't too fast but that turned out to be a top sire of working horses. That stallion was known as Old Poco Bueno, and one of his daughters, a mare named Miss Taylor, produced the younger, more-famous Poco Bueno.

"So, I've always been around good horses and have always admired them."

With his deeply rooted ties to both the land and good horses, it was only natural that young Gonzales would eventually search for an opportunity to become involved with both.

After high school and a four-year stint in the military, just such an opening presented itself. Hired by Estephanita Canales, his father's sister, to work on her La Perla ranch near Premont, Gonzales was able to hook up with horses in a new and exciting way.

"Aunt Stephanie's son, Ed, was living on the ranch when I came to work there," Alfonso says. "Ed liked racehorses and had been dabbling in them for a while. Oil had been discovered on La Perla years before, so money was not an issue. Beginning in the late 1950s, Ed began breeding racehorses in earnest, and I began training them."

Lalito Canales (QH), a 1962 sorrel stallion by Danger Boy II and out of Monina by Slow Motion, was one of the first champions for the Canales/ Gonzales team to turn out. Sent to the track, he attained an official AAA rating. Retired to stud, he became a top race sire.

Gonzales served as the La Perla racehorse trainer for more than two decades, and, throughout that time, helped field a competitive string of such runners as Lalito Canales, Canales Dody, Monina 2, Canales Falcon, Canales Fandango, Miss Canales Jet, Canales Darbone, Canales Missy, Canales Tipico and Canales Twist.

At around the same time as Ed and Alfonso were starting up their Quarter racehorse program, Ed's brother Armando was doing the same with a family of spotted sprinters. The two top representatives of this line were Dual Image (see chapter 4) and Crystal Eye.

Sentimiento, a 1965 sorrel overo colt by Bank Bob (QH) and out of Crystal Eye, first went to the tracks as a long yearling. Here he is after winning a 220-yard yearling futurity held Nov. 21, 1966 at Lost Valley Downs, Bandera, Texas.
Courtesy APHA

In the Blink of an Eye

"I bought Dangerous Girl's Paint filly from Armando Canales when she was a weanling," Gonzales says, "and registered her with the APHA when she was 4. I named her Crystal Eye because she had one blue eye.

"By the time I registered her, I had already raced Crystal Eye quite a bit. She was probably the fastest racehorse I ever trained. I matched her against quite a few AAA-rated Quarter Horses, and she won more than she lost.

"On one occasion," he continues, "I was running Crystal Eye at Del Camino Downs in Edinburg, Texas.

I put her in a race against a bunch of Quarter Horses, and she won it.

"The horse that came in second in that race was named Jiggs' Cap Bar, and he was AAA-rated. After the race, 'Cap Bar's' owners came over and offered me $10,000 for Crystal Eye. I turned them down.

"My father got really mad at me. He told me I was nuts to turn down that kind of money for a horse. He was probably right."

As much money as they did offer Gonzalez for Crystal Eye, the owners of Jiggs' Cap Bar might have offered even more if they had realized the mare who took the measure of their

Sentimiento was also match-raced. Here he defeats a Bubba Cascio-trained Quarter Horse in a July 1967 race at Carencro, Louisiana. The rail between the two runners was put there to ensure a fair contest. **Courtesy APHA**

AAA sprinter had already been slowed down by motherhood.

Sentimental Journey

In 1964, Gonzalez had bred Crystal Eye to a Three Bars (TB) grandson named Bank Bob. The cross resulted in a mostly white overo colt who was named after a Gonzalez family member.

"Shortly before Crystal Eye had her first foal," Gonzalez says, "one of my brothers came to visit me. We were sitting around one evening, reminiscing about our childhood. At one point, my brother got very emotional—so much so that we got into an argument and he stalked off to bed.

"When Crystal Eye had her foal a few days later, I decided to name it after my brother. I named the colt, Sentimiento, or 'Sentimental.' "

Like his Paint predecessors, Sentimiento was given the chance to prove himself on the racetrack. And like Texas Paint, Dual Image and Crystal Eye, the colorful stallion proved up to the challenge.

"I first ran Sentimiento when he was a long yearling," Gonzalez says. "Normally, I would not do that, but he was a big colt and I felt he could handle the early work.

"He won one futurity and placed second in another. They were both open to the world, and the second one, which was run in Laredo, Texas, had more than 200 entries.

In this rare historic photo – taken July 30, 1967 – Sentimiento is shown after defeating early APHA show greats Dial A Go Go and Yellow Mount in a 350-yard race at Manor Downs in Manor, Texas. Owner/trainer Alfonso Gonzalez stands at the rear of his champion runner.

Courtesy APHA

"Sentimiento ran second in it, beaten by a nose by a mare that went on to be AAA-rated and the dam of an All-American Futurity winner.

"I raced Sentimiento all over Louisiana and South Texas," he continues. "I always had a lot of fun when I raced in that Louisiana 'Cajun Country.'

"One time, I matched Sentimiento against a Cajun horse. A couple of the Cajuns and I were on our way to the track for the race when I overheard them talking in French about what they were going to do to Sentimiento to mess him up so he'd lose the race.

"They didn't realize that I had learned French years earlier, when I was stationed overseas in the military. I spoke back to them in their own language, telling them that I didn't think they should do that to my horse.

"When they realized that I had understood them, their mouths dropped open and they said, 'Oh, we weren't really going to do any of that stuff. We knew you spoke French, and we were just having a little fun with you.'

"As it turned out, the race was run clean and Sentimiento won it."

After successfully campaigning Sentimiento on the tracks for several years, in May of 1968 Gonzalez sold half-interest in him to the B&B Stud Farm of Baton Rouge, Louisiana. Unfortunately, the promising young stallion died in Louisiana before even covering a mare, and the breed lost what potentially could have been one of its early superstars.

The loss of Sentimiento was a devastating blow to Alfonso Gonzalez' embryonic Paint program. Despite that fact, he continued to move forward with it.

The Dark Horse

"In 1966," Gonzalez says, "I retired Crystal Eye for good. The following year, I bred her to Lalito Canales. In 1968, she produced a sorrel overo colt that I named Slow Danger."

As he had with Sentimiento, Gonzalez broke, trained and ran Slow Danger as a 2-year-old. Having gotten wind that APHA was sponsoring a

National Championship race futurity in Pueblo, Colorado, in the fall of 1970, the South Texas horseman decided to head north with his speedy charge.

"I had never raced in Colorado before," Gonzalez says, "so I didn't know what to expect. When I got there, they weren't going to let me run because Slow Danger didn't have a charted race record.

"I told them I'd come a long way not to run, and they finally told me that if I would make up some sort of chart record for Slow Danger, they'd let me in the race.

"A tobiano stallion by the name of Spoiler was the overwhelming favorite to win the futurity. He was officially AAA-rated and had won five of his seven starts. Nobody up north really knew anything about me or my horse, and I don't think they took me too seriously."

By the end of the futurity finals, a lot of people knew who Gonzalez was, and most of them learned to take both he and his horses seriously.

"Slow Danger was in pretty good racing condition for the futurity," Gonzalez says. "I lined up a catch rider for him and had the guy work him the morning before the race, to get used to him.

Slow Danger, a 1968 sorrel overo stallion by Lalito Canales (QH) and out of Crystal Eye, was the winner of the first APHA National Championship Race —held August 30, 1970, in Pueblo, Colorado.

Photo by George Martin

"We took Slow Danger out and the 'jock' breezed him down the track," Gonzales recalls. "After he was finished, he rode up to me and said, 'You might as well leave this horse in the barn. He's not fast enough to beat anybody.'

"Well, that guy wasn't carrying a bat, so I borrowed one and gave it to him. 'Don't hit the colt with this,' I said. 'Just show it to him and you'll get all the speed you need.'

"He did what I told him and rode up to me again. 'There's not a horse here that can touch him,' was all he said."

In the futurity finals, the jockey's assessment turned out to be quite prophetic. Breaking alertly in the 350-yard race, Slow Danger led from wire to wire, defeating Spoiler and a full field of spotted sprinters by a minimum of two lengths. It would be his only official start of the year.

Back in South Texas, with one National Champion Paint racehorse to his credit, Gonzalez set his sights on fielding another.

Party On

"I had rebred Crystal Eye to Lalito Canales in 1968," he said. "In 1969, she had a loud-colored overo filly that looked better at birth than Slow Danger."

Gonzalez named his new filly Party Gal and, like the rest of her family, she proved to be a speed burner.

"I put Party Gal in race training when she was a long yearling," Gonzalez says. "A local horseman came by that fall and talked me into matching her against an older, experienced race mare.

"I probably shouldn't have let the guy bait me into it, but I did. Like Sentimiento, Party Gal was big for her age.

"The day of the race came and we lined the two horses up. Party Gal broke on top and was never headed. She ran that race like a scared jackrabbit. Her ears never did come up. She just flat took off and left that old mare. She won the race going away, by three lengths."

Party Gal, a 1969 sorrel overo full sister to Slow Danger, made it two in a row for Crystal Eye and Alfonso Gonzalez when she won the second edition of the Championship Race.
Courtesy APHA

PARTY GAL
ALFONSO GONZALEZ, OWNER   BILL MAHER, TR.
350YDS. :18.65 4 NOV 72 CHARLEY HUNT, U
SHADRACH 2ND   GREY WONDER 3RD
THE APHA NATIONAL FUTURITY TROPHY BY
THE AMERICAN PAINT HORSE ASSN.
CENTENNIAL RACE TRACK

Danger Spots, a 1972 sorrel overo stallion by Slow Danger and out of Canales Missy 2, completed the Crystal Eye "three-peat" when he raced to victory in the 1974 APHA National Championship Race.
Courtesy APHA

In the summer of her 2-year-old year, after being campaigned on a limited basis in South Texas, Party Gal was turned over to Bill Maher of Augusta, Kansas, for training. Hauled by him to Denver, Colorado, for the second edition of the APHA National Futurity, Party Gal responded with a one-length victory over Shadrach and Grey Wonder.

The Alfonso Gonzalez/Crystal Eye record in the National Championship race now stood at two-for-two. And the possibility of a three-peat loomed on the horizon.

Danger Times Two

"Party Gal turned out to be Crystal Eye's last foal," Gonzalez says. "In 1971, though, Ed Canales bred one of his best mares to Slow Danger. Her name was Canales Missy 2, and she was sired by Lalito Canales and out of Canales' Missy by Parr Passum.

"The result of this cross was a colt that had just enough color to get registered. I bought him from Ed as a weanling and registered him as Danger Spots."

In keeping with the formula that had bred success for him with his previous Paint runners, Gonzalez broke and started Danger Spots himself.

After seasoning him as an early 2-year-old on the South Texas tracks, he turned him over to Bill Maher to be readied for the APHA futurity. Back in Pueblo for its fifth installment, the big race took place on August 31, 1974. With a purse of $16,546, it was the richest race in Paint Horse history.

Like his sire and half-sister before him, Danger Spots emerged victorious in the 350-yard sprint, finishing a neck ahead of Tom Mix and Charge Card, and collecting $8,273 for his effort.

A Paint Pair of Import

For both Gonzalez and Crystal Eye, the race turned out to be something of a swan song.

Following the death of both Stephanie and Ed Canales in the mid-1970s, the La Perla racehorse program was dispersed. Gonzales, his wife, Imelda, and their five children relocated to a 70-acre farm just north of the small community of Palito Blanco—a holding that was originally part of Ferman Lopez' Loma Alta estate.

After winning the 1970 APHA Futurity and being named the Champion Running 2-Year-Old, Slow Danger took a year off. Campaigned by Gonzalez as a 4-year-old, he finished second in the Kansas and

Retired to stud after his racing days were over, Slow Danger went on to enjoy a moderately successful career as a speed sire. **Courtesy APHA**

Missouri maturities, and third in the Oklahoma and Texas maturities. From 12 approved starts, he finished with a record of two firsts, six seconds and three thirds. He also achieved a speed index of 86 and earned 30 racing points.

Retired to stud, the Crystal Eye son sired two world champions: Danger Spots and Mr Danger Three, the 1985 Champion Running Stallion and Aged Horse. In addition, he sired such ROM performers as Red Bee Goette, Divijo Danger, King A Danger, Miss Danger Six, Hunka Danger and Skippa Danger.

A halter-point earner himself, Slow Danger was also the sire of Miss Danger Ship, APHA Champion and Superior Halter, and Van Dandy,

Van Dandy, a 1974 palomino overo gelding by Slow Danger and out of Van Alice (QH), was both a race winner and an APHA Champion show horse.
Courtesy APHA

Skipa Charge, a 1986 sorrel overo stallion by Skipa Star Jr. and out of Go Gal Go, was a Slow Danger descendant who carved out a highly successful career as a show horse sire.

**Courtesy
Gloria Bollier**

Youth APHA Champion and the earner of five ROMs and 180 points.

Party Gal was the dam of two foals: Go Gal Go, a 1980 solid sorrel mare by Mr Kid Charge, and My Little Mule, a 1986 sorrel overo mare by Super Swift. Of these two, it was the oldest, solid-colored sister who did the most to keep the line in the limelight.

Bred to Skipa Star Jr, Go Gal Go produced Skipa Charge, a 1986 sorrel overo stallion. A halter-point earner himself, "Charge" contributed to the breed such first- and second-generation Superior halter horses as Rainbos Brite, Skipa Dee Sonny, Dee Skipa Son, Skipa Dee Money, Skipa Dee Sonny Jr, CL Dreamin Of You and CL Dance Til Dawn.

Getting back to the matriarch of the family, Crystal Eye and her line have slowly faded from memory.

Like the legendary South Texas racehorses whose tracks she followed, the spotted speedster had her moment in the sun. As first a performer and then a producer, she made her mark on the landscape and the breed. And both are better off because of it.

Skipa Dee Money, a 2002 chestnut overo stallion by Skipa Charge and out of Fancy Sundee Money (QH), earned an APHA Superior Halter award and was also the 2006 PtHA World Champion Amateur Aged Stallion.

Photo by Jeff Kirkbride

6 PAINTED BREEZE BAR #2144

This classic speed-bred stallion sidestepped an untimely end and went on to found a show and breeding dynasty.

Painted Breeze Bar, a cropout stallion with impeccable breeding, was started on the road to greatness by legendary North Country horseman A.J. "Jack" Campbell. Jack's "37" brand is visible in this unique night shot.

Courtesy APHA

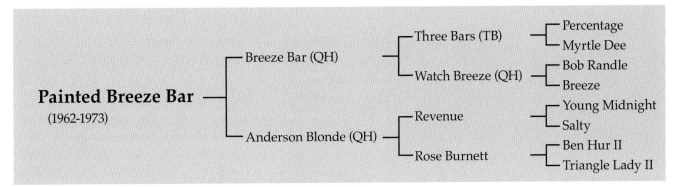

Painted Breeze Bar
(1962-1973)

- Breeze Bar (QH)
  - Three Bars (TB)
    - Percentage
    - Myrtle Dee
  - Watch Breeze (QH)
    - Bob Randle
    - Breeze
- Anderson Blonde (QH)
  - Revenue
    - Young Midnight
    - Salty
  - Rose Burnett
    - Ben Hur II
    - Triangle Lady II

PAINTED BREEZE BAR was bred to take a place among the names of straightaway racing royalty. But that plan was scrapped when the colt came out not as the solid-colored Quarter Horse he was intended to be, but as a loud-colored Paint Horse, instead.

Because of those unwanted excessive white markings, the flashy youngster could easily have been gelded and sold, relegated to a back pasture somewhere, or worse. As luck would have it, however, he was foaled the same year that the American Paint Stock Horse Association (APSHA) was founded, and that single coincidence transformed him from a black sheep to a favored son.

Well-Connected

Painted Breeze Bar, a 1962 palomino overo stallion by Breeze Bar (QH) and out of Anderson Blonde (QH), was bred by George McGinley of Keystone, Nebraska. That the stallion was bred to run was readily apparent.

Breeze Bar was a 1956 chestnut stallion by Three Bars (TB) and out of Watch Breeze by Bob Randle. The 1961 AQHA Champion Quarter Running Stallion, he won 16 races, including the 1960 State Fair Stallion Stakes in Albuquerque, New Mexico, and the 1961 Lightning Bar Stakes and Chicado V Handicap in Los Alamitos, California.

In addition to being endowed with blazing speed, Breeze Bar was also blessed with model conformation and working ability. Taken off the track and turned into a show horse, he earned an AQHA Championship.

Finally, when retired to stud he was the sire of 197 race starters that earned $379,600 and four Superior race awards and 83 ROMs; and 17 show performers that earned three AQHA Championships, three Superior performance awards and 10 ROMs.

Although Breeze Bar was a colorful horse who sported a blazed face and three stockings, it was probably not his genetics that were most responsible for Painted Breeze Bar's loud overo coat pattern. That honor most rightfully belongs to the foundation Paint stallion's dam, Anderson Blond.

Breeze Bar – the sire of Painted Breeze Bar – was the 1961 AQHA Champion Quarter Running Stallion. Once owned by renowned racehorse man Walter Merrick, the good-looking stallion carries Merrick's "14" brand on his left hip.
Courtesy Walter Merrick Estate

Easter Rose, the 1956 AQHA Honor Roll Racehorse, was from the same mare line that produced Painted Breeze Bar.

Courtesy Walter Merrick Estate

A Color-Coded Producer

Anderson Blond, a 1950 palomino mare by Revenue and out of Rose Burnett, was bred by legendary racehorse man Walter Merrick of Cheyenne, Oklahoma. Revenue, a 1942 chestnut stallion by Young Midnight and out of Salty, was Merrick's main herd sire for six years during the mid- to late 1940s, before being sold to Pete Becker of Hyanina, Nebraska.

Rose Burnett, a 1947 palomino mare by Ben Hur II and out of Triangle Lady II, was bred by the Burnett Ranch of Guthrie, Texas, and purchased by Merrick as a yearling for $150. She was, in the renowned horseman's own words, "a light-colored palomino with some small spots on her neck and a lot of roan hairs at the base of her tail."

However she was colored, the Burnett-bred mare was said to have too much "buck in her to make a racehorse" and was placed in the Merrick broodmare band as a 2-year-old. Bred to Revenue in 1949, "Rose" foaled Anderson Blond the following year.

Bred to Monterrey in 1952, Rose produced the redoubtable Easter Rose in 1953. The 1956 AQHA Honor Roll Racehorse, Easter Rose went to the post an amazing 168 times, winning 33 races, finishing second 30 times and third 34 times.

In either 1955 or 1956, Merrick gave Rose Burnett to a local horseman. This man, in turn, sold her to Raymond Drake of Sallisaw, Oklahoma. In 1960, Drake bred the mare to a son of Leo named Sixteen Tons, and in 1961 she foaled Sallisaw Rose, a loud-colored palomino overo and one of the Paint Horse breed's most noteworthy foundation mares (see *More than Color, Vol. 1*).

Getting back to Anderson Blond, she was sold as a 3-year-old to Walter Anderson of Turpin, Oklahoma, for $50. Anderson, who was the owner of the well-known race stallion Snip Raffles, kept the mare for four years before including her in his complete dispersal sale that was held on November 2, 1957.

Ed Honnen of Denver, Colorado,

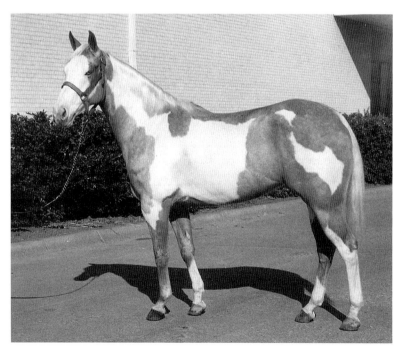

Sallisaw Rose, the great foundation Paint Horse performer and producer, was from the same influential mare line.   **Courtesy Jack Campbell**

then purchased Anderson Blond through the sale. In 1958, while in his ownership, she foaled a cropout palomino overo mare named Yellow Flame, who will be discussed in detail in the following chapter.

Honnen owned "Blond" for less than two years. While a member of his Quincy Farms broodmare band, she produced Mustache, a 1959 sorrel gelding by Jaguar. Then, in September of 1959, the mare was sold to George McGinley of Keystone, Nebraska. In the spring of 1960, she produced Hoot Gibson, a dun gelding by Jaguar.

McGinley, a Sandhills rancher with an eye for speed, promptly hauled Anderson Blond to the court of the AAAT-rated speedster Quick M Silver. This mating resulted in Yokahama Mama, a 1961 sorrel mare who went on to become a racing Register of Merit race qualifier.

That same year, Anderson Blond was transported to Wray, Colorado, to be bred to Breeze Bar. The result of this cross was Painted Breeze Bar, a well-made palomino colt who was all George McGinley and his son Terry had hoped for … and then some.

No Laughing Matter

Painted Breeze Bar wasn't immediately welcomed into the world. In fact, according to Terry McGinley of Chandler, Arizona, he just about didn't stay around long enough to be anything at all.

"We bred Anderson Blond to Breeze Bar the year he was the world's champion running horse," he says, "and she foaled a palomino colt on April Fools Day, 1962. Up to that point, everything was all right. Where the problem came in was, we were in the Quarter Horse business, and the colt came out as loud a colored Paint as you could ever imagine.

"Dad took one look at the colt and turned back to the house. 'Where are

Under Jack Campbell's ownership, Painted Breeze Bar chalked up an enviable early-day show record. Here he is after earning grand champion stallion honors at the 1968 National Western Stock Show, Denver, Colorado.

Photo by Darol Dickinson

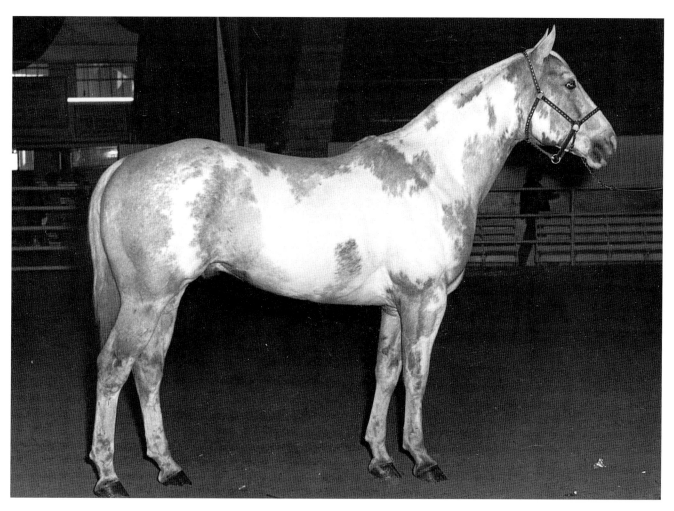

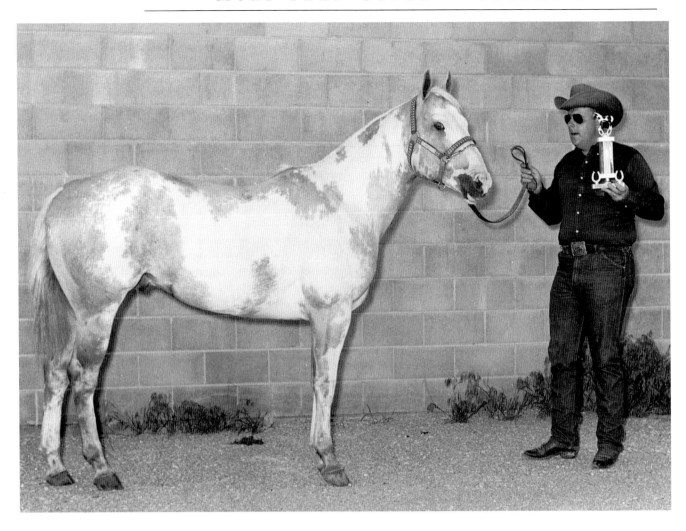

Painted Breeze Bar was shown by Mike Campbell, Jack's son, to the grand champion stallion title at the 1969 Wyoming State Fair.

Courtesy APHA

you going?' I asked. 'To the house to get the gun,' he said. 'I'm going to shoot him.'

"To make a long story short, I convinced dad that we had a lot in the colt and maybe we would be better off seeing if there wasn't some way we could recoup a little of our investment."

The "way" happened along several months later in the form of well known North Country horseman and auctioneer A.J. "Jack" Campbell of Gillette, Wyoming.

"Dad and I had known Jack Campbell for years," Terry McGinley says. "He cried horse sales all over the Mountain and Plains regions, and he would often drive up Highway 26 past our ranch on his way back home from a sale.

"One day in the late summer or early fall of 1962, Jack paid us a visit. He looked at all our horses, like he usually did. When he saw the

palomino Paint colt, he inquired about how he was bred. After he found that out, he asked dad to price him. Dad said he'd take $800 for the colt and all Jack said was, 'Mark him sold.'

"He came and got him after he was weaned, and then went on to do pretty well with him."

From Pauper to Prince

Jack Campbell was, of course, the pioneer Paint Horse breeder who would be forever identified with the Painted Robin line of horses (see *More than Color Vol. 1*). Campbell actually acquired Painted Breeze Bar a year before he happened on Painted Robin. Both stallions did, however, share space at the savvy horseman's 37 Ranch for a number of years.

From the very beginning, Campbell's plans seemed to be to utilize Painted Robin as his main breeding animal and Painted Breeze Bar as his main show horse.

Paint Horse shows were few and far between in the Rocky Mountain region during the breed's formative years. Still, during a four-year show career that began in 1966 and ended in 1969, Painted Breeze Bar managed to earn seven grand championships, one reserve championship and 15 points at halter.

In August of 1966, he won the aged stallion class and was named reserve champion stallion at the Wyoming State Fair in Douglas. In 1967, he took grand champion honors at the Glendive Spring Exposition in Glendive, Montana, and the Wyoming State Fair.

In January of 1968, the big palomino stallion scored his most prestigious show ring victory when judge Jimmie Randals of Montoya, New Mexico, named him the grand champion Paint Horse stallion of the National Western Stock Show in Denver, Colorado, over a star-studded halter lineup that included such early day notables as Baldy Raider, Flying Fawago, Tinky's Spook and Snip Bar.

In June of 1968, Painted Breeze Bar earned grand champion stallion honors in Wheatland, Wyoming, and in August he placed second in a class of 11 aged stallions at the Colorado State Fair in Pueblo. Adding further luster to his already sterling show record, he capped the year off by being named the 1968 Rocky Mountain Paint Horse Association High-Point Halter Stallion.

Miss Bar Light, a 1970 buckskin tobiano mare by Painted Breeze Bar and out of Poco Patch, was a Superior Halter Horse with 58 points to her credit.
Courtesy APHA

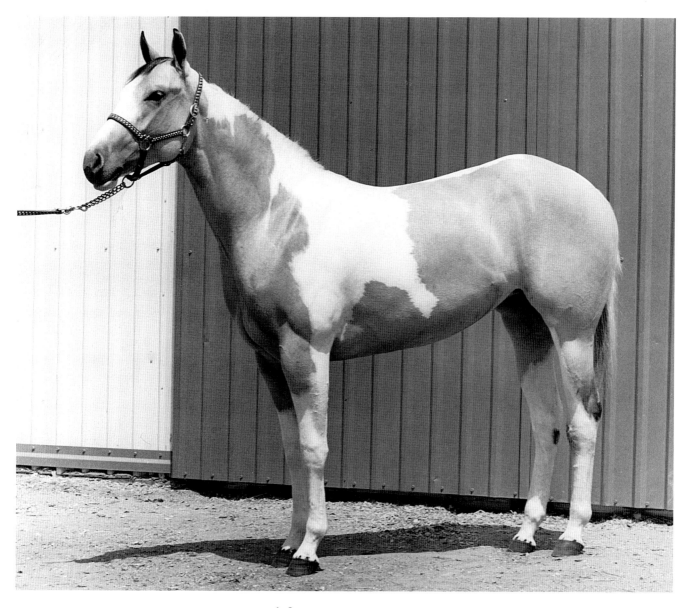

"Breeze Bar's" last foray into the show arena occurred on August 9, 1969, when he was once again named the grand champion stallion at the Wyoming State Fair.

By now, the palomino cropout was generally recognized as one of the region's top show stallions. It was time to find out if he could duplicate that level of accomplishment in the breeding shed.

An Early Start

Painted Breeze Bar actually had an early start to his breeding career when, as a yearling, he bred and settled a Quarter Horse mare named Mill Iron Susie. Painted Bar Jr, a 1964 palomino overo stallion, was the result of this unplanned cross.

In 1965, two planned Painted Breeze Bar foals made their appearance. Donna Bars, a bay tobiano mare, who eventually earned three halter points, and Squirmin' Irma, a blue roan (gray) overo mare out of Red Susie Blue (QH), who became one of the breed's most influential early day matrons.

The following year saw two more Painted Breeze Bar foals hit the ground. Wades Miss B Bar, a 1966 sorrel overo mare out of Miss Miles, was the earner of 12 halter and eight performance points in open and youth competition. Cupid Bar, a 1966 sorrel overo stallion out of Yellow Flame, went on to be an all-time leading sire. He is profiled in the following chapter.

During the years 1967 through 1970, 20 more "Breeze Bars" found their way into the APHA registry. Of these, Pine Breeze, Sue Bar McCue, Miss Bar Light and Breeze Mountain were the most accomplished.

Pine Breeze, a 1967 dun overo stallion out of Miss Pine Bar, was an APHA Champion with 28 halter and 82 performance points to his credit; and Sue Bar McCue, a 1968 sorrel overo mare out of a Matador Mare, was an APHA Champion and the earner of five ROMs, 20 halter and 139 performance points in open and youth competition.

Miss Bar Light, a 1970 palomino tobiano mare out of Poco Patch, earned a Superior award and 58 points at halter. Breeze Mountain, a 1970 buckskin overo gelding out of Ila, was an APHA Champion and the earner of 36 halter and 52 performance points.

In February of 1970, Painted Breeze Bar was sold for the second and final time. Purchased by Lowell Eitle of Willard, Ohio, the powerfully built Three Bars grandson immediately made his presence felt on the Midwestern Paint Horse scene.

Breeze Bar's first Ohio-based foal crop hit the ground in 1971. It numbered five and included among it was the horse who would go on to be his sire's top point-earning offspring.

B Bar Badger, a 1971 buckskin overo gelding out of noted Badger's Lou, was bred by Sam Kinsley of Mt. Sterling, Ohio. Under the ownership of six different people, the versatile performer was the 1977 Reserve National Champion Hunter Under Saddle, earner of one Youth Versatility award; Youth Superiors in showmanship, Western horsemanship and hunter under saddle; nine ROMs and 369 points in open and youth competition.

Tonto Breeze and Tough Breeze—full brothers by Painted Breeze Bar and out of Miss Pepper Lou (QH)—were among the next members of the family to make their mark as performers.

Tonto Breeze, a 1972 sorrel overo stallion, was initially sent to the racetrack. From six starts as a 2- and 3-year-old, he tallied four firsts, two seconds and a respectable 81 speed index. Pulled off the track and made ready for the show ring, he earned 11 halter points, 30 performance points and ROMs in reining and Western pleasure.

Tough Breeze, a 1973 palomino overo stallion, was also initially campaigned on the straightaway track. Sent to the post five times, he earned two firsts, two seconds, one third and a 77 speed index. Trained and conditioned for the show ring, he went on to earn an APHA Supreme Championship, APHA Championship, Superior Halter award, six ROMs, and 168 halter, performance and racing points.

Breeze Mountain, a 1970 buckskin gelding by Painted Breeze Bar and out of Ila, was an APHA Champion and the earner of 36 halter and 52 performance points.
Courtesy APHA

After being sold to Lowell Eitle of Willard, Ohio, in February of 1970, Painted Breeze Bar continued his champion siring ways. Cocoa Breeze Bar, a 1973 buckskin overo mare out of Gypsy Car Bet, was a two-time APHA Champion.
Courtesy APHA

Tough Breeze, a 1973 palomino stallion by Painted Breeze Bar and out of Miss Pepper Lou (QH), achieved the highest honor the Paint show industry had to offer when he earned APHA Supreme Championship #30.
Photo by Lee Locke

was headlined by Sir Barton Breeze, a 1974 sorrel overo stallion out of Sassy Miller Bar (QH) who went on to become an APHA Champion and the earner of 30 halter and 51 performance points.

According to APHA records, Painted Breeze Bar was the sire of 49 foals. Of these, 25 were performers that earned one reserve national championship, one APHA Supreme Championship, one Versatility award, seven APHA Championships, six Superior awards, 44 ROMs and 1,610 points in all divisions combined.

While this is not an overwhelming production record by any means, the Painted Breeze Bar line remains a viable one to this day. Cupid Bar went on to become an all-time leading sire, and Squirmin Erma became the cornerstone matron of a line of award-winning Paint Horses that included Mardelle Dixon, Ratchett and Sockett.

Tough Breeze enjoyed moderate success as a sire. Among his top get were Breeze A Leo, a 1977 palomino gelding out Miss Traveleo (QH), earner of 712 halter and 863 performance points; and Aladar, a 1980 sorrel overo stallion out of Ima Sparkler, earner of 76 halter and 51 performance points.

Painted Breeze Bar's APHA production record reveals him to be the sire of 32 mares, 10 stallions and seven geldings. Subtracting the geldings from the mix, this left only 42 breeding animals to perpetuate the line.

That doesn't seem like very many, but judging from the number of current Painted Breeze Bar descendants that are making their presence felt as champion show and breeding animals, it's turned out to be more than enough.

Cocoa Breeze Bar, a 1973 buckskin overo mare by Painted Breeze Bar and out of Gypsy Car Bet, was yet another of her sire's Midwestern-born performers. Bred by Carl Ross of Mount Gilead, Ohio, she became an APHA Champion, APHA Youth Champion, Superior Youth Barrel Racing award winner and the earner of 45 halter and 309 performance points in open and youth competition.

In September of 1973, Painted Breeze Bar died unexpectedly. His 11th and final foal crop hit the ground in 1974. Numbering only three, it

The versatile Tough Breeze amassed 168 points in 11 events, including jumping.   **Courtesy APHA**

Sir Barton Breeze, a 1974 sorrel overo stallion by Painted Breeze Bar and out of Sassy Miller Bar (QH), was an APHA Champion and his sire's last noteworthy performer.

Courtesy APHA

7

CUPID BAR
#7118

The product of two cropout parents, this line-bred overo founded one of the breed's top families of all-around athletes

Cupid Bar, the "Superior All-Around Sire."
Courtesy APHA

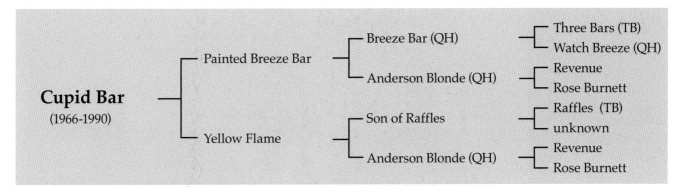

CUPID BAR, A 1966 sorrel overo stallion by Painted Breeze Bar and out of Yellow Flame, may have been born on the front end of APHA's formative years, but the loud-colored stallion was nevertheless the end product of generations of work by horsemen and the breeding of top horses.

A Murky Past

As noted in the previous chapter, Painted Breeze Bar, Cupid Bar's sire, was a speed-bred cropout stallion. Bred by George McGinley of Keystone, Nebraska, Painted Breeze Bar was purchased as a weanling by pioneer Paint Horse breeder Jack Campbell of Gillette, Wyoming. The stallion went on to become a prominent early day show horse and sire.

Yellow Flame, Cupid Bar's dam, was a 1959 palomino mare sired by a son of Raffles and out of Anderson Blond— and therefore a maternal half sister to Painted Breeze Bar.

There is considerable controversy surrounding Yellow Flame's pedigree as recognized by APHA. Also noted in the previous chapter, Anderson Blond was bred by Walter Merrick of Cheyenne, Oklahoma. Acquired by Walter Anderson of Turpin, Oklahoma, in 1953, "Blond" was among the horses auctioned off in Anderson's complete dispersal sale held in Hooker, Oklahoma, on November 2, 1957.

The then-7-year-old mare was listed on page 41 of the sale catalog as: *Lot 49 Dun Mare – Anderson Blond P-43,061 – Foaled 1950 – "Here is a beautiful palomino mare that is bred to run and do things. Her half sister Easter Rose set a new track record at Raton this year. Easter Rose out of Rose Burnett earned more points racing in 1956 than any other Quarter Horse...This*

mare's conformation is right to raise show colts and her breeding is right to raise running colts. Sells bred to Diamond Joe."

The service sire referred to in the sale description was Diamond Joe Anderson, a 1944 sorrel stallion sired by Joe Moore and out of Frankie by Paul Ell. Bred by Bernard Adams of Alice, Texas, "Diamond Joe" was owned at the time of the 1957 sale by W.E. Nickeson of Turpin, Oklahoma.

If Anderson Blond carried her 1958 foal full term, it would have been born on Ed Honnen's renowned Quincy Farms, located on the eastern edge of Denver. Be that as it may, no Anderson Blond foal born in 1958 was ever registered in either AQHA or APHA.

Yellow Flame was the next of Anderson Blond's produce to be accounted for. Registered with APHA in 1966, she is listed as being a 1959 palomino overo mare, bred by Walter Anderson and sired by a "Son of Raffles."

And so begins the tinge of controversy surrounding Cupid Bar.

To begin with, there is the ambiguity of Yellow Flame's sire, as stated. Whenever and wherever the mating that produced Yellow Flame occurred, it would have happened under controlled circumstances in Turpin or Denver. In other words, Ed Honnen and/or Quincy Farms manager Leonard Milligan would have known the exact name of the service sire.

The controversy surrounding Yellow Flame, then, centers around two points of contention.

Given that she is listed as being bred by Walter Anderson, her foaling date would have to be 1958. This theory is substantiated by the fact that Anderson Blond is credited with producing an Ed

After being purchased from Jack Campbell by Earl Jones of Ogden, Utah, Cupid Bar saw some winning chariot racing action.

Courtesy APHA

Honnen-bred foal in 1959—Mustache, a sorrel gelding sired by Jaguar.

Second, if the notes in the 1957 Anderson sale catalog were accurate and no information to the contrary was ever presented to Ed Honnen, then Yellow Flame's sire was not a "Son of Raffles," but was Diamond Joe Anderson.

In any event, all three of the principles involved—Walter Anderson, Ed Honnen and Leonard Milligan—are all long gone. Yellow Flame's correct pedigree, it would appear, is yet to be determined.

A Coy Connection

However Yellow Flame was bred on top, she apparently had enough quality to be kept around until she could be marketed. The wheels for this transaction were set in motion in the spring of 1958, when pioneer Quarter Horse breeder, trainer and exhibitor Bill Coy of Torrington, Wyoming, decided to haul his champion all-around mare down to Denver to be bred to Jaguar.

The resulting foal from this cross was, of course, the renowned AQHA High-Point Halter Stallion and All-Time Leading Sire Coy's Bonanza.

While visiting Quincy Farms, Coy spied Honnen's cropout palomino Paint filly. At some point within the next year, he bought the filly, took her home and gave her to his son B. Joe Coy.

Bill Coy succumbed to cancer in 1974, at the age of 52. His son, who resides in Cody, Wyoming, remembers Yellow Flame well.

"As near as I can recall," he says, "Yellow Flame was a late weanling or an early yearling when Dad brought her home. This was before there was any registry for Paint Horses, but he thought she was a good enough filly to give to me.

"I was pretty young at the time, but I broke her to ride with Dad's help.

" 'Flame' was an average-sized mare; not overpowering in any aspect, but she could do anything. We match-raced her, roped off her and ran barrels on her. She had a lot of speed

Cupid Bar's real worth was not on the track, however; it was as a sire. Cupid's Cody Bar, one of his first sons, was an APHA Supreme Champion and the 1975 National Champion Aged Stallion.

Photo by LeRoy Weathers

and a lot of 'try,' and she kept me and my sisters horseback for years."

In 1963, B. Joe decided to breed Yellow Flame for the first time. With his father being one of the Rocky Mountain region's most-respected pioneer Quarter Horse breeders, selecting a stallion proved to be no problem at all.

"When my dad was in his late twenties and early thirties," B. Joe says, "Charley and Elmer Hepler of Carlsbad, New Mexico, kind of took him under their wing. Beginning in the mid-1940s, the Hepler brothers sold dad some of their best stock. Among them were Little Joe Wrangler, a top son of Joe Hancock; Sparky, an older foundation broodmare; and Jackie McCue and Little Jackie, two of Sparky's best daughters.

"The Hepler horses were an integral part of Dad's foundation breeding program and they did a lot to help both him and the Quarter Horse breed get established in this area."

In the mid-1960s, Bill Coy acquired yet another top Hepler horse. This was Mileaway Hep, a 1956 sorrel stallion sired by Aldeva (TB) and out of Hagle Hep. "Hep" had been lightly raced as a 2- and 3-year-old, and had won the 1958 New Mexico-Bred Futurity at Ruidoso Downs.

In 1963, young B. Joe Coy bred Yellow Flame to Mileaway Hep. Speckaway, a 1964 sorrel overo mare, was the resulting foal. In 1965, B. Joe bred Yellow Flame once more. This time, he decided to take her to the court of Jack Campbell's Painted Breeze Bar.

"My dad and Jack Campbell were close friends for as far back as I can remember," he says. "My earliest recollections of Jack date back to when he lived near Gillette, Wyoming. Later on, though, he moved down to Douglas. That's where the state fair was held every August, and when our family went down there to participate in it, we always stayed at Jack's place on the east edge of town.

"In 1965, I bred Yellow Flame to Painted Breeze Bar and Cupid Bar was the resulting foal."

Up to this point, Yellow Flame and her two foals were not registered. In April of 1966, B. Joe registered Yellow Flame and Speck Away; two years later, he did the same with Cupid Bar.

Cupid's Waggoner, a 1974 sorrel tobiano gelding by Cupid Bar and out of Sue Osage Gill, was an APHA Champion and carried Brad Jones to numerous youth wins.
Courtesy APHA

Cupid's Slave Boy, a 1977 sorrel overo stallion by Cupid Bar and out of Duster's Slave (QH), was one of the first of his sire's get to qualify for Open Versatility and Superior All-Around awards.

**Photo by
Don Shugart**

B. Joe held on to his Painted Breeze Bar colt for two years. During that time, he broke him to ride and had him trained for racing.

"By this time, Dad had started to dabble a little bit in racing," Coy says. "We trained Cupid Bar for racing and did all right with him. We won some local matches and even ran him in the 1968 Rocky Mountain Paint Horse

Cupid's Hanketta, a 1977 sorrel overo mare by Cupid Bar and out of 7C Hank, was likewise an Open Versatility and Superior All-Around award winner. In addition, the talented performer earned reserve national champion titles in halter, reining and western riding.

**Photo by
Don Shugart**

Cupid's Casino, a 1980 full brother to Cupid's Slave Boy, joined his older sibling as an Open Versatility and Superior All-Around award winner.

Courtesy APHA

Futurity that was held during the Colorado State Fair in Pueblo. It was a 250-yard race and we placed fourth in our trial heat and sixth in the finals, three-quarters of a length off the pace. The colt was fast enough, but we did have trouble getting him to run straight."

Cupid Bar's true calling was not to be a racehorse though, it was to be a sire. And the door to success in that realm was opened when the stallion was still a 2-year-old.

"Of course, as close as our two families were, Jack knew all about our Paint Horses," Coy says. "By this

Cupids Honey, a 1980 palomino overo mare by Cupid Bar and out of Honey Rey, was an APHA Champion with 39 halter and 25 performance points to her credit.

Photo by Rich Reimann

time, I had Yellow Flame and her two foals, Speckaway and Cupid Bar, and my sister Judy had a top cropout mare named Mitzy O'lee and one of her foals, Mileaway Mitzy. In the fall of 1968, Jack came up and bought Cupid Bar and Speckaway from me. Then, a couple of years later, he bought Mileaway Mitzy from Judy.

"Of course, Jack just bought Cupid Bar to re-sell, but that was all right with me. He did keep the two mares, though, and they went on to become a couple of his better producers."

Utah Bound

With Painted Robin and Painted Breeze Bar sharing the herd sire duties at Jack Campbell's 37 Ranch, Cupid Bar was purchased to re-sell. In early 1969, Earl Jones of Ogden, Utah, came to the Campbell Ranch in search of a young stallion and left with Cupid Bar.

Jones, who was one of the founding fathers of the Utah Paint Horse Club and an early day APHA director, passed away in December of 1986. His son Kent, who was active in the Paint Horse industry throughout the 1970s and 1980s, still recalls the circumstances surrounding the acquisition of Cupid Bar.

"My dad was a great horseman," Kent says. "He had a good eye for a horse, and he always had good horses around. Initially, he had Quarter Horses, but he always liked something different so he got into Paints.

"In March of 1969, Dad made the trip from Ogden to Jack Campbell's ranch in search of a Paint stallion. Dad took one look at Cupid Bar and decided he would do.

"He had to have seen something in him that most of the rest of us couldn't. Cupid Bar was not a particularly good-looking horse. He was a little rough and you couldn't look at him and think that he was going to be a standout in any particular field.

"He'd proven that he couldn't get it done as a racehorse. We tried to chariot race with him and he did fairly well, but, like Bill and B. Joe Coy, we had trouble getting him to run straight.

"We did show Cupid Bar at halter once, at an Ogden, Utah, show in the

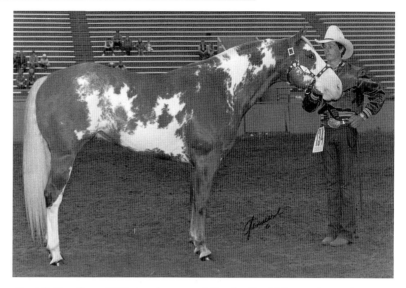

Cupid's Bandit, a 1976 sorrel overo gelding by Cupid Bar and out of Bandit's Sorrel (QH) earned 17 halter and 84 performance points en route to his APHA Championship. **Courtesy APHA**

Here's Cupid's Caballine, a 1980 palomino overo mare by Cupid Bar and out of Cowboy's Blondy (QH). Bred by Clegg Livestock Company of Erda, Utah, "Caballine" was the earner of two APHA Championships. **Courtesy APHA**

Cupid's Slave Girl, a 1976 sorrel mare, was the third member of the Cupid Bar/Duster's Slave "golden cross" to achieve stardom in the show ring.

Photo by Glenncarol

summer of 1969. He placed second that day, but he wasn't a halter horse and everybody knew it.

"As it turned out, though, Dad had the last laugh because Cupid Bar did

go on to make it as a sire—one of the top sires of his day, really."

A Sire for all Seasons

At the time he purchased Cupid Bar, Earl Jones owned several mares, including Twin Valley Tawny, one of the Intermountain region's earliest ApHA Champions and the reserve champion mare of the 1969 Golden Spike International Livestock Show, held in Ogden, Utah.

Beginning in 1969, he bred Cupid Bar to his own mares and a modest number of outside mares. Cupid Bar's first foal crop, numbering eight, hit the ground in 1971. From it came one the stallion's top get and a horse that served as a portent for what was to come.

Cupid's Cody Bar, a 1970 sorrel overo stallion out of Lucy Q. Mark (QH), was campaigned by Jones as a racehorse. "Cody Bar" won one stakes race, placed second in another and achieved an 84 speed index.

Campaigned as a show horse, he was named grand champion stallion at the Colorado State Fair in Pueblo, reserve champion stallion at the Golden Spike International Show and earned his APHA Championship.

Cupid's Lindy J, a 1976 sorrel overo mare by Cupid Bar and out of Wham Bam Phoebe (QH), was the earner of an Open Versatility, APHA Championship, seven Superior awards and 22 ROMs.

Photo by RTrudeau

In June of 1975, Jones sold Cody Bar to Gary Gatsby of Bellvue, Colorado. In August of that year, Gatsby showed the then-5-year-old stallion to honors as the 1975 National Champion Aged Stallion.

Sold to a succession of owners, Cupid's Cody Bar became APHA Supreme Champion #36, a Superior halter horse, and the earner of 104 halter and 97 performance points.

Getting back to Cupid Bar – "Cody Bar's sire – he remained at stud in the Ogden, Utah, area from 1970 through 1973. During this time he firmly established himself as one of the breed's up-and-coming young sires. Among his top performers during this time were:

• Cupid's Holly J, a 1972 sorrel overo mare out of Miss Missie Bars (QH): Open Versatility, Superior All-Around, APHA Champion, 84 halter and 255 performance points.

• Cupid's Waggoner, a 1974 sorrel tobiano gelding out of Sue Osage Gill: APHA Champion.

• Cupid's Mona, a 1974 sorrel tobiano mare out of Mazie Mount: Superior reining, seven halter and 139 performance points.

In short order, the Cupid Bar story took on a decidedly Jones family flavor. Earl Jones began showing the stallion's get at halter and in performance, aided by his son Kent, daughter and son-in-law Connie and Jim DeSimon, and Noel Skinner.

In addition, Earl's grandchildren— Brad Jones, Lori DeSimon and Ricky DeSimon—began showing in both the open and youth divisions.

By the mid-1970s, Jones had tired of standing a stallion, so entered into a partnership with J. Bruce Clegg, owner of Clegg Livestock Company of Erda, Utah.

The Clegg family had been involved in ranching in Tooele County, Utah, for generations and was well known for its top line of ranch horses.

Beginning in 1974, Cupid Bar spent his springs and summers running with a band of Clegg-owned mares sporting such top bloodlines as Seven Bars, J.B. King, Star Duster, Tonto Bars Hank and Tinky Joe. Under the terms of the partnership, Jones and Clegg split the resulting foals right down the middle.

During the Clegg era, which lasted until 1984, Cupid Bar rose to prominence as the Paint Horse breed's Number 1 All-Time Leading Sire of Superior All-Around award winners. Among his top performers were:

• Cupid's King, a 1976 sorrel overo stallion out of Wayward Mitzy (QH): 1986 World Champion Heading, 1987 Reserve National Champion Calf Roping, Open Versatility, APHA Champion, 34 halter and 307 performance points. Sire of Kings Copy Cat, earner of 3,908 points.

• Cupid's Slave Boy, a 1977 sorrel overo stallion out of Duster's Slave: 1981 and 1984 National Champion Heading, 1984 National Champion Heeling, Open Versatility, Superior All-Around, APHA Champion, 52 halter and 544 performance points.

Cupid's Cowgirl, a 1976 palomino overo mare by Cupid Bar and out of Cowboy's Blondie (QH), was yet another Clegg Livestock Company-bred all-around champion. **Photo by Harold Campton**

Cupids Valentine, a 1980 sorrel overo mare by Cupid Bar and out of 7C 23 (QH), was a two-time APHA Champion and the 1986 Amateur Reserve National Champion Goat Tying Horse.
Courtesy APHA

- Cupids Hanketta, a 1977 sorrel overo mare out of 7C Hank 6: 1981 Reserve National Champion Reining, 1982 National Champion Western Riding, 1983 Reserve National Champion Broodmare, Open Versatility, Superior All-Around, APHA Champion, five Superiors, 10 ROMs, 367 halter and 644 performance points.
- Cupids Bar Mount, a 1978 sorrel overo gelding out of 7C 13 (QH): Open Versatility, Superior All-Around, APHA Champion, 96 halter and 234 performance points.
- Cupids Casino, a 1980 sorrel overo stallion out of Duster's Slave (QH): Open Versatility, Superior All-Around, APHA Champion, 79 halter and 333 performance points.
- Cupids Gold Bar, a 1982 palomino overo stallion out of Honey Rey: Open Versatility, Superior All-Around, APHA Champion, 53 halter and 173 performance points.
- Cupids Mindy, a 1983 sorrel overo mare out of 7C Hank 6 (QH): Open

Versatility, Superior All-Around, APHA Champion, 153 halter and 460 performance points.

In addition, Cupid Bar added an impressive array of APHA Champions to his siring resume, among them Cupids Darby, Cupids Sundae, Cupids Classic, Cupids Honey, Cupid's Caballine, Cupid's Valentine, Cupid's Bandit, Cupid's Cowgirl, Cupid's Sizzler, Cupid's Slave Girl, Cupid's Wind Song, Cupid's Holly J and Cupid's Qewpie Doll.

Known as the sire of top youth horses, Cupid Bar also sired five Youth Versatility award winners: Cupid's Cowgirl, Cupid's Lindy J, Cupid's Slave Girl, Cupid's Holly J and Cupid's Qewpie Doll; and nine APHA Youth Champions: Cupids Classic, Cupids Caballine, Cupid's Cowgirl, Cupid's Lindy J, Cupid's Sizzler, Cupid's Holly J, Cupid's Echo Bars and Cupid's Qewpie Doll (2).

And finally, although his siring career mostly preceded the advent of the APHA Amateur era, Cupid

Bar sired three APHA Amateur Champions, including Cupids Gold Bar, Cupids Sundae and Cupids Valentine.

Cupid Bars' glory years as a sire were definitely those in which he stood in Utah, first at Earl Jones' and then at Clegg Livestock.

From 1984 through 1990, the aged stallion stood at three different breeding establishments, those of Jerry Antrim of Lexington, Oklahoma; Ray and Arley Decker of Arlington, Washington; and Circle G Quarter Horses of Fort Morgan, Colorado.

While the Paint Horse breeders in each region brought mares in modest numbers to the venerable sire, he could manage only three final single-digit point earners.

By the fall of 1990, Cupid Bar's health had begun to decline. He suffered from arthritis and was having trouble getting up and down, so the decision was made to have him humanely euthanized.

Cupid Bar's passing signaled the end of an era; not only for his, but for the Paint Horse industry, as well. The age of the all-around horse would soon give way to the age of the specialized horse. Gone would be the days when a horse would be expected to show at halter in the morning and then come back and show in numerous performance classes in the afternoon—rail, cattle and speed among them.

APHA records show Cupid Bar to be the sire of 182 registered foals. Of these, 60 performers earned one World Championship, five National Championships, four Reserve National Championships, one Supreme Championship, 13 Versatility awards, seven Superior All-Around awards, 35 APHA Championships, 54 Superior Event awards, 231 ROMs and 10,191 points in all divisions combined.

Cupid Bar may have come from a cloudy past, and he might have left something to be desired as an individual performer, but as an all-around sire, he was absolutely one of the best.

Cupid Bar and Earl Jones – a pair of Utah Paint pioneers that re-wrote the breed's history
Courtesy the Earl Jones family

8 LEO SAN MAN
#2400

Teamed with a pioneer Paint Horse breeder and three top mares, this early-day sire founded a golden family of champions.

Leo San Man, the founder of a truly golden family of Paints

Courtesy Kaye Kuhn

REBECCA TYLER'S ROLE in the founding of the American Paint Stock Horse Association (APSHA)—how she originated the concept of a breed registry for Paint stock horses, gathered the original 17 members of the association together in a restaurant in Gainesville, Texas, and how she served as the fledgling registry's first secretary—has been well documented.

In addition to being the driving force behind APSHA's formation, however, the savvy horsewoman was also a gifted organizer and motivator. Throughout the association's early years, she called upon these talents to encourage scores of family and friends to join the cause.

Included among Tyler's recruits were two men—Dick Barrett of

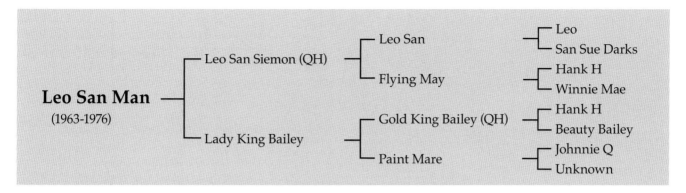

```
                                                         ┌─ Leo
                                          ┌─ Leo San     └─ San Sue Darks
                  ┌─ Leo San Siemon (QH) ─┤
                  │                        └─ Flying May  ┌─ Hank H
Leo San Man ──────┤                                       └─ Winnie Mae
 (1963-1976)      │                        ┌─ Gold King Bailey (QH) ┌─ Hank H
                  └─ Lady King Bailey ─────┤                        └─ Beauty Bailey
                                           └─ Paint Mare  ┌─ Johnnie Q
                                                          └─ Unknown
```

Ryan, Oklahoma, and Dale Lukens of Medicine Lodge, Kansas—who played pivotal roles in the development of a foundation stallion by the name of Leo San Man.

A Family Affair

Dick Barrett of Ryan, Oklahoma—Rebecca's first cousin—became involved with the Paint Horse breed shortly after the association's formal birth in February of 1962. He did so in a big way by locating, acquiring and registering the foundation stallion Pretty Boy #4 and nine foundation mares.

Included among the mares was Lady King Bailey #62, a 1955 dun tobiano by Gold King Bailey and out of a "brown and white mare" by Johnnie Q. Placed into production and bred to a variety of Quarter Horse and Paint stallions, she was the dam of five registered foals.

Of these, Leo San Man was both the first-born and the one who would go on to exert the most positive influence on the Paint Horse breed.

Royally-Bred on Top

Leo San Man, a 1963 dun tobiano, was by Leo San Siemon (QH).

Leo San Siemon was a 1959 sorrel stallion by Leo San and out of Flying May. Leo San, the sire of cutting horse legends Peppy San and Mr San Peppy, was a 1949 sorrel stallion by Leo and out of San Sue Darks. Flying May, an AQHA Champion producer, was a 1951 chestnut mare by Hank H and out of Winnie Mae Tyler.

Leo San Siemon was bred by Rebecca Tyler and conditioned and shown by George Tyler to a Superior Halter award. En route to that honor, the stallion won 40 of the 44 halter classes in which he was entered. Included

among his wins were victories at such prestigious Texas stock shows and fairs as Dallas, Fort Worth, Houston and San Antonio.

Utilized to a limited degree in the Tyler Paint Horse breeding program, Leo San Siemon sired Cherokee War Chief, an APHA Supreme Champion; Lone Wolf, a four-time national champion; and Sage Siemon, a three-time national champion.

On the topside of his pedigree then, Leo San Man traced to such Quarter Horse royalty as Leo, Hank H, King P-234, Zantanon, Traveler, Chief P-5 and Peter McCue.

According to "San Man's" breeder, the bottom side of the Paint stallion's pedigree was full of outstanding horses, as well.

A Powerful Bottom Line

As noted in *More than Color Vol. 1*, chapter 7 (Calico Waggoner), Dick Barrett was a top rodeo competitor and the 1951 and 1952 World Champion

Leo San Siemon (QH), "San Man's" sire, was the earner of a Superior halter horse award.

Courtesy
Western Horseman

Lady King Bailey, Leo San Man's dam, was a direct daughter of famed Quarter Horse sire Gold King Bailey.
Courtesy APHA

All-Around Intercollegiate Cowboy. In addition, he was an astute stockman with a natural eye for a horse.

Having been encouraged by Rebecca Tyler in the spring of 1962 to start up a Paint Horse breeding program of his own, Barrett acquired and registered Lady King Bailey in May of that year.

"As I recall," Barrett says, "I paid George and Rebecca Tyler a visit that spring. I was looking over their mares when I spied a typey dun tobiano mare. She was only around 14.1 hands high, but she was a stout little mare with a lot of muscling and an outstanding head.

"I asked George about her and he said she was a daughter of Gold King Bailey. I remember telling George that, as good as she was, I figured she had to have some sort of breeding behind her.

"Gold King Bailey came from our country; he was bred by the Smith Brothers of Indianola, Oklahoma. They sold him to Guy Ray Rutland of Pawhuska, Oklahoma, and Guy Ray turned him into a top racehorse and sire. And then his daughters went on to make him a leading broodmare sire.

"So I asked George what he wanted for the tobiano mare. He asked me either $600 or $700, I can't remember which, and I bought her. I've always figured that, in order to be a top breeding horse, a stallion should be out of a top mare. Lady King Bailey fit that bill; she was good enough to be a stud's mother.

"And she proved that by producing Leo San Man."

Leo San Man was foaled on May 25, 1963. For the first two years of his life, he was allowed to simply grow up. In April of 1965, he was sold to Dale Lukens of Medicine Lodge, Kansas, for $2,500.

A Horseman and His Mares

Dale Lukens, although relatively new to APHSA, was not new to horses.

Here's the Lukens family and some of their first Paint show horses – daughter Kaye on White Man; Dale and granddaughter Natalie on Snowball, with Poco Snowflake in tow.
Courtesy Kaye Kuhn

A native Kansan, he was born in 1922 on the family farm in Barber County. Beginning at an early age, he helped farm with teams of horses and mules.

In 1940, he married his high school sweetheart, Marjorie Baier of Medicine Lodge. The young couple set up house in the Eagle Township of Barber County and began a family that eventually included a son, Roger, born in 1941, and a daughter, Kaye, born in 1948.

Horses were a mainstay of the Lukens household, with Dale becoming active in saddle club and rodeo calf roping circles in the 1940s, and cutting horse competition in the 1950s. Kaye Lukens also became deeply involved with horses, first as a 4-H and Little Britches Rodeo competitor, and later as her father's horse showing partner.

Paint Horses entered the scene in 1947, when Dale purchased a small tobiano Paint mare of unknown breeding. The mare, "Lady," taught several generations of Lukens children to ride and also became the maternal cornerstone of the Lukens Paint Horse breeding program.

Dale Lukens passed away in December of 1995. His daughter, Kaye Lukens Kuhn, still resides in the area in which she grew up, with her husband, well-known Western artist Earl Kuhn, and three sons, Kelly, Kerry and Kory. She retains vivid memories of the family's early involvement with the Paint Horse breed.

"My father was an outstanding horseman," she says. "He grew up with horses and used them from the time he was a young boy to farm and ranch with.

"And he was a knowledgeable horse breeder. He had an instinctive feel for which crosses would result in superior offspring.

"Our original Paint mare was not that much to look at, and she was a little on the small size. But dad bred her to some pretty good using ranch Quarter Horses owned by his neighbor and friend Ott Beagley, and got a couple of nice mares that we kept. And then he bred those mares to some more good Quarter Horses and got several more good mares.

"And it was these mares, the daughters and granddaughters of old Lady, that put us in the Paint Horse business."

At the time APSHA was founded, Dale Lukens had been breeding tobiano Paint Horses for close to a decade. In 1953, he bred Lady to Buckshot's Pride (QH), a 1948 dun stallion sired by Buckshot McCue and out of Dunn Lady. A product of the legendary Matador Ranch of Vega, Texas, on both sides of his pedigree, "Pride" was a multiple ROM performance sire.

Snowball, a 1954 dun tobiano mare, was the result of this first cross, and she was followed two years later by a full brother, White Man, a 1956 dun tobiano gelding.

However, the Lukens Paint program was almost derailed before it was able to build up any steam when Snowball suffered a life-threatening injury.

"It was during the winter of 1965–66," Kaye Kuhn says. "Snowball had already produced Miss Cooper Dee and Poco Snowflake, and was carrying her first Leo San Man foal when she got a severe wire cut. My brother, Roger, was close to graduating from the Kansas State School of Veterinary Medicine, so dad hauled Snowball up to Manhattan for treatment.

"The vets there treated Snowball for a while, but weren't making much progress. So Roger asked permission

To prove the adaptability of his ranch-bred Paints, and to show his grandchildren how he had lived as a boy, Dale Lukens often broke his ranch and show horses to the harness.

**Courtesy
Kaye Kuhn**

*Dale Lukens' primary
breeding program goal
was to raise "good
working ranch and
performance horses."*
**Courtesy
Kaye Kuhn**

to try his own remedy. He pulled some of the infection out of the leg, mixed it with some antibodies and came up with a remedy.

"He began treating her with the concoction and she started to get better. He treated her at the college for a while, and then dad and I continued the treatments here at home.

"In the end, we saved Snowball and her unborn foal. That foal was Snow Man, one of Leo San Man's first great performers.

"Snowball had seven more foals for us, and Roger graduated from college that spring and went on to start up the vet tech programs at Colby Community College in Colby, Kansas, and Purdue University in West Lafayette, Indiana."

By the summer of 1964, Dale Lukens was aware that a Paint stock horse registry had been founded. In April of that year he registered his first two horses with the association—White Man #1545 and Snowball #1546. Both horses were listed as being sired by Buckshot's Pride and out of an unknown mare.

Then the word went out that the association had scheduled its first national show, to be held at the Kansas State Fairgrounds in Hutchinson, November 27–28, 1964.

Lukens rushed to get the papers on Poco Snowflake, a 1964 dun tobiano mare by Kansas Red (QH) and out of Snowball. At the same time, he registered Lady, the family's original Paint riding mare. Because the name "Lady" was already taken, the cornerstone producer was registered as Susy #1903. (Note: APHA records were never corrected to show that Susy was, in fact, the dam of Snowball and White Man.)

In late November, Dale and Kaye loaded Snowball, White Man and Poco Snowflake and headed for Hutchinson. Kaye was, by this time, a seasoned rodeo and horse show competitor.

"Dad was a big believer in Little Britches Rodeo," she says, "And he was one of the founders of the Medicine Lodge Little Britches Rodeo. I attended my first rodeo in 1960, when I was 12. By the middle 1960s, White Man and I were pretty tough competitors in barrel racing, pole bending and trail. I won the trail at the Little Britches Rodeo Finals in Littleton, Colorado, in 1964 and 1966, and was the 1966 Runner-up Cowgirl.

"Dad and I got in a little trouble with mom over the 1964 National," she continues. "It was held late in November, and we missed the family's Thanksgiving meal. But we wound up doing real well at the show."

Exhibited at the Nationals by Kaye, Poco Snowflake was the Reserve National Champion Weanling Filly and White Man was the National Champion Barrel Racing Horse. Snowball was shown in the cutting by Dale, but failed to win a title.

The following summer, Leo San Man was acquired to head up the rapidly expanding Lukens Paint Horse program.

A Show Horse and Sire

After getting his 2-year-old Paint Horse stallion home in April of 1965, Dale Lukens' first order of business was to test-breed him to a handful of mares.

The stallion's first foal crop, which numbered four, hit the ground in 1966, and from it came Snow Man and Tippy Sue, the first two champions from the "golden cross" of Leo San Man and the Snowball family of mares.

Snowman, a 1966 dun tobiano gelding out of Snowball, became the 1969 Reserve National Champion 3-Year-Old Gelding, the 1970 Reserve National Champion Aged Gelding and the 1971 Reserve National Champion Youth Gelding and Youth Showmanship Horse. In open and youth competition, he earned two APHA Championships, two Superior Halter awards, seven ROMs and 364 points.

Tippy Sue, a 1966 dun tobiano mare out of Miss Cooper Dee, was also a product of the golden cross, with her dam being a 1963 solid sorrel mare by Kansas Rusty (QH) and out of Snowball. Shown alongside her sire during her short lifetime, "Tippy" earned numerous firsts and championships before her untimely death as a 3-year-old.

As far as the show records for Leo San Man and his early get are concerned, APHA records are sketchy.

It is a matter of record that the Dale Lukens-owned stallion earned grand champion stallion honors in Franklin, Nebraska, and Atwood, Kansas, in

Snow Man, a 1966 dun tobiano gelding by Leo San Man and out of Snow Ball, was a three-time reserve national champion at halter.

Photo by Dolcater

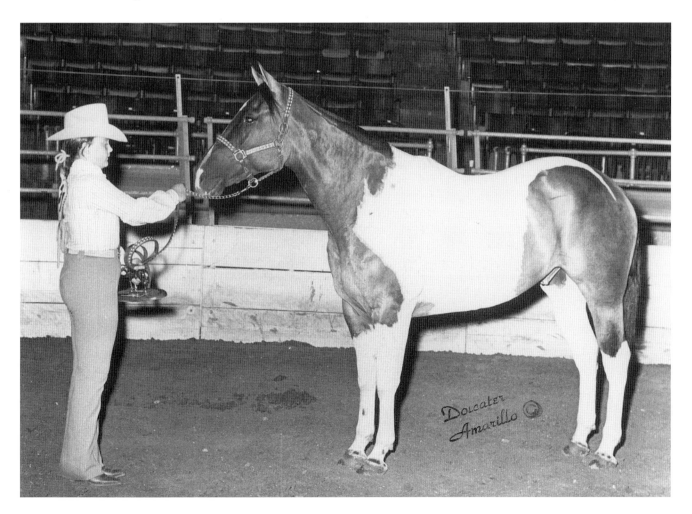

At the 1964 APSHA National Show in Hutchinson, Kansas, Kaye Lukens showed Poco Snowflake to the Reserve National Champion Weanling Filly title.

Courtesy Kaye Kuhn

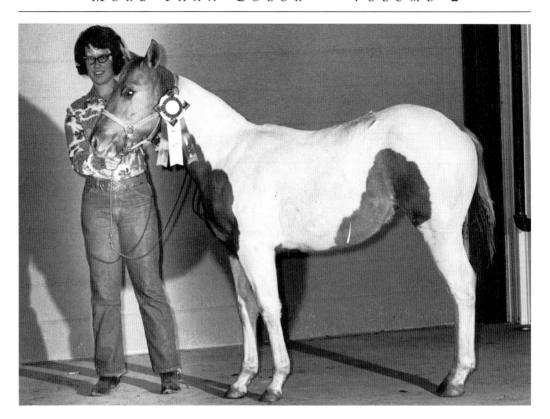

Prissy Sue, a 1969 dun tobiano mare by Leo San Man and out of Miss Cooper Dee, was the winner of the weanling halter futurity at the World Wide Paint Review in Hutchinson, Kansas.

Courtesy Kaye Kuhn

1967; and McCook, Nebraska, and Grinell, Kansas, in 1968.

Likewise, Tippy Sue earned 1967 grand champion mare honors in Franklin, and won the yearling filly class in Atwood the same year. Half Pint, a 1967 dun tobiano stallion by Leo San Man and out of Poco Snowflake, was named the reserve champion stallion at the Atwood show in 1967 and finished the year as the Kansas Paint Horse Club High-Point Weanling Stallion.

At the 1967 APHA National Show, which was held September 23–24 in Oklahoma City, Oklahoma, Leo San Man was the Reserve National Champion Get of Sire winner and Miss Cooper Dee finished in a two-way tie for Reserve National Champion Produce of Dam honors.

Miss Leo San, a 1967 dun tobiano filly by Leo San Man and out of Snowball, was the National Champion Weanling Filly; Tippy Sue placed third in the yearling filly class and Half Pint finished fifth in the weanling stallion class.

Over a span of six years—from 1966 through 1971—the get of Leo San Man and the Snowball mares established Dale Lukens as one of the industry's leading breeders.

Half Pint, Snowman's three-quarter brother who was gelded as a 2-year-old, became the line's next top performer. Among his many accomplishments were earning two APHA Championships, a Superior Trail award, five ROMs and 225 points.

Still other Leo San Man get out of Snowball and her two daughters became top performers. Among them were:

• Prissy Sue, a 1969 dun tobiano mare out of Miss Cooper Dee—winner of the weanling filly halter futurity at the World Wide Paint Review, held November 1–2, 1969, in Hutchinson. Earner of 38 halter and performance points.

• Missy Ann, a 1969 sorrel tobiano filly out of Poco Snowflake—1973 Reserve National Champion Youth Halter and Western Pleasure, 1974 Reserve National Champion Youth Western Pleasure and Broodmare, 1976

Reserve National Champion Produce of Dam, earner of two APHA Championships, six Superior event awards, eight ROMs and 660 points.

• Snowflake's Girl, a 1970 dun tobiano mare out of Poco Snowflake—1973 Reserve National Champion Youth Western Pleasure; 1974 Reserve National Champion Hunter Under Saddle, Youth Hunter Under Saddle and Youth Mares; earner of one Versatility award; three APHA Championships; five Superior event awards; 10 ROMs and 599 points.

• San Man's Frosty, a 1971 dun tobiano mare out of Poco Snowflake—1975 National Champion Youth Western Horsemanship and Reserve National Champion Youth Mares, one Versatility award, three APHA Championships, eight Superior event awards, 11 ROMs and 952 points.

• San Man's Snowfire, a 1972 dun tobiano mare out of Poco Snowflake—APHA Champion, Superior Western Pleasure award and 127 points.

Miss Leo San, shown here with Kaye Lukens, was the 1967 National Champion Weanling Filly.
Courtesy APHA

Half Pint, a 1967 dun tobiano gelding by Leo San Man and out of Poco Snowflake, was a top open and youth show horse.

Photo by Marge Spence

And Leo San Man's champion get were not all out of the Snowball-bred mares. Among the stallion's other top performers during this era of his life were:

• Miss Sprite Siemon, a 1968 bay tobiano mare out of White Diamond—APHA Champion.
• Miss Lynn, a 1969 sorrel tobiano mare out of Judy Lynn—1976 National Champion Broodmare, 1980 National Champion Produce of Dam, 1976 and 1978 Reserve National Champion Produce of Dam, two APHA Championships, Superior Halter, four ROMs and 171 points.
• Nugetta San, a 1970 buckskin tobiano mare out of Nugget S River (QH)—1976 National Champion Senior Reining, Superior Western Pleasure,

three ROMs and 218 points.
• Leo's Ginger, a 1972 sorrel overo mare out of Flee O Girl (QH)—APHA Youth Champion, Superior Halter, one ROM and 113 points.

By the end of 1971, Dale Lukens and his Leo San Man/Snowball Paint Horses were among the nation's elite.

That year's APHA Leading Sires, Dams and Breeders List saw Leo San Man as the No. 1 Leading Sire of Halter Point Earners (most points won and most point earners), finishing ahead of such top sires as Yellow Mount, Painted Robin, Skippa Streak, Sr. Don Juan, Adios Amigos and Mister J. Bar.

Dale Lukens occupied the No. 1 slot on the 1971 Leading Breeders of Halter Point Earners (most points won), and the quartet of Lukens, Leo San Man, Snowball and Poco Snowflake appeared somewhere on 15 of the remaining 21 lists.

Lukens' success did not go unnoticed and, as a result, it wasn't long before the heart and soul of his Paint breeding program simply became too valuable to hold on to.

A Change in Venue

In the fall of 1970, Darrell and Shirley Bilton of Berrien Springs, Michigan, were in the market for some Paint youth horse prospects for their three children—John, Darla Gene and Mary. Half Pint, the first top performer from the Leo San Man/Poco Snowflake cross, was acquired in September for John.

The Bilton family was so pleased with the gelding's looks and performance potential that they contacted Dale Lukens in Kansas and arranged with him to add some additional prospects of the same breeding to their show string.

And then they acquired the factories.

By the end of 1972, the Biltons and their Double B Ranch were the new home of Leo San Man, Poco Snowflake, Miss Cooper Dee, Half Pint, Prissy Sue, Missy Ann, Snowflake's Girl, San Man's Frosty, Prissy Ann and San Man's Snowfire.

And a new chapter in the Leo San Man story was begun.

"I know it was hard for my father to sell his very best horses," Kaye Kuhn

says. "But the prices he was offered for them were just too good to turn down. And he also knew that the Bilton family was gearing up to make a big splash on the show horse scene and that they would see to it that the horses would have to opportunity to test their mettle against the very best competition that the breed had to offer.

"And dad was ready to slow down a little. He was involved with such ongoing community events such as the Medicine Lodge Peace Treaty Pageant and the Medicine Lodge Riding and Rodeo Club, and such family endeavors as showing off his driving horses and antique horse-drawn farm implements, wagons and buggies. So, he stayed busy even though much of his Paint Horse breeding program had been relocated to Michigan."

Best of Breed

As the headliners of the Double B Ranch's show and breeding operation, Leo San Man, his mares and his get were indeed catapulted onto the national stage. Placed in the hands of ranch manager/trainer C.L. Andrews, the horses and their youthful exhibitors began to carve out impressive show careers.

As noted earlier, Half Pint, Missy Ann, Snowflake's Girl, San Man's Frosty and San Man's Snowfire were all shown to multiple national championships.

A sixth full sibling soon joined them. This was Poco Snowcap, a 1974 dun tobiano mare, who earned 1978 Reserve National Champion Youth Reining honors, two Versatility awards, two APHA Championships, 10 Superior event awards, 25 ROMs and 1,839 points.

Leo San Man earned honors as the Reserve National Champion Get of Sire winner at the 1967 National Show in Oklahoma City, Oklahoma.
Photo by Dolcater

Poco Snowflake was the 1971 and 1973 National Champion Produce of Dam winner, represented by the Leo San Man daughters Missy Sue and Snowflake's Girl.
Photo by George Martin

Snowflake's Girl carried John Bilton to the 1973 Reserve National Championship title in Youth Western Pleasure (14-18).
Photo by George Martin

As a result of the Leo San Man/Poco Snowflake cross, Dale Lukens and his horses remained in the public eye.

On the 1972 APHA Leading Sires, Dams and Breeders Lists, Leo San Man had ascended to the No. 2 position on the Leading Sires of Halter Point Earners 1966–1972 (most points won) and the Leading Sires of APHA Champions 1966–1972.

Poco Snowflake was the No. 1 Leading Dam of Halter Point Earners 1966–1972 (most point earners), and Snowball was the No. 2 Leading Dam of Halter Point Earners 1966–1972 (most points earned).

By 1975, Poco Snowflake was the No. 1 All-Time Leading Dam on four of the five APHA lists, and she was No. 2 on the fifth. Leo San Man occupied the No. 2 or No. 3 position on four of

the six All-Time Leading Sire lists, and held down the No. 4 and 5 slots on the remaining two lists.

Dale Lukens, the originator of the Leo San Man/Snowball line appeared on three of the six All-Time Leading Breeders lists, and Double B Ranch, the unabashed promoter of the same cross, appeared on two of the remaining three lists.

Leo San Man also managed to sire top performers out of other mares. Included among them were:

• Dorleska San, a 1974 black tobiano mare out of Navajo Ann—APHA Champion, Superior Halter, four ROMs and 155 points.

• Dirty Sally, a 1974 dun tobiano mare out of Lazy J Cinnamon—Youth APHA Champion, Superior Youth Mares, four ROMs and 199 points.

- Sophisticated Lady, 1975 brown tobiano mare out of Dana Buck (QH) – APHA Champion.

Prior to the 1976 breeding season, Leo San Man succumbed to a malady that had plagued him for most of his life.

"Back when dad was showing Leo San Man," Kaye Kuhn says, "his goal was to make him an APHA Champion. We knew he was good enough to get his halter points, and he showed a lot of promise in performance. He was blessed with outstanding speed and athletic ability.

"But he suffered with recurring foot problems. We never knew for sure, but dad always suspected that he had been foundered prior to coming to live with us. Dad tried everything to get him sound. He even had Don Baskins, the well-known New Mexico farrier, work on him for more than a year.

"We got him sound enough to ride around the ranch, but he never got to the point where dad thought he would hold up under a lot of training and hauling. And we heard that it was the foot problems that led to his death at the age of 14."

Poco Snowflake—the premiere producer of her era—also succumbed prematurely.

" 'Snowflake' had impaired vision in one eye," Kaye Kuhn says. "One day in late 1975 or early 1976, she and another mare apparently got loose and wandered onto a highway. As we understand it, a vehicle struck and killed her."

The Final Tally

APHA records show Leo San Man to be the sire of 138 registered foals. Of these, 48 performers earned eight National Championships, 16 Reserve National Championships, four Versatility awards, 23 APHA Championships, 38 Superior event awards, 114 ROMs and 6,790 points in all divisions combined.

Of the 6,790 points that the get of Leo San Man earned, the produce of the Dale Lukens-bred trio of mares—Snowball, Poco Snowflake and Miss Cooper Dee—accounted for an amazing 4,974 points.

In addition, all three mares were the recipients of national honors as producers. Snowball was the 1970 Reserve Champion Produce of Dam winner, Miss Cooper Dee was the 1981 National Champion and 1967 Reserve National Champion Produce of Dam winner, and Poco Snowflake was the 1971 and 1973 National Champion Produce of Dam winner.

History records Leo San Man as one of the most influential sires of his era. Much of the credit for his many successes can be attributed to the Lukens family of Medicine Lodge, Kansas, and the Bilton family of Berrien Springs, Michigan.

Some recognition, however, must be reserved for the Leo San Man/Snowball cross. In terms of both coat color and accomplishments, it was truly a golden one.

Darla Bilton showed Missy Ann to the 1973 National Championship in Western Pleasure and the Reserve National Championship in Western Horsemanship. **Photo by George Martin**

9

JOECHIEF BAR
#3658

As the breed's first tobiano APHA Supreme Champion, this race-bred stallion set the standard for generations to come.

Joechief Bar, the race-horse-bred Supreme Champion.
Courtesy APHA

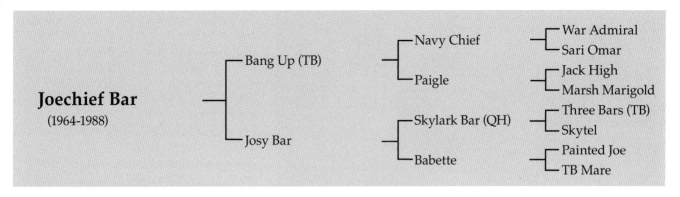

Joechief Bar
(1964-1988)

Bang Up (TB)
— Navy Chief
— War Admiral
— Sari Omar
— Paigle
— Jack High
— Marsh Marigold

Josy Bar
— Skylark Bar (QH)
— Three Bars (TB)
— Skytel
— Babette
— Painted Joe
— TB Mare

ON JANUARY 1, 1969, APHA inaugurated its Supreme Champion award. To earn this most prestigious of all honors, a horse had to earn 70 points—40 at halter and 30 in performance. In addition, all of the points had to be earned in the toughest of competition, "A" shows, and the performance points had to include earning Register of Merit (ROM) certificates in four distinct categories.

Needless to say, the competition to be among the breed's first APHA Supreme Champions was fierce. Within 15 months, three horses had successfully answered the challenge: Snip Bar, Yellow Mount and Joechief Bar.

Snip Bar, a 1966 sorrel overo stallion owned by Bill Maher of Augusta, Kansas, was trained and shown by Joy Rose and Bill James, two of the industry's top professional trainers. Yellow Mount, a 1964 dun overo stallion owned by Stanley Williamson of Iowa Park, Texas, was trained and shown by Vickie Adams and Lanham Riley, another pair of top trainers.

Joechief Bar, the breed's third Supreme Champion, differed from his two predecessors in two key ways. To begin with, he was not an overo; he was a tobiano. Second, he was not handled at any stage of his championship run by a professional. He was trained and shown solely by his owner, Mott Headley Jr. of Port Gibson, Mississippi.

Because of these differences, Joechief Bar and his owner wound up being standard bearers for generations to come. More specifically, they served as living proof that there was a spot for both tobiano Paints and non-professional horsemen and -women in the APHA show world.

Born into Royalty

Joechief Bar, a 1964 chestnut tobiano stallion by Bang Up (TB) and out of Josy Bar, was bred by Paul and Carolyn Crabb of Winfield, Kansas. Born as he was at the dawn of the Paint Horse movement, "Joechief" was nevertheless a member of a royal family.

Bang Up was a 1956 bay stallion by Navy Chief by War Admiral and out of Paigle by Jack High. The sire of only five APHA-registered foals, Bang Up still managed to contribute one Supreme Champion, one National Champion, one year-end champion racehorse and three APHA Champions to the breed.

Josy Bar, Joechief Bar's dam, was a 1955 chestnut tobiano mare by Skylark Bar (QH) by Three Bars (TB) and out of Babette (see *More than Color, Vol. 1*) by Painted Joe.

On the APHA inaugural Leading Dams List (1966–1970), "Josy" headed up all three categories: Leading Dams of Halter Point Earners, Leading Dams of Performance Point Earners and Leading Dams of Register of Merit Qualifiers. In addition to Joechief Bar, she was also the dam of APHA Champion and Superior Halter horse Bon Bon, the 1969 National Champion 3-Year-Old Mare, and APHA Champion King Bee.

At the time of Joechief Bar's birth, the Crabbs were primarily Thoroughbred breeders. At their facility near Winfield, they stood both Bang Up and Mr. Harrison (TB).

Carolyn Crabb had a fondness for Paint Horses, however, and that fondness eventually led her to acquire Babette, the renowned early day race

Even as a gangly yearling, Joechief Bar's conformation hinted of the greatness that was to come. **Courtesy APHA**

mare, Babette's two daughters Josy Bar and Jody Bar, and the mare's grand-daughters Sky Bar and Bright Bar.

Beginning in 1963, the Crabbs made the Thoroughbred/Paint crosses that resulted in a trio of spotted superstars—Joechief Bar, Painted Jewel and Powder Charge—who would re-write Paint Horse history.

Tragically, the Crabbs would not reap the full benefits of what they had created. In late 1965, financial difficulties forced them to disperse their horses. Art Beall of Broken Arrow, Oklahoma, took possession of the best of the Paints and wasted little time in brokering them to new owners.

Babette, Josy Bar, Jody Bar and Sky Bar were acquired by Paul Harber of Jenks, Oklahoma; Bright Bar was purchased by Jo-An Soso of Live Oak, California; Painted Jewel wound up in the hands of Bud and Betty Crump of Wynnewood, Oklahoma; Powder Charge went to Cleon Cope of McAlester, Oklahoma; and Joechief Bar went to Mott Headley Jr. of Port Gibson, Mississippi.

As a mature horse, the stallion's structural correctness and over-all balance was good enough to garner 11 grands, three reserves and 32 points at halter.
Photo by Marge Spence

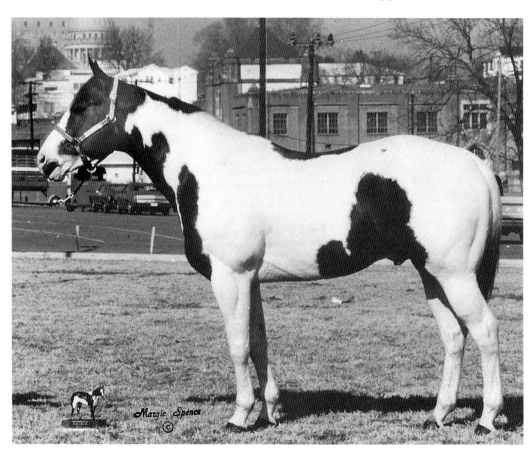

Southern Bound

The relocation of Joechief Bar from the Osage Country of northeastern Oklahoma to the River Delta Country of southeastern Mississippi was originally slated to be a group effort.

In early 1966, word had reached a group of Mississippi Paint Horse fanciers that Art Beall had some fancy young stud prospects for sale. After some back-and-forth negotiating, the group decided to purchase Joechief Bar, then a 2-year-old, and syndicate him.

For various reasons, however, the final arrangements for a multiple-owner transfer were never finalized. Instead, Joechief wound up being sold and transferred on April 11, 1966, to a single new owner—16-year-old Mott Headley Jr. of Port Gibson, Mississippi.

The Headley family encompassed three generations of Mississippi farmers and ranchers. Far from being newcomers to the breed,

family members could trace their involvement with "spotted Indian ponies" to the late 1890s. Mott Headley Sr. was the Magnolia State's first APHA director and went on to be elected APHA president in 1973.

But in April of 1966, the Headleys were simply in the process of putting together an APHA-registered Paint Horse program. As their first sire, they chose Joechief Bar. It proved to be a wise choice.

From the very beginning, Joechief was slated to be young Mott's responsibility. It was he who broke and trained the 3-year-old, and it was he who began showing the promising Paint.

The duo's first foray in the world of Paint competition came in October of 1966, at the National Show in Baton Rouge, Louisiana. There, Joechief Bar placed third in the highly competitive 2-year-old stallion class, behind Yellow Mount and Skippa Streak, but

Shown at the 1970 Dixie National in Jackson, Mississippi, "Joechief" helped owner/trainer Mott Headley Jr. earn the trophy saddle for being the High Point Adult Exhibitor.

Photo by Marge Spence

On March 17, 1971, Joechief Bar became the breed's third Supreme Champion.

Photo by Marge Spence

ahead of J Bar Flash, J Bar Junior and Hy Diamond Bailey.

Shortly after the National Show, Joechief was sent to Oklahoma for race training. The classically speed-bred stallion went to the post twice, winning one race and going unplaced in the other.

Throughout the spring and summer of 1967, the younger Headley continued to school Joechief in a variety of performance disciplines. Exhibited at Alexandria, Louisiana, on August 12, the stallion earned multiple honors as the grand champion stallion and first-place 3-year-old stallion. Shown in performance, he placed first in the barrel race and pole bending, and second in the junior reining.

Exhibited the next day at Port Gibson, Joechief again placed first in the barrel race and pole bending, and second in the junior reining. His only other outing in 1967 was at the National Show in Oklahoma City, where he finished third at halter behind Yellow Mount and Skippa Streak, and third in the junior reining.

Shown only three times in 1968, Joechief Bar notched halter grand

championships at Port Gibson and Natchez, Mississippi, and a first in a strong junior Western pleasure class at McKinney, Texas. The latter win completed the requirements needed for Joechief to be named APHA Champion #22. At that time, he had earned 14 halter and 17½ performance points

In 1969, the then-5-year-old tobiano was relegated to being mainly a breeding animal. Shown only twice, he added two halter and three performance points to his résumé.

In February of 1970, the inaugural Dixie National Paint Horse Show was held in Jackson, Mississippi. By this time, Joechief Bar and Mott Headley had molded themselves into a highly competitive team. The result was their most impressive showing to date. Shown at halter, Joechief was named grand champion stallion and first-place aged stallion. Brought back in performance, he placed first in a barrel racing class of 18, first in a pole bending class of 15, and fifth in a Western pleasure class of 36.

It was after this strong showing that the decision was made to go after the newly created APHA Supreme Champion title.

"Several people encouraged us to go for the Supreme," Mott Headley Jr. recalls. "But it was difficult for me because, by this time, I had graduated from high school and was attending Mississippi State University at Starkville, 250 miles away. But we decided the goal was an attainable one, so we went after it."

After the Dixie National, Mott Jr. and Joechief Bar headed for a series of "A" shows—at Lafayette, Louisiana, in May; Edwards, Mississippi, in June; Baton Rouge, Louisiana, and Port Gibson, Mississippi, in July; the National Show in Amarillo, Texas, in August; and Shreveport, Louisiana, in October.

Each show yielded points to the seasoned exhibitors and, by the end of the year, all Joechief lacked was his required ROM in a cattle event. Mott Sr. suggested sending the horse to a professional trainer for his remaining points at the end of the 1970 show season, but young Mott refused.

"Joechief and I had gotten all of his points together," Mott Jr. says, "and I felt strongly that we should stick together and finish the championship off ourselves.

"So, I took Joechief to the roping chutes and schooled him on some cattle. I'd kind of grown up with ropes and cattle, and Joechief and I had done a lot of cattle work around the ranch over the years, so it didn't turn out to be all that difficult to bring him up to speed."

Exhibited in calf roping at two shows, Joechief failed to earn any points. Exhibited in working cow horse, though, the results were far better. So much better that, on March 28, 1971, in Roswell, Georgia, the then-7-year-old stallion finished off his ROM in working cow horse and completed all of the requirements needed to earn honors as the third APHA Supreme Champion.

As frosting on the cake, Joechief was the first horse in the five-and-one-half year history of the APHA performance department to win an ROM in working cow horse. By the time it was all over, the versatile performer had attended 13 "A" shows and amassed 32 halter and 65 performance points. In addition, he earned Register of Merits in barrel racing, Western pleasure, working cow horse, pole bending and reining.

After such a stellar show ring career, the next challenge for the Mississippi marvel was to prove that he could achieve a similar level of success in the breeding shed.

A Southern Sire of Note

Joechief Bar's first test foal crop hit the ground in 1968. It numbered only four and included two point earners. Joe's Star Snip, a dun tobiano stallion out of Short Dixie, earned 34 performance points in seven events. Kiowa Girl, a bay tobiano mare out of Dakota, earned two halter points.

Joechief's next foal crop numbered nine and included two APHA Champion show horses: Joechief's Image, a sorrel tobiano stallion out of Charro's Doll; and Joechief Bar Jr, a 1969 bay tobiano gelding out of Gypsy Moore.

Joechief's Image, a 1969 sorrel tobiano stallion by Joechief Bar and out of Charro's Doll, was his sire's first APHA Champion.
Courtesy APHA

From this point on, the foal crops got larger and the champions more numerous.

APHA records reveal that Joechief Bar sired a total of 272 registered foals. Of these, 98 were performers that earned two national championships, one world championship, two reserve national championships, one Youth Versatility award, 12 APHA Championships, 14 Superior awards, 92 ROMs and 3,560 points in all show divisions combined. In addition, the speed-bred stallion also sired six race starters that earned 54 racing points and $11,820.

Among the stallion's top performers was a quartet of national or world champions: Vaquero Bar, Chief Dakota Bars, Can-Ya-Beat-Er and Chief's Moore Bars.

Vaquero Bar, a 1970 sorrel tobiano gelding out of Charro's Doll, was the 1975 Youth English Equitation Reserve National Champion; while Chief Dakota Bars, a 1971 sorrel tobiano stallion out of Dakota, was the 1974 National Champion 3-Year-Old Stallion and Junior Calf Roping Horse, an APHA Champion and the earner of a Superior Western Pleasure award.

Can-Ya-Beat-Er, a 1973 bay tobiano mare out of Geddes Twist (QH), was the 1978 Reserve National Champion Broodmare, an APHA Champion and the earner of Superior Halter and Trail awards. Chief's Moore Bars, a 1971 red roan tobiano out of Gypsy Moore, was the 1988 Youth World Champion Working Hunter, a Youth Versatility award winner and the earner of a Superior Youth Hunter Hack award.

Known throughout his own show career as a "good-looking" performance horse, Joechief Bar

consistently sired in his own image. Among his remaining performers were three who earned both APHA Championships and Superior Halter awards: Joe's Pat Hand, a 1975 sorrel tobiano stallion out of Honey Bee Pink (QH); Little Joey B, a 1976 buckskin tobiano gelding out of Snow Moore; and Luscious Lil, a 1976 sorrel tobiano mare out of Kings Golden Glo (QH).

In addition, Seventh Heaven, a 1979 sorrel tobiano mare by Joechief Bar and out of Nance's Best, earned both an APHA Championship and a Superior Western Pleasure award.

Four more of Joechief's get qualified as APHA Champions. They were: So-Big-Cody, a 1973 sorrel tobiano stallion out of Well I'll Be Durn; The Magnolia Miss, a 1974 sorrel tobiano mare out of Geddes Twist (QH); KMR Magic Bar, a 1976 sorrel tobiano mare out of Magic Mount; and Squaw Baby Brock, a 1978 chestnut overo mare out of Mistippee Bars.

And, finally, four of the Supreme Champion's get earned Superior awards. They were Joe Snow—halter, Prissy Jean—trail, Bar's Ko Ko Boy—trail and Chiefs Casanova—Western pleasure.

As a final touch to his superlative siring record, Joechief Bar added a national title to his own record by being named the 1976 Reserve National Champion in the Get of Sire class.

High-Speed Connection

As noted earlier, Joechief Bar even managed to sire some racehorses. Olympia Joe, a 1977 sorrel tobiano stallion out of Olympia Babe, was by far the most accomplished.

Sent to the post 13 times, "Joe" finished first eight times, second twice and third twice. He achieved a speed index (S.I.) of 96, won the Spring Paint Horse Derby and the PSBA Derby, and earned $11,661.

Retired to stud, Olympia Joe proved to be an outstanding sire of straightaway speed. From 190 starters, he sired four world champions, 13 stakes winners, 54 winners, eight Superior award winners, 56 ROM qualifiers and the earners of 1,844 racing points and $674,943.

Joechief Bar Jr, a 1969 bay tobiano stallion by Joechief Bar and out of Gypsy Moore, was an APHA Champion with a Superior in Western Pleasure. Here, he carries Edith Shoemaker to a first in the jr. western pleasure class at the Fort Worth Stock Show. **Photo by Don Shugart**

At the 1976 APHA National Show in Baton Rouge, Louisiana, Joechief Bar earned honors as the Reserve Champion Get of Sire winner.
Courtesy APHA

Olympia Joe, a 1977 sorrel tobiano by Joechief Bar and out of Olympia Babe (QH), was a top racehorse and sire.
Courtesy APHA

Among his most durable performers were:

- Bow And Arrow, a 1984 sorrel tobiano gelding out of Miss Yellow Arrow (QH)—1987 Champion Running 3-Year-Old Gelding; 1988 Champion Running Aged Horse and Champion Running Aged Gelding; S.I. 100; $53,302; six stakes wins.
- Simba Bar Joe, a 1986 sorrel tobiano stallion out of Simba Bars (QH)—1989 Champion Running 3-Year-Old Gelding; S.I. 99; $35,606; one stakes win.

- Olympic Dancer, a 1990 bay tobiano gelding out of Sleepy Dancer—1992 Champion Running 2-Year-Old Gelding; S.I. 93; $47,710; two stakes wins.
- Joe Mammy, a 1988 sorrel tobiano gelding out of Easy Dozen (QH)—1991 Champion Running 3-Year-Old Gelding; S.I. 90; $15,506.
- Bit O Olympia, a 1983 sorrel tobiano stallion out of Bit O-Easter (QH)—S.I. 94, $66,270; three stakes wins.
- Bright Flo Jo, a 1988 sorrel tobiano mare out of Lady Bright Win—S.I.

BOW AND ARROW

BONNIE HUNT/MELBA TALIAFERRO OWNERS   JOREEDA JET 2ND
6 Blue Ribbon Downs MIKE RALIAFERRO TRAINER   10-29-88   EASILY SMASHED 3RD
   SALLISAW OKLAHOMA MARK MOORE UP   440 YDS   TIME :22.09
                       A.P.H.A. NATIONAL CHAMPIONSHIP MATURITY Photo by: Gene WILSON & Associates © 1988
                                                                            POND CREEK, OK 73766

Bow And Arrow, a 1984 sorrel tobiano gelding by Olympia Joe and out of Miss Yellow Arrow (QH), was the 1987 Champion Running 3-Year-Old Gelding, 1988 Champion Running Aged Horse and Champion Running Aged Gelding. **Courtesy APHA**

90; $42,691; one stakes win.

• Easyanajoe, a 1985 sorrel tobiano mare out of Easyana—S.I. 90, $40,602; one stakes win.

And like his famous sire, Olympia Joe managed to cross over and contribute such world-class performance horses as Slide A Way Sally and Pick A Winner to the breed.

Slide A Way Sally, a 1992 sorrel tobiano mare out of Spice N Ice, was bred by David Luckett of Brandon, Mississippi, and is owned by Shelton Headley of Port Gibson. Shown in open, amateur and youth competition, the Joechief Bar granddaughter has earned an amazing 11 world championships and six reserve world championships in barrel racing, stake racing and pole bending. In addition, the talented arena speedster has earned seven Superior awards, 12 ROMs and 1,417 performance points in all divisions combined.

Pick A Winner, a 1989 sorrel tovero gelding out of Win A Bunny, was bred and is owned by Peggy Cummings of Sedalia, Colorado. Shown in amateur competition, he was the 1996, 1998 and 1999 Amateur Reserve World Champion Working Cow Horse. In addition, he has earned a Superior award in Amateur Working Cow Horse, six ROMs in working

cow horse and reining, and 167 performance points in all divisions combined.

Getting back to Joechief Bar, the patriarch of the clan, his last three foal crops hit the ground in 1987, 1988 and 1989. Numbering three, three and one, respectively, they contributed one final performer to their sire's production resume.

Miss Cowboys Jet, a 1987 sorrel overo mare out of Cowboy's Miss Jet, was the earner of 42 points—six in trail; and 36 in youth halter, showmanship, Western pleasure, hunter under saddle, hunt-seat equitation, Western horsemanship, showmanship at halter and trail.

In 1989, the last of the first generation Joechief Bars made her appearance. This was Diamond Josy, a 1989 solid sorrel mare out of Diamond Rosalee (QH). Bred by Mott Headley, "Josy" lived out her life on the ranch where she and so many of her half-siblings were born.

For more than a quarter of a century, Joechief Bar and the Mott Headley family were an integral part of the pioneering Paint Horse story. They remain so to this day through the successive generations of both families, who still contribute to the lore of the breed.

Joe Mammy, a 1988 sorrel tobiano gelding by Olympia Joe and out of Easy Dozen (QH), was the 1991 Champion Running 3-Year-Old Gelding.
Courtesy APHA

10 SKY BUG BINGO
#22,000

As both a show horse and sire, this "Generation Next" champion was a standard-bearer for one of the breed's top tobiano lines.

Sky Bug Bingo, a Supreme Champion show horse and sire.
Courtesy Cindy Gattis

THE BABETTE FAMILY of tobiano Paint Horse champions found its way into the APHA registry in the mid-1960s and, by the end of the decade, was one of the best known in all the land.

It was a line of race and show horses that had been developed by three top breeders—Ralph Gardiner of Ashland, Kansas; Paul and Carolyn Crabb of Winfield, Kansas; and Paul Harber of Jenks, Oklahoma—and it included such early day great race and show performers as Painted Jewel, Joechief Bar (see chapter 9), Powder Charge, By Jingo, Bright Bar, Bon Bon, King Bee and Million Heir.

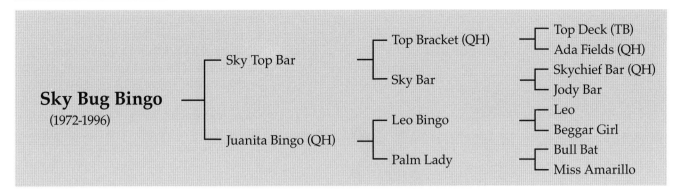

Sky Bug Bingo (1972-1996)
- Sky Top Bar
  - Top Bracket (QH)
    - Top Deck (TB)
    - Ada Fields (QH)
  - Sky Bar
    - Skychief Bar (QH)
    - Jody Bar
- Juanita Bingo (QH)
  - Leo Bingo
    - Leo
    - Beggar Girl
  - Palm Lady
    - Bull Bat
    - Miss Amarillo

In the early 1970s, a new member of the clan was foaled who would add considerable luster to the line. His name was Sky Bug Bingo.

Bred to be Good

Sky Bug Bingo, a 1972 chestnut tobiano stallion by Sky Top Bar and out of Juanita Bingo (QH), was bred by H. M. Roark of Vega, Texas. From a genetic standpoint, he was nothing short of a powerhouse.

Sky Top Bar was a 1967 bay tobiano stallion by Top Bracket (QH) and out of Sky Bar. Top Bracket was a AAA-rated racehorse by Top Deck (TB), an all-time leading racehorse sire, and out of Ada Fields, a multiple AAA producer. Sky Bar was a 1961 chestnut tobiano mare by Skychief Bar (QH) and out of Jody Bar, the daughter of Skylark Bar (QH) and Babette.

Skychief Bar and Skylark Bar, both of whom were bred by Ralph Gardiner, were full brothers by Three Bars (TB) and out of Skytel. Three Bars remains, to this day, the most influential sire in the history of the Western horse, and Skytel was a AAA and AQHA Champion producer. Babette was by Painted Joe and out of a Thoroughbred mare of unrecorded breeding.

On the top half of his pedigree, then, Sky Bug Bingo was a masterful blend of three of the greatest race sires of all time—Top Deck, Three Bars and Painted Joe.

And the bottom side of the genetic equation was just as potent.

Juanita Bingo was a 1968 chestnut mare by Leo Bingo and out of Palm Lady. Leo Bingo was a AAA AQHA Champion sired by Leo, an all-time leading broodmare sire, and out of

Beggar Girl, a multiple AAA producer. Palm Lady, a My Texas Dandy-bred mare, was likewise a race Register of Merit producer.

The Line Lengthens

As noted in the previous chapter, pioneer Paint Horse breeder Paul Harber, then of Jenks, Oklahoma, acquired Babette, Jody Bar, Josy Bar and Sky Bar in the mid-1960s.

Sky Bar, the youngest member of the quartet, became a top producer and the dam of four great fourth-generation Babette descendants—Powder Charge, By Jingo, Sky Top Bar and Million Heir.

Powder Charge, a 1965 chestnut tobiano stallion by Mr. Harrison (TB), was the winner of the 1967 Oklahoma, Kansas and Rocky Mountain

Sky Top Bar, "Bingo's" sire, was the winner of the 1967 Oklahoma Paint Horse Maturity.
Courtesy APHA

Sky Bug Bingo, shown here with Cindy (Nelson) Gattis, was an ROM western pleasure horse.
Courtesy Cindy Gattis

bred horses to be foaled on Harber's Blue Chip Farms. Sold to Ray Graves of Duncan, Oklahoma, as a yearling, he became a stakes-winning racehorse and a highly successful race and show sire.

On the tracks, his get included the earners of two world championships, 21 ROMs, two Superiors and $194,498. Sky Jet, his top straightaway performer, was the 1983 World Champion Running Paint Horse and Champion Running 3-Year-Old. The winner of seven stakes races, he achieved a 101 speed index and earned $43,392.

In the show arena, Sky Top Bar's get earned five national championships, one world championship, one Supreme Championship, three Versatility awards, six APHA Championships, 13 Superior awards, 79 ROMs and 2,862 performance points in all divisions combined. Lady Sky Top, his top show performer, earned two Versatility awards, three APHA Championships (one Open and two Youth), six Superior awards, 19 ROMs and 957 points in all divisions combined.

And Sky Top Bar also sired Sky Bug Bingo.

The Early Years

Ray Graves remembers both Bud Roark and Sky Bug Bingo very clearly.

"Bud was a farm implement dealer," Graves says. "He passed away several years ago, but during his heyday he had quite a nice set of horses and bred some outstanding Paints.

"Bud liked running blood, and during the 1960s and 1970s had some well-bred granddaughters of Leo and Three Bars. Juanita Bingo was one of the Leo-bred mares and I remember her as a nice, well-balanced mare that had that 'Leo look' about her.

"He bred 'Juanita' to Sky Top Bar in 1971 and then brought her back and re-bred her the following year.

"When I laid eyes on Sky Bug Bingo as a foal, I knew he was going to be a good one. So I bought half-interest in him when he was a yearling. The following year, we sent him to the tracks.

futurities. By Jingo, a 1966 chestnut tobiano stallion by Bang Up (TB) was an APHA Champion.

Sky Top Bar, a 1967 bay tobiano stallion by Top Bracket (QH), was the winner of the 1970 Oklahoma Paint Horse Maturity, while Million Heir, a 1969 sorrel tobiano stallion by Three Jets (QH), won the 1971 Kansas, Oklahoma and APHA National Championship futurities and APHA Champion honors, as well.

All four stallions enjoyed successful careers as sires, with their get experiencing success both on the racetrack and in the show arena.

Sky Top Bar, the sire of Sky Bug Bingo, was one of the first Babette-

"Charlie Murrah of Lexington, Oklahoma, broke the colt and trained him for racing," Graves continues. "Charlie schooled him a lot at Apache Downs, a small racetrack located 20 miles north of Lawton. It was a nice track, with an eight-horse starting gate and a surface that you couldn't hardly get a colt hurt on.

"The competition there could get a little tough though. Top racehorse men like Walter Merrick used to test their young horses there, and, on any given race day, you might find yourself in the gates with horses that would go on to be world champions.

"We ran Bingo 10 times as a 2-year-old. He showed some promise to begin with and finished third in the Paint futurity at Midway Downs in Stroud, Oklahoma. Then he suffered some bone chips in his knees and we never could get him right after that. He did achieve a 78 speed index, but I think if we'd handled his recovery a little different, we could have brought him back out and done a little better."

In June of 1975, Roark bought back

Cindy also competed in barrel racing on the big tobiano stallion.

Photo by Roger Graves

With Bill Horn in the saddle, "Bingo" earned an ROM and 16 points in cutting.

Photo by Roger Graves

OKLAHOMA CITY 1984

Sky Lite, a 1977 sorrel tobiano mare by Sky Bug Bingo and out of Rock-A-Lite, was the 1982 National Champion Broodmare.
Photo by Don Shugart

Graves' interest in Bingo. That fall, he turned the then-3-year-old stallion over to Kenneth Switzer of Minco, Oklahoma, to be made ready for a second career as a show horse.

In January of 1976, Switzer showed Bingo to grand champion stallion honors at the San Antonio Livestock Show and the Dixie National Livestock Show in Jackson, Mississippi. At the latter show, the big stallion caught the attention of Tom and Cindy Nelson of Shelbyville, Indiana. The result of this encounter was a third change of ownership for Bingo and a trip for all concerned to the very pinnacle of the Paint Horse show horse world.

Simply Supreme

The Nelsons were, at the time, two of the Paint Horse industry's most promising young professionals. They were fresh off an impressive showing at the 1975 APHA National Show, where they had exhibited five halter horses to National titles, and they were midway through an equally

successful winter stock show run.

Cindy—now married to Don Gattis and living near Sorrento, Florida— remembers the day she got her first look at Sky Bug Bingo.

"Tom and I had gotten married in 1973," she says. "Both he and his dad, Tom Sr., were already involved with Paint Horses, and they just sold their blue roan tobiano stallion Mr. Red Bar to Jerry Antrim of Maroa, Illinois.

"I don't know that we were really looking for a stallion when we happened across Sky Bug, but once we saw him, we both knew we needed to own him. He was tall and elegant, but also very heavily muscled, with the biggest forearms and gaskins that you could imagine. And, remember, this was before the Impressive horses and the HYPP gene took over the halter industry.

"Immediately after getting our first good look at Sky Bug, we hunted up Kenneth Switzer and asked him if the horse was for sale," Cindy continues. "He replied that he probably was, but he'd have to check with the owner to make sure.

"We asked what he thought it would take to buy him, and he replied, '10 or 15 thousand.' Well, we got excited and called Tom's dad. He listened to our description of the stud and said, 'count me in.'

"The next day, we hunted up Switzer again to close the deal. He told us that he'd been a little light on his price estimate and that Mr. Roark wanted $25,000. That came as kind of a shock, but we held an impromptu 'war council' and decided to buy him anyway. It was one of the better decisions that we ever made."

To begin with, the Nelsons decided to continue Sky Bug Bingo's show career, with the ultimate goal of making him a Superior halter horse. Early on in that campaign, they also opted to take a run at some performance events.

"Bingo had so much talent and was so willing," Cindy Gattis says, "that training him for performance just seemed to be the logical thing to do. So, Tom trained and campaigned him in Western pleasure and reining, and Bill Horn of Cable, Ohio, rode him in cutting. By mid-year, Bingo had earned his APHA Championship and had ROMs in Western pleasure and cutting.

"By the end of the year, Bingo had nailed down his Superior Halter

Shady Sam, a 1977 sorrel tobiano stallion by "Bingo" and out of Miss Lynn, earned an Open Versatility, Superior All-Around and APHA Championship.

Photo by Harold Campton

Buggetta, a 1978 red dun tobiano mare by Sky Bug Bingo and out of Nugetta San, was another of her sire's top all-around performers.

Photo by Bob Heidlage

award. Then, after looking over his complete show record, we realized that he only needed three more ROMs to qualify for his Supreme Championship.

"So, Tom went after and got his ROM in reining, I showed him to ROMs in hunter under saddle and barrel racing, and we got the job done."

On July 3, 1977, Bingo was honored as APHA Supreme Champion #27. His final APHA show record reveals him to be the earner of a Superior award, 10 grand championships, seven reserve championships and 52 points at halter. In performance, the talented all-around athlete amassed six ROMs and 81 points: 16 cutting, 15 Western pleasure, 14 hunter under saddle, 13 reining, 12 racing and 11 reining.

All of his show ring goals had been attained and it was now time to see what he could do as a sire.

Like Begets Like

Sky Bug Bingo's first foal, Passum Bug Bingo, hit the ground in 1976. Bred by H. M. Roark, he was not a point earner.

Beginning with the stallion's first Midwestern-born foal crop, however, the point earners came fast and

Here's Bingo's Game Point, a Sky Bug Bingo son and the 1979 Reserve National Champion Yearling Stallion.

Courtesy APHA

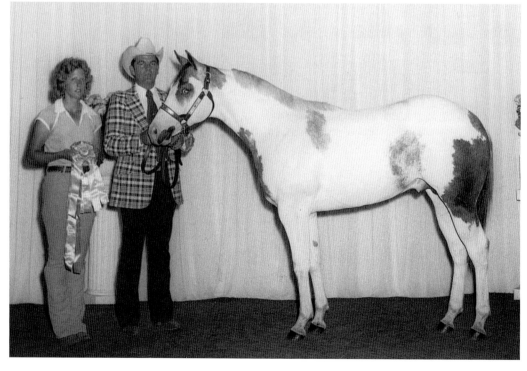

furious. And, before long, there wasn't much doubt in anyone's mind that the Nelsons' young tobiano was going to be a sire.

During the next nine years—from 1977 through 1985—the "Sky Bugs" were a dominant force in APHA shows rings throughout the country. Among the stallion's top performers during this era were:

- Sky Lite, a 1977 sorrel tobiano mare out of Rock-A-Lite—1980 Reserve National Champion 3-Year-Old Mare, 1982 National Champion Broodmare, 1984 Reserve National Champion Broodmare, APHA Champion, Youth Versatility and APHA Youth Champion.
- Shady Sam, a 1977 sorrel tobiano stallion out of Miss Lynn—Open Versatility, Superior All-Around and APHA Champion.
- Miss Sky High, a 1978 bay tobiano mare out of Miss Lynn—APHA Champion, Youth Versatility and APHA Youth Champion.
- Buggetta, a 1978 red dun tobiano mare out of Nugetta San—Open Versatility, APHA Champion, 1983 Youth National Champion Halter and English Equitation, Youth Versatility (2) and APHA Youth Champion.
- Bingo's Game Point, a 1978 gray tobiano stallion out of Jay Cee Lucky (QH)—1979 Reserve National Champion Yearling Stallion and APHA Champion.
- Sky Bugs Lad, a 1979 chestnut tobiano gelding out of Scenic Takela Bars—1986 and 1987 World Champion Sr. Trail; APHA Champion; 1986 Amateur World Champion Trail; 1986 Amateur Reserve National Champion Trail; 1987 Amateur Reserve National Champion Showmanship; 1985 Youth World Champion, English Equitation and Trail; 1985 Youth Reserve World Champion Hunter Under Saddle, Halter, Reining, Showmanship and Western Pleasure; Youth Versatility and APHA Youth Champion (2).
- Skip A Bug, a 1980 sorrel tobiano stallion out of Skip A Zero—1985 Reserve World Champion Jumping, Open Versatility, APHA Champion, 1985 Amateur World Champion Trail, 1989 Amateur National Champion Hunter Hack and 1991 Amateur World Champion Working Hunter.
- Mighty Royal, a 1981 sorrel tobiano gelding out of Hi N' Mighty Miss—1982 National Champion Yearling Gelding, APHA Champion, Youth Versatility and APHA Youth Champion.
- Ima Lou Too, a 1982 sorrel overo mare out of San Juan Lou—1988 Reserve National Champion Calf Roping.
- Popa Smurf, a 1983 sorrel overo gelding out of Lea Sorrel Mac (QH)—APHA Champion, 1990 World Champion Youth Western Riding, 1991 Reserve World Champion Youth Western Riding and 1992 Reserve World Champion Youth Western Riding.

Sky Bug's Lad, a 1979 chestnut tobiano stallion out of Jay Cee Lucky (QH), was a multiple world champion in Amateur and Youth competition.

Photo by Bob Heidlage

At the 1980 National Show in Oklahoma City, Sky Bug Bingo placed first and second in the Get of Sire class. (above photo and below photo) **Courtesy APHA**

In July of 1984, Sky Bug Bingo was transferred solely into Tom Nelson's name. Two months later, the stallion was sold to Doug and Vivian Newton of Keller, Texas, and installed as a senior sire at their Rocky Top Ranch.

The Newtons were very familiar with Sky Bug Bingo and his get due to the fact that their daughter Dana had compiled an exemplary youth record on Sky Bugs Lad.

Sky Bug Bingo was warmly received in the Lone Star State, and throughout the remainder of the decade stood to a full book. Among his top performers during this stage of his life were:

- Hug Me Sky Bug, a 1986 bay tobiano gelding out of Hug Me Doc—Superior Bridle Path Hack.
- RT Texas Bug, a 1988 sorrel tobiano gelding out of HF Skip N Lilly—Superior Western Pleasure, Bridle Path Hack and Trail.
- Bingos Sweetdreams, a 1988 red dun tobiano mare out of Patsy Cline—1992 Reserve World Champion Working Cow Horse; 1993 Reserve World Champion Team Penning and 1993 World Champion Working Cow Horse.

At the dawning of the 1990s, Sky Bug's breeding responsibilities were eased. His last three foal crops hit the ground from 1993 through 1995 and numbered two, five and two, respectively.

Kristens Bug Bingo, a 1991 bay tobiano mare out of Howdys Doery (QH), was her sire's last point earner. Bred by Joe and Sandy Ferguson of Lowell, Arkansas, the versatile performer earned 101 points and three ROMs.

APHA records reveal that Sky Bug Bingo sired 255 registered foals. Of these, 104 performers earned seven World Championships, 13 Reserve World Championships, six National Championships, nine Reserve National Championships, 14 Versatility awards, one Superior All-Around award, 29 APHA Championships, 80 Superior event awards, 258 ROMs and 15,230 points in all divisions combined.

1980 OKLAHOMA CITY

Also at the 1980 National, Miss Lynn won the Produce of Dam class with the Sky Bug Bingo get Shady Sam and Miss Sky High.
Courtesy APHA

111

Hit Man, a 1979 chestnut tobiano stallion by Sky Bug Bingo and out of Mien Yucca (QH) was a top show horse and sire in his own right.
Photo by Don Shugart

A number of the Sky Bug sons and daughters became top breeding animals in their own right. Two—Hit Man and Im An Eighty Lady—are worthy of special mention.

Hit Man, a 1979 chestnut tobiano stallion by Sky Bug Bingo and out of Mien Yucca (QH), was bred by Joanne Whitcomb of Oxford, Michigan. Sold to Ron Hooker of Apopka, Florida, he earned an APHA Championship, and Superiors in halter and Western pleasure.

Retired to stud, he sired 44 performers that earned one National Championship, four Reserve World Championships, six Versatility awards, one Superior All-Around award, one Superior Youth Champion, 11 APHA Championships, 42 Superior event awards, 127 ROMs and 6,480 points in all divisions combined.

Im An Eighty Lady, a 1980 sorrel tobiano mare out of Jane's Flit Bar (QH), was bred by Don Lehman of Defiance, Ohio. The earner of 22 halter points, she went on to produce 13 foals and six performers.

Impressive Eighty, a 1988 sorrel tobiano stallion by Eternal Impressive (QH) and out of Im An Eighty Lady, was the 1991 World Champion 3-Year-Old Stallion and the 1992 Amateur Reserve World Champion Aged Stallion. Retired to stud, he also became a top sire.

Sky Bug Bingo, the patriarch of the strain, passed away of natural causes in 1995. One of the top performers and sires of his era, he did his part to ensure that the Babette line of foundation Paint Horses remained a driving force within the industry to this very day.

VR Master Bug, a maternal grandson of Sky Bug Bingo, was likewise a top show horse and sire.
Courtesy APHA

Here's Impressive Eighty, a 1988 sorrel tobiano stallion by Eternal Impressive (QH) and out of Im An Eighty Lady. A Sky Bug Bingo grandson, Impressive Eighty was the 1991 World Champion 3-Year-Old Stallion.

Photo by Larry Williams

11 SKIPPA STREAK
#3818

A product of the Rocky Mountain region's most storied program, this stallion went on to become a Lone Star State superstar.

Skippa Streak, a model of color and conformation.
Photo by George Martin

SKIPPA STREAK, A 1964 sorrel tobiano stallion by Skip Hi #8 and out of Cheyenne Lil #2627, was a product of the H. J. "Hank" Wiescamp program of Alamosa, Colorado. Skip Hi was the cornerstone stallion of the Wiescamp Paint Horse breeding program, and his life is chronicled in *More than Color, Vol. 1.*

Cheyenne Lil, "Streak's" dam, was a 1959 sorrel tobiano mare of unknown bloodlines. Bred by the N W Cheyenne Ranch of Cheyenne, Wyoming, she is listed as being sired by a Paint stallion and out of a Thoroughbred mare.

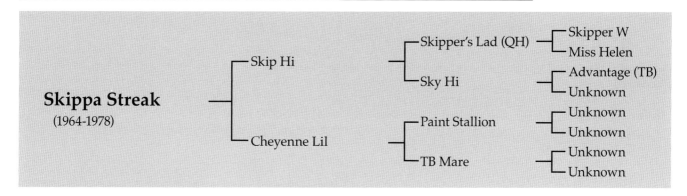

			Skipper's Lad (QH)	Skipper W
				Miss Helen
	Skip Hi		Sky Hi	Advantage (TB)
				Unknown
Skippa Streak (1964-1978)			Paint Stallion	Unknown
				Unknown
	Cheyenne Lil		TB Mare	Unknown
				Unknown

Although Wiescamp owned Cheyenne Lil at the time Skippa Streak was foaled, it was not until Joe Morris of Denver, Colorado, acquired her in the spring of 1965 that she was registered with APHA. Skippa Streak was her only registered foal.

Two Rungs Up

Hank Wiescamp's Skip Hi family of horses officially became part of the Paint Horse movement in the fall of 1963, when APSHA founder Rebecca Tyler Lockhart convinced the venerable horseman to register his then-3-year-old tobiano stallion and three mares with the association.

By this time, Wiescamp had been breeding, showing and selling horses for close to 40 years. Beginning as an auctioneer and a dealer in cavalry, carriage and polo horses in the mid-1920s, he built an empire around a family of Peter McCue/Old Fred horses so singular in type and coloring that they came to be known simply as "Wiescamp horses."

At the time APHSA was founded, Wiescamp was at the top of his game as a Quarter Horse breeder. His Nick Shoemaker/Skipper W. line of horses—most of whom sported liberal amounts of chrome—were known throughout the land and their breeder's name appeared at or near the top on virtually every breeders list that the AQHA show department published at the time.

When "The Dutchman," decided to expand his Paint Horse breeding program, it was only natural that he utilize the potent family of horses he already had.

"When I got serious about breeding Paints," Wiescamp said in a mid-1990s interview, "I had a battery of stallions that I kept penned on 'Millionaire's Row.' There were horses there like Skipper's Lad, Skipper's King, Skip's Reward and Skip 3 Bars, and I put them on a foundation set of Paint mares that carried a lot of Remount Thoroughbred and Coke Roberds blood.

"Having those good Quarter Horse studs to use on my Paint mares kind of gave me a leg up on a lot of the other breeders. I didn't have to start at the bottom; I was several rungs up the ladder, I'll grant you that."

Skip Hi, a 1959 sorrel overo stallion by Skipper's Lad (QH) and out of Sky Hi #793, was a grandson of the legendary Skipper W. on top and a remount Thoroughbred stallion named Advantage on the bottom. His first two APHA-registered foal crops, numbering just six, hit the ground

A show horse in the making, here's Skippa Streak as a yearling.
Courtesy APHA

Shown here with Lisa Jones, "Streak" was a three-time national champion in Western Pleasure and a three-time reserve national champion at halter.
Courtesy APHA

in 1962 and 1963. Among those was one performer, Skip-A-Dollar, a 1963 palomino stallion out of Gold Dollar # 836, who earned 13 halter points, eight performance points and an ROM in Western pleasure.

Skip Hi's first significant foal crop was born in 1964. Although it, too, was small in number, it included five of the foundation stallion's most noteworthy sons: Skipper's Dude, out of Schoolgirl; Skipover, out of Silver Sash (QH); Skip's Lad, out of Skip Joy (QH); Skip On, out of Slippers; and Skippa Streak.

APHA began compiling its own Leading Sires, Dams and Breeders lists, and by 1974 Hank Wiescamp and his son Larry occupied the Number 1 position on seven of the 11 lists.

As far as the first six Skip Hi sons are concerned, all went on to influence the breed in one way or another. Skip-A-Dollar and Skipover made names for themselves in the show pen, while Skipper's Dude, Skip's Lad and Skip

On did the same in the breeding shed.

Skippa Streak, however, made significant contributions as both a show horse and sire. In fact, no single Wiescamp-bred Paint was more responsible than he for the family's early rise to prominence.

A Kansas Connection

Had it not been for Paul and Carolyn Crabb, Skippa Streak might have lived his life out in relative obscurity as a Wiescamp Paint herd sire. It was the Crabbs who, in the fall of 1965, transported the yearling stallion from Alamosa to their home near Winfield, Kansas, to be made ready for sale.

The Crabbs, who were deeply involved in the racehorse industry at the time, had become acquainted with Hank Wiescamp in 1960, when he purchased a Thoroughbred son of Three Bars named St. Bar D. from them. The Kansas husband and wife team was also well known in Paint Horse circles, having located,

Skippetta, a 1967 sorrel tobiano mare by Skippa Streak and out of Jackie Van (QH), was her sire's first show ring superstar.
Photo by Marge Spence

The talented mare won the western pleasure futurity at the 1969 World Wide Paint Review at Hutchinson, Kansas, en route to becoming APHA Supreme Champion #10.
Courtesy APHA

purchased and registered the legendary Babette family of race-bred Paint Horses in 1964 (see *More than Color, Vol. 1*).

On May 4, 1966, Carolyn Crabb facilitated the sale of Skippa Streak to Paul R. Burnett of Wichita, Kansas. The 2-year-old stallion was registered with APHA that same month and turned over to a local trainer named Clyde Brandon to be conditioned for a show career.

On July 30 of that year, Skippa Streak placed first in the 2-year-old stallion class in Fredonia, Kansas. This win was followed by a short but successful eight-show freshman campaign that saw him earn four grands, two reserves and seven first places at halter. Shown in Western pleasure twice, he recorded two firsts.

The high point of the stallion's show year occurred in mid-October, when he was named Reserve Champion 2-Year-Old Stallion at the 1966 APHA National Show in Baton Rouge, Louisiana.

In 1967, Skippa Streak continued his winning ways. In June, he earned grand champion stallion honors in Salina, Kansas, ahead of such well-known halter stallions as Adios Amigos and Blackhawk Leo.

On September 19, he placed first in the 3-year-old stallion class at the Kansas State Fair in Hutchinson. One week later, he acquired his second national title by being named the Reserve Champion 3-Year-Old Stallion at the 1967 APHA National Show in Oklahoma City, Oklahoma.

The stallion's second appearance on the national stage signaled the end of the Kansas stage of his career. Advertised for sale in the Paint Horse Journal, he was purchased in February of 1968 by Robert T. Jones of Smithfield, Texas—the man under whose name he would remain for the balance of his life.

A Lone Star State of Mind

Jones and his family—wife, Chris, and daughters, Linda and Lisa—had been involved with horses for a number of years before making the switch to Paints. Both girls had learned to ride in 4-H and had owned and shown Quarter Horses. Linda

Winning Streak, a 1969 sorrel gelding by Skippa Streak and out of Levi Miss (QH), earned more than 700 points during his illustrious show career. Here, he and Linda Jones accept an award at the 1973 Houston Livestock Show. That's APHA Executive Secretary Sam Spence on the left.

Photo by Jim Keeland

Jones Gleaves, who currently resides with her husband, Sam, on the family ranch near Olney, Texas, recalls the circumstances surrounding the family's entry into the Paint Horse business.

"When it came to the horses," she says, "my father was always very supportive. Be that as it may, it was really my mother, myself and my sister who were really connected. We did most of the buying, selling and showing through the years.

"But my dad did buy Skippa Streak. Jim Pearson, one of the top trainers in the Paint industry at the time, talked dad into it. Jim was related to us through marriage and he had trained and shown Yellow Mount, the first APHA Champion, and Q Ton San Catt, the first APHA Champion mare.

"Skippa Steak was broke to ride when we got him, and he had been started right. Jim worked with him a little bit and then we turned him over to Ellis Caster of Euless, Texas, to finish. Ellis was the man who had taught both of us girls to ride, and he also taught me how to show Skippa Streak."

Beginning in the spring of 1968, the team of Skippa Steak and 16-year-old Linda Jones took the Texas Paint Horse show scene by storm. Competing in both halter and Western pleasure in places such as Wimberly, Big Spring, Richland Hills, Keller, Fort Worth and Timpson, Texas; and Wagoner and Duncan, Oklahoma, the pair began racking up the points.

By July 4th, Skippa Steak had earned the required halter and performance points to be named APHA Champion #13.

In late September, it was on to the 1968 APHA National Show in Oklahoma City, where the then-4-year-old stallion and his teenaged rider pulled off a double coup.

"Back then," Linda Gleaves says, "we didn't even have an arena to practice in. My aunt and uncle had a big, chain-link dog pen that was big enough for me to get Skippa Streak inside and work him on what filled in for a rail.

"I think 1968 was the last year they

let us show stallions in the youth performance classes. We went up to Oklahoma City and placed first in a class of 53 junior Western pleasure horses, and then came back and placed first in a class of 32 youth Western pleasure horses."

In 1969, Skippa Streak and Linda once again hit the show trail, starting out the year by earning grand champion stallion honors at the Lone Star State's "Big Three"—the Southwestern Livestock Exposition and Fat Stock Show in Fort Worth, the San Antonio Livestock Exposition and the Houston Livestock Show.

Linda graduated from high school in the spring of 1969. That summer, both she and sister Lisa went to work for Hank Wiescamp, riding young horses and showing in the Rocky Mountain region. Linda also continued showing Skippa Streak, and that fall added

Skippa Leo, a 1969 sorrel tobiano gelding by Skippa Streak and out of Sioux Bingo, was a Register of Merit racehorse.
Courtesy APHA

Deborah McLaughlin of Grapevine, Texas showed Sugar Streak to the title of Reserve National Champion Youth Showmanship at Halter (13 & Under) at the 1973 National Show in Denver, Colorado.

Photo by George Martin

a quartet of accomplishments to his already sterling record.

In mid-August, Skippa Streak was named Reserve Champion Aged Stallion and Champion Sr. Western Pleasure Horse at the APHA National Show in Kansas City, Kansas. One week later, he earned grand champion stallion honors at the Colorado State Fair in Pueblo, and in September he earned grand champion stallion honors and placed first in the senior Western pleasure at the Oklahoma State Fair in Oklahoma City.

In 1970, with Linda showing him in Western pleasure, English pleasure and reining, and Lanham Riley of Aledo, Texas, handling him in calf roping, Skippa Streak earned All-Around Champion honors at both the San Antonio and Houston Livestock Shows.

In addition, he finished the year as the South Texas Paint Horse Club's All-Around Champion, and

High-Point Stallion, Aged Stallion, Sr. Western Pleasure Horse and Sr. Reining Horse.

In February of 1971, Skippa Streak once again took grand champion stallion honors and won the calf roping at the San Antonio Livestock Exposition. In May, he stood grand in Seminole, Oklahoma, and was retired from competition shortly thereafter.

Skippa Streak's final show record was one to be proud of. According to APHA records, he was a three-time national champion in Western pleasure (counting Linda Jones' youth championship), a three-time reserve national champion at halter and an APHA Champion.

At halter, he earned 25 grand championships, 12 reserve grand championships, 100 points and a Superior halter award.

In performance, he amassed 178 points: 129 Western pleasure, 22 English pleasure, 14 calf roping, eight reining, four trail and one heeling. In addition, he earned a Superior Western pleasure award, and ROMs in Western pleasure, English pleasure, reining and calf roping.

Having established that he was, indeed, one of the top show horses of his era, the next challenge for the Wiescamp-bred tobiano was to see if he could consistently reproduce himself.

A Sire of Substance

Skippa Streak was test-bred to several mares as a 2-year-old, and his first foal crop of three tobiano fillies hit the ground in 1967.

Streak Away, a 1967 sorrel tobiano out of Susie Charge (QH), was bred by Guy Thomson of Winfield, Kansas. Sold to Larry Wiescamp in 1969, she went on to produce Skipalou, the 1973 National Champion 2-Year-Old Stallion; and APHA Champion Skipaway.

Skippetta, a 1967 sorrel tobiano mare out of Jackie Van (QH), was also bred by Thomson. Sold first to Forrest Williamson of Arkansas City, Kansas, and then to Larry and Linda Symkowski of Michigan City, Indiana, Skippetta earned honors as the 1969

National Champion 2-Year-Old Mare and the 1971 National Champion Calf Roping Horse. She also earned an APHA Supreme Championship, Superior All-Around award, APHA Championship, Superior Halter award, Superior Western Pleasure award, five performance ROMs, and 101 halter and 161 performance points.

Skippa Streak's second Kansas foal crop hit the ground in 1968. It consisted of three more tobiano fillies, none of which were performers.

The following spring, the show stallion's first Texas foals were born. From this point on, it became obvious that Skippa Streak was destined to be an extremely consistent show horse sire. Among his most noted performers were:

- Winning Streak, a 1969 sorrel gelding out of Levi Miss (QH): Versatility and Superior All-Around awards; APHA Champion; Superior Halter, Western Pleasure and Trail; seven ROMs; and 52 halter and 662 performance points. Youth: one National and one Reserve National Championship; two Versatility awards; APHA Youth Champion; eight Superior awards; 15 ROMs; and 158 halter and 973 performance points.
- Skippa Leo, a 1969 sorrel tobiano gelding out of Sioux Bingo: Speed Index 83; race ROM; 12 starts resulting in three 1sts; one second and four thirds.
- Sugar Streak, a 1970 sorrel tobiano mare out of Pocos Melody Bar (QH): 1970 National Champion Weanling Filly; APHA Champion; Superior Halter, Western Pleasure and Trail; three ROMs; and 112 halter and 211 performance points. Youth: two National and two Reserve National Championships; Youth Versatility; APHA Youth Champion; five Superior awards; six ROMs; and 109 halter and 426 performance points.
- Gold Streak, a 1970 palomino tobiano stallion out of Gold Dust Penny (QH): 1970 Reserve National Champion Weanling Stallion;

Alpo, a 1975 sorrel tobiano gelding by Skippa Streak and out of Stage Girl, was a two-time national champion and a three-time reserve national champion.

Photo by Harold Campton

Skip Oro, a 1971 dun tobiano mare by Skippa Steak and out of Del Oro (QH) earned 40 halter and 58 performance points en route to becoming APHA Champion #367.　　**Courtesy APHA**

Miss Flit, a 1973 sorrel tobiano mare by Skippa Streak and out of Calico Flit, was an APHA Champion and earned a Superior Western Pleasure award.
Photo by George Martin

APHA Champion; Superior Western Pleasure; two ROMs; and 16 halter and 87 performance points.

- Skippa Stitch, a 1971 palomino tobiano stallion out of Yellow Gold Baby (QH): APHA Champion; Superior Western Pleasure; 20 halter and 63 performance points. Amateur: three Superior awards; four ROMs; and 246 performance points.
- Skip Oro, a 1971 dun tobiano mare out of Del Oro (QH): APHA Champion.
- Tamu Skip Bug, a 1972 sorrel tobiano gelding out of Berty Bug: Youth Versatility; APHA Youth Champion; five Youth Superior awards; five Youth ROMs; and 28 halter and 317 performance points.
- Scooter Streak, a 1973 sorrel tobiano stallion out of Kitchawa Kutie (QH): APHA Champion; two ROMs; and 20 halter and 71 performance points.
- Miss Flit, a 1973 sorrel tobiano mare out of Calico Flit: 1976 Reserve National Champion Jr. Western Pleasure; APHA Champion; Superior Western Pleasure; two ROMs; and 18 halter and 136 performance events.
- Eternal Streak, a 1973 sorrel tobiano gelding out of Del Oro (QH): 1976 National Champion 3-Year-Old Gelding; 1976 National Champion Jr. Calf Roping; 1979 National Champion Sr. Calf Roping; APHA Champion; Superior Halter and Calf Roping; three ROMs; and 67 halter and 152 performance points.
- Easy Streak, a 1973 dun tobiano mare out of Latest Fashion (QH): APHA Champion; Superior Halter, Western Pleasure and Trail; two ROMs; and 129 halter and 156 performance points. Youth: Youth Versatility; two Youth APHA Championships; five Youth Superior awards; 10 Youth ROMs; and 300 halter and 624 performance points.

In 1973 and 1974, Skippa Streak was leased back to Hank Wiescamp. Crossed on a number of top Old Fred-bred Quarter Horse mares and Skip Hi-bred Paint Horse mares, Streak contributed such top broodmares as Skippa Mona, Skippa Bright, Skip's

Trick, Skippa Secret, Skippa's Babe and Steak After to the Wiescamp Paint Horse program.

He also sired Skip's Artist, who went on to become one of the breed's first great pleasure horse sires, and whose contributions are detailed in the following chapter.

Although Skippa Streak spent most of another two years in the San Luis Valley of south-central Colorado, the Jones family managed to get several of their own mares in foal to him.

Skip N Streak, a 1974 sorrel tobiano gelding out of Nickette (QH), was the 1980 National Champion Heeling Horse. He also earned Superiors in heeling and Western pleasure, three ROMs, and four halter and 195 performance points.

Alpo, a 1975 sorrel tobiano gelding out of Stage Girl, was the 1979 National Champion Western Riding. In open competition, he was an APHA Champion and the earner of Superiors in Western pleasure and trail, three ROMs, and 19 halter and 282 performance points.

In amateur competition, he earned a Versatility award, a Superior in Western pleasure; seven ROMs and 269 performance points. In youth competition, he earned three National Championships, one Reserve National Championship, two Versatility awards; two APHA Championships, five Youth Superior awards, 13 ROMs, and 44 halter and 609 performance points.

Skippa Streak returned home to Texas for the 1975 breeding season.

Eternal Streak, a 1973 sorrel tobiano gelding by Skippa Streak and out of Del Oro (QH), was the 1976 National Champion Jr. Calf Roping Horse.
Courtesy APHA

Easy Streak, a 1973 dun tobiano mare by Skippa Streak and out of Latest Fashion (QH), was an APHA Champion and earner of Superiors in Halter, Western Pleasure and Trail.

Photo by Don Shugart

Also an accomplished youth mount, Easy Streak earned a total of 300 halter and 624 performance points.

Courtesy APHA

Bred lightly over the course of the next six years, he sired an average of only five foals per year. Included among these were his last two noteworthy performers:

• Skip's Coaster, a 1977 sorrel tobiano gelding out of Lorun's Lady Ace: Superior Western Pleasure and Heeling; three ROMs; and 205 points.

• Chickadoo Streak, a 1979 chestnut tobiano gelding out of Miss Banna Chick (QH): ROM Western pleasure; and six halter and 11 Western pleasure points.

By the time the 1980s rolled around, Skippa Streak was winding down what had been a most illustrious life. Shortly after returning to Texas in 1975, the then-11-year-old stallion suffered a pair of physical setbacks.

"By this time," Linda Gleaves says, "Sam and I were out on our own, training and showing for the public. My mom and dad had Skippa Streak with them and, one day while they were gone, he kicked through a fence and cut the front of one of his rear legs pretty bad.

"It healed, but then he foundered. It wasn't a severe founder, but it was enough that mom thought he would do better if he were not stalled all the time.

"Dr. Roy Lee of San Saba, Texas, was a friend, and he agreed to first lease Skippa Streak and then buy him. 'Doc' had some really nice coastal Bermuda pastures that he turned Streak out on for around five years as near as we can remember, and then had him humanely put to sleep.

"I understand he never transferred the horse into his name, and I guess that was the way it should have been. Skippa Streak was always our horse, and we will always have fond memories and a deep sense of appreciation for what he contributed to both our family and the Paint Horse industry."

Skipalou, a 1971 sorrel tobiano stallion by Skipa Skip (QH) and out of Streak Away by Skippa Streak, was the 1973 National Champion 2-Year-Old Stallion.

Photo by George Martin

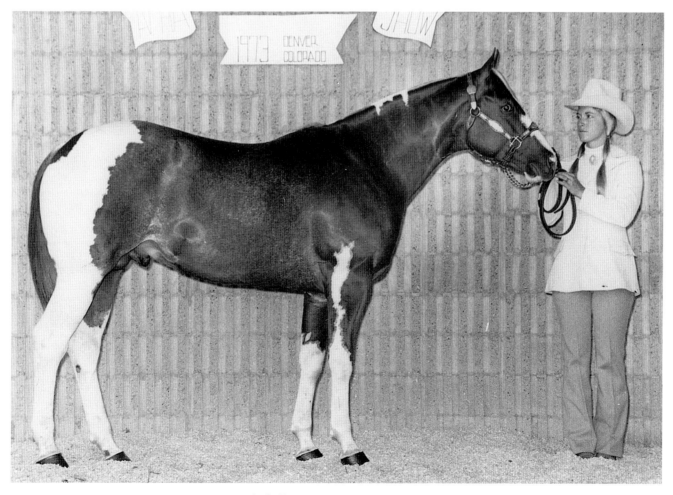

12

SKIP'S ARTIST
#38,550

*As Skippa Streak's top-siring son, this tobiano
Wiescamp-bred stallion has kept the line alive.*

SKIP'S ARTIST, A 1975 sorrel tobiano stallion by Skippa Streak and out of Skip's Aid by Skip's Lad, was bred by the late H. J. "Hank" Wiescamp of Alamosa, Colorado.

Just as Skippa Streak was one of the first sons of Skip Hi to make his presence felt on the national Paint Horse scene, Skip's Artist was one of the first sons of Skippa Streak to similarly impact the breed.

Rocky Mountain Royalty

Like so many of the Wiescamp Paints of his era, Skip's Artist was the product of an intense line-breeding program. Sired by a Skip Hi son and out of a double-bred Skip Hi granddaughter, "Art" also traced once to Skipper W. on the top side of his pedigree and five times on the bottom. In addition, he also traced to the top Wiescamp show horses Sir Teddy,

Skip's Artist, founder of a Paint Pleasure Dynasty.
Photo by Harold Campton

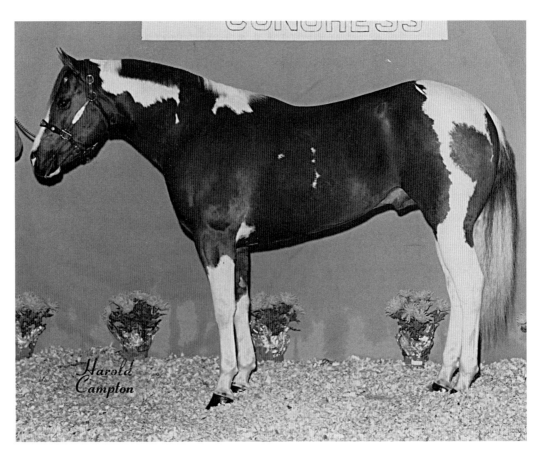

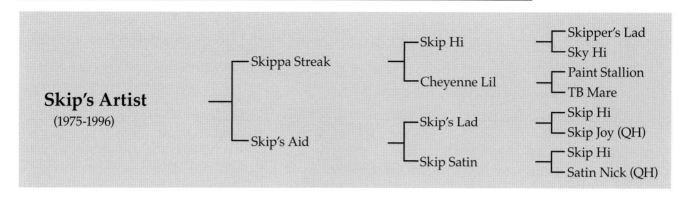

Skip's Artist (1975-1996)	Skippa Streak	Skip Hi	Skipper's Lad
			Sky Hi
		Cheyenne Lil	Paint Stallion
			TB Mare
	Skip's Aid	Skip's Lad	Skip Hi
			Skip Joy (QH)
		Skip Satin	Skip Hi
			Satin Nick (QH)

an AQHA Champion, and Skip's Joy, the grand champion mare at the 1958 Denver National Western Livestock Show.

As detailed in the previous chapter, by the mid-1970s the Wiescamp/Skip Hi family of Paint Horses was ranked among the nation's best. It was into this acclaimed family of horses that Skip's Artist was foaled, and had he remained under the Wiescamp family's ownership, it's doubtful that he would have gone on to exert much of an influence on the Paint Horse breed. He was, after all, just one good horse in a program that was churning out hundreds of good horses a year.

But Art's fortunes took a turn for the better in the fall of 1975, when he was purchased by Marsha McGovney and Clarence Helm of Helm Farms in Penalosa, Kansas.

"Helm Farms is first and foremost a working farm," remarked McGovney in a mid-1990s interview. "It's a family operation, founded almost 50 years ago by my parents, Clarence and Marjorie Helm.

"We farm about 3,200 acres, spread over a 15-by-6 mile area. Our crops are mainly irrigated grains—corn, soybeans and milo—and irrigated alfalfa hay on about half the acres, with the other divided between pasture, dry-land winter wheat and ground currently in the Conservation Reserve Program."

As far as the Helm Farms Paint Horse breeding program goes, its roots trace back to 30 years ago, when Marsha was a typical horse-crazy girl.

"We had a Quarter Horse mare that we raised foals from during my 4-H years," she recalled. "She was sired by Poco Birthday, by Poco Bueno, and she always had colts until her last three foals, and they were all fillies.

"They were three of the first five mares we had as broodmares, and their descendants can still be found in our current broodmare band.

"In 1975, my husband, Bill, and I took a vacation trip to Colorado en route to a Hereford sale and the Quarter Horse World Show. We stopped at Hank Wiescamp's in Alamosa and spent all one afternoon looking at horses by ourselves.

"After we were through, I went to Hank's home to thank him for allowing us to look around. I wound up visiting with him for two hours while poor Bill waited in the truck.

"I told Hank about our five broodmares, and he advised me to forget about the Quarter Horse World Show and to go back home, instead, and attend the Paint Horse Congress in Hutchinson, Kansas. He told me that I would have more of a chance of accomplishing something in Paints than I would in Quarter Horses, and I figured he was one man who ought to know what he was talking about.

"So, we came home, went to the Paint Congress show and sale, and bought a tobiano mare named Skippers Tone and a tobiano yearling, and that's how we got into the Paint business."

Two years later, Marsha got in touch with Wiescamp once more.

"I called Hank on the phone," she said. "I told him who I was and where I was from. He broke in and told me about the five broodmares I had. I was amazed at his recall.

"I asked him if he had any stallions who would work on my mares. I told him I just wanted to raise some ranch

HF Skip N Lace, a 1981 sorrel tobiano mare by Skip's Artist and out of Scot N Skip (QH), earned 1,190 points in open, amateur and youth competition.
Photo by Don Shugart

HF Skips Starlette was also a top competitor in all three divisions and had 667 points to her credit. **Photo by K.C. Montgomery**

horses with good dispositions. He said he might, and told me to come on out and take a look.

"Neither Dad nor I had ever handled a stallion, and we weren't sure we wanted to," Marsha continued. "But we made the trip anyway. We didn't even take a trailer.

"The horse Hank had picked out for us was Skip's Artist, then a 2-year-old. We looked him over, bought him, and arranged to leave him in Alamosa for three months for some handling.

"When we went back out to get him," she continued, "I wanted to know what they had accomplished with him. They took him to some cross-ties and put a saddle and snaffle-bit bridle on him. Then they took him to an exercise pen and started trotting him in a circle.

"While he was trotting, Hank threw a hired hand up on him. After Art had made a few rounds, the hand jumped off. That was the extent of Art's training to that point."

To the Land of Oz

Back home in Kansas, the Helms went about building a stallion pen that adjoined their broodmare pasture. They planned to put Skip's Artist in the pen, open the gate in the spring to let him out with the mares, and then sucker him back into the pen the following fall, handling him as little as possible.

Upon arriving at his new home, however, "Art" threw a monkey wrench into that plan by promptly injuring a leg severely enough to require daily treatment.

"By the time we got Art's leg healed," Marsha said, "we were all pretty used to each other. And we learned some things about him and his personality that have remained constant in the ensuing years, and that hold true for his offspring, as well.

"Art and most of his get have a very strong 'flight or fight' instinct. Their first reaction to you is one of flight. It's not that they won't listen to you, or won't try to do what you want them to. On the contrary, they have a very deeply instilled desire to please. It's just that they are a little bit 'goosy.'

They must first learn to not be afraid of you before they can listen to you.

"If they are truly panic-stricken, they will remember the scare for a long, long time. If, however, they can draw their confidence from you and perceive you as their protector, they will try anything."

In many ways, the Helm Farms horses are mirror images of the classic Wiescamp-bred horse. Hank was oft quoted as saying that "a Wiescamp horse has to be treated with integrity. You can ask him to do anything and he'll try his darnedest. If you demand that he do it, though, and try to strong-arm him into obedience, you're in for a long day."

The same holds true for the Skip's Artists.

"These horses have proven over the years how hard they'll try to do what you ask of them," McGovney said. "But if you teach them to fight, you'd better pack a lunch. They will hang in there all day and will give the fight their best effort, too."

The winning Amateur team of HF Skip N Copper and Melanie Cox were named as the 1986 Reserve World Champion in Sr. Western Pleasure. In addition, they earned a Versatility award, five superiors, five ROMs and 602 points.

Photo by Melissa

HF Runfortheroses carried youth rider Jennifer Leitow to five world championships and six reserve world championships.
Photo by Don Shugart

HF Skips Ms Twain, a 1970 sorrel tobiano mare by Skip's Artist and out of Skip Twain, was the first of her sire's get to make a big splash in the show ring.

**Photo by
Harold Campton**

HF Skip N Plaudit, a 1981 buckskin overo gelding by Skip's Art and out of Dude Plaudit, was a Superior Open and Amateur Western Pleasure horse that also earned three halter and 343 performance points.

**Photo by
Don Shugart**

At the 1990 Pinto Horse Association National Championship Show in Tulsa Oklahoma. HF Skip N Freckle won the 3-Year-Old Western Pleasure Futurity and HF Skip N Shine was named as Champion of Champions Stock Seat Pleasure and also won the 2-Year-Old Western Pleasure Futurity. Helm Farm trainer Spike Ruhnke piloted both fillies to their victories.

Photo by Melissa

"Skip N Shine" and Spike returned to the Pinto National in 1991 to earn dual honors as Supreme Champion Pleasure Horse and Champion of Champions Stock Seat Pleasure. That's Spike's blue heeler "Bama" taking her turn in front of the curtain.

Photo by Melissa

HF Skip Tizzy and Elizabeth Roberts of Urbana, Ohio, teamed up in western riding to earn honors as the 1994 Youth World Champion and the 1995 Reserve World Champion. **Photo by Melissa**

Here's HF Skips Cassanova, earner of a Versatility award, APHA Championship, nine Superior awards, 23 ROMs, 44 halter and 1,742 performance points in open, amateur and novice amateur competition. **Photo byDon Shugart**

As they continued to work with Art and his get from the late 1970s on, Helm Farms developed a successful breeding and show program that had a far-reaching effect.

"We never had any conscious intent to make it in the show horse deal," Marsha says. "We took our first spotted 2-year-old—a 1979 sorrel tobiano mare named HF Skips Ms Twain—to Karen Russell of Hutchinson, Kansas, to ride for 30 days.

"Karen told us the filly was kind of fancy, so we left her in training to show at the Kansas State Fair and Paint Congress. When it came time for the state fair, Karen had a scheduling conflict and asked Chris Barnes to catch ride for us.

"Chris and "Twain" won their class at the fair and, later, Chris also won the first World Championship 2-Year-Old Western Pleasure Futurity on a Skip's Artist daughter named HF Skip Supreme. It was held in 1984 in Fort Worth, during the World Show.

"Then we hired Spike Ruhnke, who had done most of the riding on "Twain" while she was at Karen's, and then had gone to work for Chris. Spike was with us 10 years, and he and I managed the program together during that time period."

HF Skips Ms Twain, a 1979 sorrel tobiano mare by Skip's Artist and out of Skip Twain, did go on to become a highly successful show horse. Shown in open and youth competition, the flashy mare earned one Reserve World Championship, five Superior awards, nine ROMs and 596 points.

A Paint Horse Pleasure Sire

Over the next 15 years, numerous other Helm-bred horses followed Twain into the show ring. By the time the program scaled back both it's breeding and showing operations in the mid-1990s, the Skip's Artist family of performers was one of the breed's most accomplished.

APHA records reveal that Skip's Artist sired a total of 190 registered foals. Of these, 81 performers have earned 22 National and World Championships, 20 Reserve National and World Championships, 23 Versatility awards, 154 Superior awards, nine APHA Championships, 445 ROMs and 28,340 points in all divisions combined.

From a points-earned standpoint, his most accomplished get are:

- HF Skipa Tizzy, a 1989 sorrel tobiano mare out of Skips Del: 3,675 points (76 Open, 165 Amateur and 3,434 Youth).
- HF Runforthe Roses, a 1984 sorrel tobiano mare out of Miss Peavy Twist (QH): 3,417 points (159 Open, 25 Amateur and 3,233 Youth).
- HF Skips Cassanova, a 1987 sorrel tobiano gelding out of HF Sonny Sally: 1,786 points (40 Open, 216 Amateur, 156 Novice Amateur and 1,374 Youth).
- HF Skips Grandslam, a 1988 sorrel tobiano gelding out of HF Chiefs Margo: 1,517 points (224 Open, 985 Amateur and 308 Youth).
- Skips Satin Tone, a 1980 sorrel mare out of Skipper's Tone: 1,667 points (218 Open, 687 Amateur and 762 Youth).
- Skippa Pine Bar, a 1985 sorrel tobiano gelding out of Zippos Blondie (QH): 1,378 points (253 Open, 504 Amateur, 222 Novice Amateur and 399 Youth).
- HF Skip N Copper, a 1981 sorrel gelding out of Cody's Bar Pet (QH): 1,177 points (208 Open, 106 Amateur and 863 Youth).
- HF Purely Artistic, a 1993 sorrel tobiano mare out of Lyns Sade (QH): 1,185 points (340 Open and 845 Youth).
- HF Skip N Lace, a 1981 sorrel tobiano mare out of Scot N Skip (QH): 1,190 points (238 Open, 790 Amateur and 162 Youth).
- HF Skips Starlette, a 1982 sorrel mare out of HF War Leo Baby: 667 points (79 Open, 33 Amateur, 7 Novice Amateur and 548 Youth).

The Passing of a Legend

Sometime during the evening of April 26, 1996, Skip's Artist apparently suffered a stroke. Efforts to revive him to where he could regain his feet were unsuccessful and he was humanely put to sleep the following day.

"The phrase, 'part of the family' is an overworked one," McGovney observed. "In Art's case, however, it is the only expression that adequately describes how we came to feel about him.

"He was a character, with his own little set of idiosyncrasies. But he was first and foremost a kind, capable horse, who passed on those qualities to his descendants."

Here's HF Init To Win It, a 1989 sorrel tobiano gelding by HF Skips Contender and out of HF Skip's Sarah. The double-bred Skip's Artist grandson was the earner of a Versatility award, five Superior awards, 13 ROMs and 933 points.
Shelly Larson of Kansas City, Kansas is aboard the venerable campaigner in this curtain shot.

Photo by Diane Dehane

13 BEAR CAT
#4800

One of the Midwest's first homebred champions, this colorful cropout stallion founded a family that was uniquely his own.

Bear Cat, the product of a potent cropout line, did much to bolster the Paint Horse industry in the Midwest.
Photo by Marge Spence

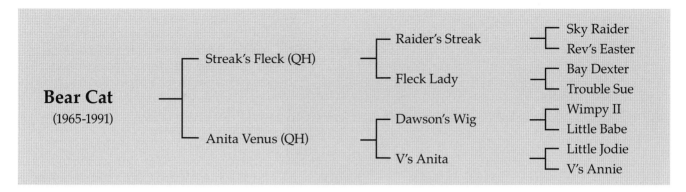

Bear Cat
(1965-1991)

- Streak's Fleck (QH)
  - Raider's Streak
    - Sky Raider
    - Rev's Easter
  - Fleck Lady
    - Bay Dexter
    - Trouble Sue
- Anita Venus (QH)
  - Dawson's Wig
    - Wimpy II
    - Little Babe
  - V's Anita
    - Little Jodie
    - V's Annie

THROUGHOUT THE 1960s and into the 1970s, the Paint Horse movement took hold and spread from the Southern Plains region to other parts of the country. The growth of the breed was dramatic, thanks in part to "cropouts"—the Quarter Horses with excessive white markings.

Deemed unacceptable for registration by the American Quarter Horse Association (AQHA), cropouts were, in essence, horses without a country. The formation of APSHA in 1962 provided these genetic black sheep with not only a home, but also a show and race venue.

For decades it was widely known that certain Quarter Horse lines had a propensity to produce cropout color. Included among them were the Colorado-based Old Fred/Peter McCue line that later branched out to include the Wiescamp and Shoemaker horses; and the Louisiana-originated Della Moore line that grew to encompass all of the Joe Reed, Joe Moore and Leo horses.

In the mid-1960s, a Midwestern cropout line surfaced that would go on to make quite a splash in the breed. At its head was a most-promising young stallion named Bear Cat.

A Color-Coded Heritage

Bear Cat, a 1965 chestnut overo stallion by Streak's Fleck (QH) and out of Anita Venus (QH), was bred by Carl Leininger of Crown Point, Indiana. At first glance, his pedigree offers few clues as to where his excessive white markings might have come from.

Streak's Fleck was a 1961 sorrel stallion by Raider's Streak and out of Fleck Lady. An AQHA Champion, his lineage was full of such early day

notables as Star Duster, Revenue, Roan Hancock, Golden Chief and Joe Hancock. None of these horses, however, were known to be prolific excess-white getters.

Anita Venus was a 1959 sorrel mare by Dawson's Wig and out of V's Anita.

Again, Dawson's Wig was a well-bred foundation Quarter Horse with no documented cropout get. Anita Venus, through, was a different story, altogether. APHA records reveal her to be the dam of four cropout foals. What's more, her dam, V's Anita, produced one cropout, and her granddam, V's Annie, produced two.

V's Annie, Bear Cat's great granddam, was a 1946 sorrel mare by Oklahoma Star P-6 and out of Annie. Annie, in turn, was a 1939 bay mare by Bert and out of a "Bald-Faced Mare." It is this bald-faced mare of unknown breeding that appears to be the root of the entire mare line's tendency to produce horses with extra chrome.

However Bear Cat came by his color, come by it he did, and it wasn't long before both the horse and the color began to get noticed.

Into the Spotlight

When Bear Cat was a weanling or short yearling, his breeder sold him to an AQHA judge and "weekend horse trader" named Harold Baker. Shortly thereafter, Bear Cat came to the attention of John Cratty of Marion, Ohio. John and his wife, Barbara, were well known and highly respected Quarter Horse trainers who, at the time, were showing a gelding named Pecho Dexter—one of AQHA's all-time leading point earners.

Cratty, who still resides in Marion, remembers the young Paint stallion well.

Skipa Show, a cropout maternal brother to Bear Cat, was the 1968 National Champion Weanling Stallion. **Photo by Dolcater**

"I guess it was around March or April of 1966 when I saw Bear Cat for the first time," Cratty says. "He was running in a cow shed and was wearing a halter with a 20-foot lead rope attached to it so you could catch him. As soon as they ran him by me though, I knew I was going to own him.

"Back then," Cratty continues, "I wasn't very big. The colt was nice-sized, so I started riding him when he was a long yearling. I didn't ask him to do too much—just walk, trot and canter.

"I'd ridden him a dozen times or so when I decided to take him to an all-breed show in Columbus. It was being held in the indoor coliseum where the Congress got its start, and I wanted to give the colt a little indoor riding experience.

"So, I rode him around there a little, and we were getting along so well that I decided to enter him in the Western

Skipa Lea, also a cropout and also a maternal sister to Bear Cat, was the 1967 National Champion Yearling Filly.
Courtesy APHA

pleasure. Up to this point, Bear Cat had never made a wrong move. I'd had a little trouble getting him to pick up one lead, but that was it.

"Well, we were stacked up against 25 horses or so, but the colt picked up both of his leads and we won it. After that weekend, I just turned him out and never got on him again until the following spring."

In February of 1967, Cratty registered Bear Cat with APHA. In a small ad in the March-April issue of the Paint Horse Journal, he touted his new acquisition as "the greatest young combination halter and performance stallion of the breed." What's more, he advertised him as standing at stud for a fee of $75. At the end of breeding season, he turned Bear Cat over to a local family to show.

A Youth Movement

"At this time," Cratty recalls, "I had a full barn of customer horses that were paying the bills. I had to decide whether I wanted to eat or show my own horse.

"John and Jean Dixon from Middleburg, Ohio, indicated that they would like to take Bear Cat to a few shows. They had a teenaged daughter named Becky who was pretty handy with a horse. So I let them have him for the summer, and then, that fall, they decided they wanted to own him.

"And they went on and did a good job with him—in the show ring and breeding barn. As I remember him, Bear Cat was one of the nicest studs I was ever around. In fact, as manners and attitude were concerned, I can't recall ever having to correct or discipline him."

Renowned trainer John Cratty of Marion, Ohio, purchased Bear Cat as a yearling. He introduced him to the Paint Horse world through this ad that appeared in the March-April 1967 issue of the Paint Horse Journal.
Courtesy APHA

At first, the Dixon family kept their new show horse fairly close to home. In September of 1968, however, they made a trip to Oklahoma City, Oklahoma, to compete in the APHA National Show. There, Bear Cat earned National Champion 3-Year-Old Stallion honors.

The Anita Venus line of cropout Paints was particularly well represented at this event, with Skipa Show, a 1968 sorrel overo stallion by Show Cash (QH) and out of Anita Venus, being named the National Champion Weanling Stallion, and Skipa Lea, his full sister, placing third in the 2-Year-Old Mares class.

Skipa Show and Skipa Lea, while bred by Carl Leininger, were both owned by Charles Hensel of Monroe, Wisconsin. "Lea" had, the year before, earned National Champion Yearling Filly honors, and that left Anita Venus with the unique distinction of having produced three cropout national champions in a row.

Getting back to Bear Cat, the oldest member of the cropout clan, his show career continued to blossom. Exhibited by his youthful owner, he went on to earn distinction as one of the top Midwestern show horses of his era.

In 1968, he earned grand champion stallion honors in Columbus, Ohio, in July and October; and Kilbourne, Ohio, in October. At the Kilbourne show he also placed first in a Western pleasure class of 20, and at the second Columbus show he placed first in a youth Western pleasure class of 17.

The highlight of the year was, of course, his national championship win. Following close behind it was being named the Ohio Paint Horse Association's (OPHA) High-Point Stallion, 3-Year-Old Stallion, Jr. Western Pleasure Horse and Youth Western Pleasure Horse.

Teen-aged Becky Dixon of Middleburg, Ohio, showed Bear Cat to multiple honors, including APHA Championship #29.
Photo by Peasley

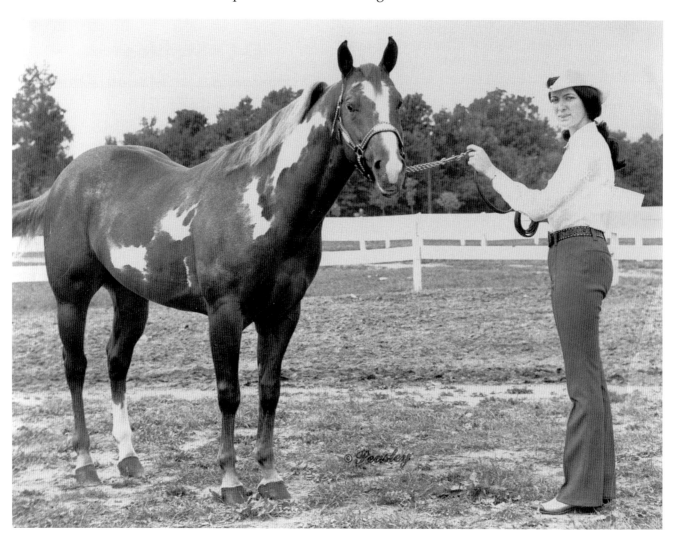

In 1969, it was more of the same—grand championships in Columbus, Randolph and Blacklick, Ohio, and Quincy, Michigan; reserves in Fremont and Columbus, Ohio; and performance wins at various locations in Western pleasure, English pleasure and reining.

On June 8, 1969, Bear Cat was awarded APHA Championship #29—the first Ohio horse to be so honored.

Exhibited at the 1969 APHA National Show, held August 14–16 in Kansas City, Missouri, the talented stallion placed fourth in a tough class of 60 junior Western pleasure horses. And, once again, he won multiple year-end honors as the OPHA High-Point Halter Stallion, Aged Stallion and Western Pleasure Horse.

The year 1970 proved to be Bear Cat's last to be heavily campaigned. And, once again, a string of championships at halter and first-place finishes in performance resulted in a three-peat as OPHA's High-Point Halter Stallion.

The stallion's official APHA show record reveals him to be the earner of 139 points—48 halter, 41 Western pleasure, 34 hunter under saddle and 16 reining—and all with teenaged Becky Dixon in the saddle.

John Dixon passed away in 1991, but his widow still resides in the Middleburg area. And, like John Cratty, Jean Dixon has fond memories of Bear Cat.

"We never advertised Bear Cat nationally," she says. "We generally kept around a dozen of our own mares around and it seemed like it was all we could handle to get them bred every year. From time to time we would take an outside mare in, but we never actively pursued that end of the business.

"Bear Cat was so easy to handle that, when my husband and I bred him to a mare, I always preferred to handle the stallion. He got to the point where during breeding season he'd get a little vocal. But, other than that, he was just the best horse to be around."

Becky Dixon Maxson, who recently retired from a career as a U.S.

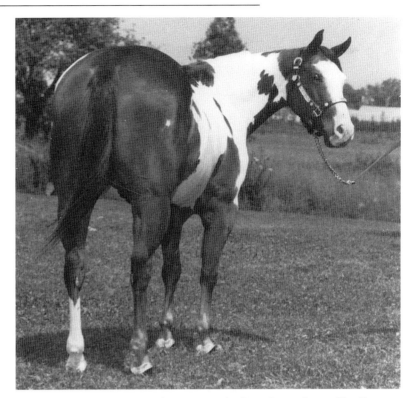

Bear Cat's June, a 1970 sorrel overo mare by Bear Cat and out of Leolita, was an APHA Champion, Superior Halter Horse with 56 halter and 18 performance points to her credit. **Courtesy APHA**

Department of Labor investigator, echoes all of her mother's sentiments and adds a few of her own.

"I started showing Bear Cat when I was 14 years old and he was 2," she says. "To begin with, I showed him in the open division. Then the APHA created the youth division and I

Charga Bear, a 1980 sorrel tobiano stallion by Bear Cat and out of Molly Powdercharge, earned 53 points and a Superior at halter. **Courtesy APHA**

Tag A Bear, a 1979 red roan overo stallion by Bear Cat and out of Miss Tag Heels, was the earner of an APHA Championship and Superior Halter award.
Courtesy APHA

showed him in that for a year or two. Finally, when the association barred youth from showing stallions, I went back to showing him in open.

"We showed mostly in Ohio. We were a small outfit and we operated on a limited budget. Still, by the time it was all said and done, the two of us did all right.

"After we had more or less retired Bear Cat," Becky continues, "I finished out my youth career on a mare named Kick-A-Poo Sioux. We bought her in February of 1971 from Dale Smith of Westerville, Ohio. She was Ohio's first APHA Champion mare, an honor she'd earned before we bought her, and then I made her the state's first Youth APHA Champion mare.

"At the 1972 APHA National Show in Columbus, Ohio, we were the national champions in youth showmanship,

and the reserve national champions in Western horsemanship and reining. We also won two trophy saddles at the 1972 World Wide Paint Horse Congress in Hutchinson, Kansas, and finished the year as the Number Two Youth in the Nation.

"Between Bear Cat and 'Sue,' I probably had about as enjoyable a youth career as anyone could ever imagine."

As for Bear Cat himself, life after the show ring rapidly turned into life as a leading sire. Here again, according to Becky Maxson, the path to success was somewhat unorthodox.

"Bear Cat never had a high-dollar broodmare band to work with," she says. "In fact, most of our mares were of the 'Saturday Night Horse Sale' variety. We tried to get good mares, but we were never in the position to go out and buy any expensive ones.

"Bear Cat was a consistent sire, though, on all types of mares. He was not a big horse himself, but he was well balanced and had such a kind, affectionate personality. He threw that in all his foals, and I think that's what made them excel as all-around horses."

A Super Sire

Bear Cat's first foal crop numbered five and included two top performers—Yogi Bear, a 1970 bay tobiano gelding out of Dixon's Trixie, who became an APHA Champion and Youth APHA Champion; and Bear Cat's June, a 1970 sorrel overo mare out of Leolita, who earned APHA Champion and Superior Halter honors.

During the next decade-and-a-half—from 1971 through 1985—the Dixon stallion sired an impressive array of halter and performance champions from colt crops that averaged in only the single digits. Among them were:
• Bear's Bonanza, a 1971 bay tobiano stallion out of Seneca Sue—APHA Champion.
• Moma Bear, a 1972 bay tobiano mare out of Shawnee Maid—APHA Champion.
• Bear Cat's Cricket, a 1973 sorrel tobiano mare out of April Fool—APHA Champion; Superior Western Pleasure and Superior Youth Western

Horsemanship.

- Apache Cat, a 1974 sorrel tovero stallion out of Shawnee Maid—APHA Champion.
- Bear's She Cat, a 1975 sorrel overo mare out of Shawnee Maid—APHA Champion.
- Extra Light, a 1978 red roan gelding out of Joker's Queen—APHA Champion, Youth Versatility, Superior Youth Western Pleasure and Hunter Under Saddle, 14 ROMs and 517 points.
- Tag A Bear, a 1979 red roan overo stallion out of Miss Tag Heels—APHA Champion and Superior Halter.
- Charga Bear, a 1980 sorrel tobiano stallion out of Molly Powdercharge—Superior Halter.

Bear Cat's last three foal crops, which totaled 11, hit the ground from 1986 through 1988. They included the foundation sire's final point earner, B C Junior, a 1986 sorrel overo gelding out of Molly Powdercharge, who ended his career with Superior Western Pleasure, Youth Versatility, and Superior Youth Showmanship and Western Pleasure honors, as well as nine ROMs and 389 points.

Super Bear, a 1978 sorrel overo stallion by Bear Cat and out of Miss Tag Heels, was an accomplished performer. Retired from the show ring, he went on to become a top sire in his own right. **Courtesy APHA**

Super Bear, shown here with trainer Mike Craig in the saddle, earned multiple national championship awards.

Photo by Don Shugart

First In Command, a 1982 sorrel stallion by Man In Command (QH) and out of Honey Bear by Bear Cat, won the weanling colt division of the Indiana Paint Horse Club halter futurity for owner Celeste Fender of Dublin, Ohio.   **Courtesy APHA**

APHA records reveal that Bear Cat sired 144 registered foals. Of these, 56 performers earned three national championships, four reserve national championships, three Versatility awards, one Superior All-Around award, 13 APHA Championships, 19 Superior event awards, 96 ROMs and 3,974 points in all divisions combined.

Two of the stallion's get—Super Bear and Honey Bear—deserve special recognition.

Super Bear, a 1978 sorrel overo stallion out of Miss Tag Heels, was bred by Becky Dixon. Sold to K Bar G Corrals of Tucson, Arizona, and Guernsey, Wyoming, the talented all-around performer was the 1984 Reserve National Champion Trail Horse, 1986 National Champion Amateur Aged Stallion, 1986 National Champion Utility Driving Horse, 1986 Reserve National Champion Pleasure Driving Horse, and 1988 and 1989 National Champion Get of Sire winner.

In addition, he earned an Open Versatility; a Superior All-Around; an APHA Championship; Superiors in halter, bridle path hack and Western pleasure; nine ROMs and 539 points.

As a mature horse, First In Command qualified for his Superior Halter award.

Photo by Melissa

Retired to stud, Super Bear sired 126 registered foals. Of these, 50 performers earned 10 World Championships, eight reserve world championships, two national championships, eight Versatility awards, seven APHA Championships, 55 Superior event awards, 186 ROMs and 3,224 points in all divisions combined.

Honey Bear, a 1973 bay overo mare out of Noble Annie (QH), was also bred by Becky Dixon. Sold first to Kelley Grossman of Lockbourne, Ohio, and later to Celeste Fender of Dublin, Ohio, the Bear Cat daughter was the 1983 National Champion Produce of Dam winner. In addition, she was an APHA Champion, and earned Superiors in halter and Western pleasure, seven ROMs and 224 points.

Placed in production, Honey Bear produced 13 foals, 11 of them performers that earned three world championships, one national championship, one reserve world championship, three reserve national championships, two Versatility awards, six APHA championships, 22 Superior event awards, 32 ROMs and 3,229 points in all divisions combined.

Bear Cat lived to a ripe old age.

"In 1991," Becky Maxson says, "my father lay critically ill in the hospital for several months. Mom and I were spread thin just dealing with this, and then Bear Cat, who was 25 years old, suffered a severe colic attack.

"He was really beginning to show his age, and we felt that his quality of life was just going to deteriorate. So we made the decision to have him euthanized.

"Mom said, 'You take care of it,' and so I did. But it was one of the hardest things I've ever had to do."

Bear Cat lies buried on the Dixon Farm near Middleburg, and this is as it should be. Ohio-bred, owned and shown, he lived his entire life in the Buckeye State and did much to establish and grow the Paint Horse breed in the region.

Right Hand Man, a 1984 stallion by Man In Command (QH) and out of Honey Bear, earned both an APHA Championship and Superior Halter award.
Courtesy APHA

14 TAURUS JING
#15,808

Born into a proven family of speed, this cropout stallion found his niche as a multi-talented show horse and sire.

LIKE BEAR CAT before him, Taurus Jing was something of a forerunner for the cropout halter horse movement that began as a trickle in the 1960s and 1970s and grew into a torrent in the 1980s and 1990s.

Making their appearance during the early years of this era were horses such as Nylon, Sallisaw Rose, Painted Robin and Painted Lasan.

The movement grew in stature and influence with the emergence of horses such as Bear Cat, Flying Fawago and Babby Skit, and it reached a level of total dominance with the arrival of Sonny Dee Bar, Red Sonny Dee and their descendants.

Sandwiched somewhere in the middle of the cropout takeover of the Paint halter horse industry was

Taurus Jing–A cropout forerunner of things to come.
Photo by Libutti

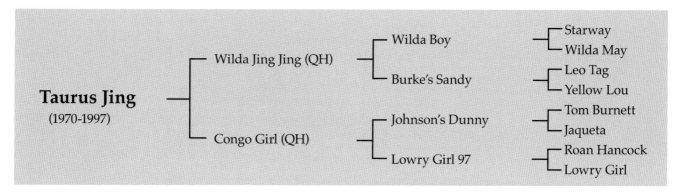

Pedigree chart for Taurus Jing (1970-1997):

- Wilda Jing Jing (QH)
  - Wilda Boy
    - Starway
    - Wilda May
  - Burke's Sandy
    - Leo Tag
    - Yellow Lou
- Congo Girl (QH)
  - Johnson's Dunny
    - Tom Burnett
    - Jaqueta
  - Lowry Girl 97
    - Roan Hancock
    - Lowry Girl

Taurus Jing. At the pinnacle of this Midwestern stallion's show and breeding career, he was one of the breed's brightest young stars. Then fate conspired to put a damper on his march toward becoming one of the industry's all-time greats.

Still, his story is an interesting one, and one that deserves to be told.

Bred to Go Fast

Taurus Jing, a 1970 sorrel overo stallion by Wilda Jing Jing (QH) and out of Congo Girl (QH), was bred by Earl and Virginia Crossman of Plantation, Florida.

The Crossmans were primarily racehorse breeders, and their senior sire ,Wilda Jing Jing, was a 1960 bay stallion by Wilda Boy and out of Burke's Sandy by Leo Tag. A Register of Merit racehorse, Wilda Jing Jing went on to sire one Superior racehorse, eight runners with speed indexes of 90 or higher, and the earners of 18 ROMs and $94,524. Included among this number were two top AQHA-registered sprinters–Jingo Girl S.I. 94 and Lowry Jing S.I. 93–who were full sisters to Taurus Jing.

Congo Girl, the dam of Taurus Jing and his speedy full siblings, was a 1959 brown mare by Johnson's Dunny and out of Lowry Girl 97 by Roan Hancock.

As far as his breeding was concerned then, Taurus Jing was speed-bred on the top and bottom through the foundation running blood of Leo, Joe Hancock and Oklahoma Star. As to where the overo stallion's excessive white markings came from, the finger points straight at his maternal grandsire, Leo Tag.

Leo Tag, a 1949 sorrel stallion by Leo and out of Tagalong, was a AAA-AQHA Champion who also won the 1953 Rocky Mountain Quarter Horse Association Stallion Stakes at Centennial Racetrack in Denver, Colorado. Retired to stud, he sired the Quarter Horse earners of 38 race ROMs and $106,729.

As a Paint Horse sire, Leo Tag was responsible for putting Sky Hi Tag, the 1975 National Champion Calf Roping Horse, and Hot Pants, the 1974 Reserve National Champion 3-Year-Old Mare, into APHA's books. The Leo son also put six cropouts into the registry: Dave's Leo Tag, Willie Tag, Frosty Tag, Janie Tag, Flicka-Tag and Painted Leo Whiz.

What's more, Leo Tag passed his cropout overo genes to his grandson Wilda Jing Jing, who sired five cropouts: Gemini Jing, Taurus Jing, Siringo Jing, Aquarius Jing and Double Jing Jing.

Leo Tag, with his blazed face and four high stockings, was a cropout sire supreme.
Courtesy *Quarter Horse Journal*

Shown here as a weanling, Taurus Jing displays the balance and refinement that remained in evidence throughout his show ring career.
Courtesy APHA

In all, the Crossmans made the Wilda Jing Jing/Congo Girl cross five times. Taurus Jing was the only cropout to come from the matings, and he was also the only one to not be a race winner.

From a very early point in the young Paint's life, it became apparent that his destiny lay not on the track, but rather in the show arena.

Buckeye State Bound

In April of 1971, Virginia Crossman hauled Taurus Jing to a series of three Paint shows in West Palm Beach, Florida. There, under judges Robert Johnson, Bud Alderson and Jack Brainard, the yearling stallion won all three outs.

Bob and Nellie Parsons of Lexington, Ohio, were in attendance at the shows and promptly negotiated to purchase the Crossmans' promising youngster.

After getting Taurus Jing home, the Parsons wasted no time in getting him out before the public. Hauled to the 1971 National Show in Tulsa,

Oklahoma, "Jing" earned the Reserve National Champion Yearling Stallion title.

In addition, he earned grand champion stallion honors as a yearling at the Indiana State Fair, New York State Fair and the Ohio State Paint Show, competing against a field of older Paint cropouts that included the likes of Bear Cat, Painted Eternal and Rockabar.

Brought back as a 2-year-old, the team of Taurus Jing and Bob Parsons continued to take the Paint show scene by storm. In July, in Columbus, Ohio, Jing was named the National Champion 2-Year-Old Stallion. By year's end, his official APHA halter record stood at eight grand championships, three reserves, 10 firsts and three seconds.

The year 1973 saw Taurus Jing add a Superior Halter award to his resume and run his halter record to 27 grands, four reserves, 27 firsts and three seconds. In 1974, Jing added a third national title to his record when he was named the reserve champion aged stallion at the National Show in Jackson, Mississippi.

By 1975, the push was on to make Taurus Jing an APHA Champion. The training and showing chores were turned over to Bob and Nellie Parsons' son Terry, and the goal was achieved on August 16, 1975.

The stallion's final show record was an impressive one. At halter, he earned 49 grand championships, 10 reserve grand championships, 66 firsts, six seconds and 148 points. In performance, he earned 44 points and ROMs in Western pleasure, hunter under saddle and reining.

By the end of his six-year show career, Taurus Jing had proven himself to be one of the nation's top show ring stars. And his career as a breeding horse, which had gotten underway several years earlier, was by now beginning to take off, as well.

Taurus Leaf, a 1974 sorrel overo stallion by Taurus Jing and out of Flagalita, was his sire's first representative in the show ring. Shown by both Bob and Terry Parsons, "Leaf" was the 1977 Reserve National Champion 3-Year-Old Stallion.

In addition, he earned an APHA Championship, Superior awards at halter and in Western pleasure, two ROMs and 135 halter and 458 performance points.

Miss Taurus Jing, a 1974 sorrel overo mare by Taurus Jing and out of Miss Jay Cash, earned an APHA Youth Championship, two ROMs and 39 halter and 72 performance points.

From Taurus Jing's second foal crop, which hit the ground in 1975, came the likes of Taurus Golde and Scorpion Smoke.

"Golde," a 1975 palomino overo gelding out of Buffy Breeze Bar, earned two APHA Championships, Youth Versatility award and Superior Youth Showmanship award, eight ROMs, and 46 halter and 254 performance points. "Smoke," a 1975 sorrel overo mare out of Miss Smokette, was the 1976 Reserve National Champion Yearling Filly. In addition, she earned an APHA Championship, two ROMs and 19 halter and 28 performance points.

During these first years, the golden cross of Taurus Jing on Barton Jewel resulted in three top performers:

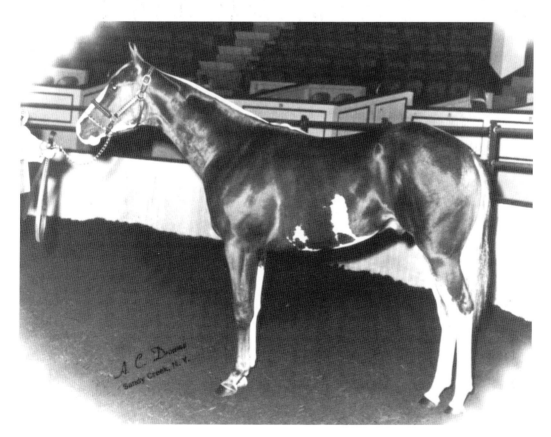

As a yearling, "Jing" earned grand champion stallion honors at the Indiana and New York State Fairs.

Photo by A.C. Drowns

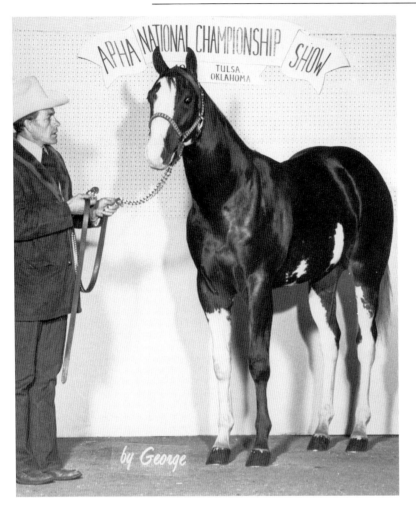

Owner Bob Parsons showed Taurus Jing to reserve champion yearling stallion honors at the 1971 APHA National Show in Tulsa, Oklahoma.
Photo by George Martin

1,275 performance points.

And there were other Taurus Jing winners during this phase of the stallion's life. Among them were:

- Mister Fantastic, a 1977 sorrel tobiano gelding out of Jingo Belle–APHA Champion, one ROM, and 19 halter and 23 performance points.
- Touch Of Taurus, a 1978 sorrel overo mare out of Lady Skip Bars–two APHA Championships, three Superior awards, eight ROMs, and 78 halter and 292 performance points.
- Taurus Bell Tone, a 1978 sorrel tobiano mare out of Half Tone–APHA Champion, Superior Halter, five ROMs, and 78 halter and 167 performance points.
- No Bull Taurus, a 1980 sorrel overo gelding out of Lady Skip Bars–two APHA Championships, 11 ROMs, and 52 halter and 212 performance points.
- Totally Taurus, a 1981 sorrel overo gelding out of Nordeena–three APHA Championships, two Superior awards, 12 ROMs, and 241 halter and 280 performance points.

In 1977, Bob Parsons succumbed to a massive heart attack, suffered while he was showing Taurus Leaf in a junior Western pleasure class.

Terry Parsons, Bob and Nellie's son, was by this time a well-established Paint Horse trainer in his own right. It was Terry who showed Jing to his last national title and it was he who showed the stallion to his APHA Championship.

To begin with, Terry and Nellie continued on with business as usual. Jing continued to stand to the public and the 1978 breeding season saw a full compliment of mares make their way to the stallion's court.

The 1979 season was slow, and as a result, the following spring saw only three Taurus Jing foals hit the ground. By early winter of 1980, the decision was made to sell Jing, and on December 31, 1980, he was transferred to Ray and Jan Barton, of Norco, California.

The Bob Parsons portion of Taurus Jing's life was now over and a new phase was in the offing.

Taurus Jewel, Hope To Shout and Ima Cover Girl.

Taurus Jewel, a 1977 sorrel tobiano mare, earned an APHA Championship, Superior awards in open and amateur Western pleasure, three ROMs, and 41 halter and 169 performance points.

Hope To Shout, a 1978 sorrel tobiano mare, earned a Superior Halter award, two ROMs, and 99 halter and 58 performance points.

Ima Cover Girl, a 1979 overo mare, was the 1982 and 1986 National Champion Trail Horse and 1986 Reserve National Champion Hunter Hack. Shown in youth competition, she was the 1983 National Champion Trail Horse, 1986 World Champion Working Hunter, 1988 World Champion Hunter Hack and 1986 Reserve World Champion Hunter Hack.

In addition, she earned two Versatility awards, three APHA Championships, 16 Superior event awards, 19 ROMs, and 69 halter and

California Dreamin'

Once in place on the Bartons' Ray Jan Paint Horse Ranch in Southern California, Taurus Jing settled back into his role as an up-and-coming Paint Horse sire. Remaining in place as the Barton establishment's senior sire for a dozen years, Jing continued to prove his worth.

To be sure, the emphasis of the Barton program was heavily weighted toward the halter end of the industry. As a result, most of Taurus Jing's West Coast performers were bred with that event in mind. Among the stallion's top performers during this stage of his life were:

- My Ladys Mercedes, a 1985 red roan overo mare out of Sassy Skip–Superior Halter and 98 halter points.
- Ima Hussy, a 1986 chestnut overo mare out of Go Lady Go–Superior Halter and 155 halter points.
- Im Bud Light, a 1988 chestnut overo gelding out of Go Lady Go–Superior Open and Amateur Halter, and 257 halter points.
- U No It, a 1990 chestnut overo gelding out of Go Lady Go–Superior Youth Halter and 150 halter points.

The team of Bob Parsons and Taurus Jing were a force to be reckoned with in the Paint show circles of the early 1970s. **Courtesy APHA**

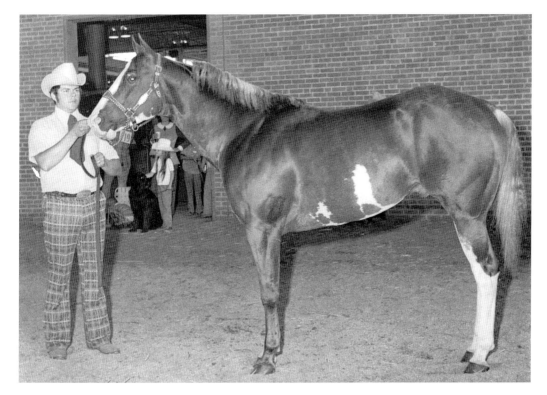

Terry Parsons showed Jing to his APHA Championship in 1975.
Courtesy APHA

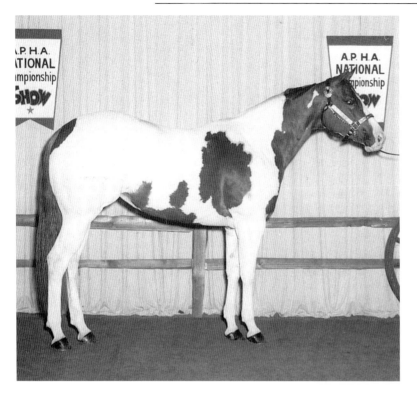

Hope To Shout, a 1978 sorrel tobiano mare by Taurus Jing and out of Barton Jewel, earned a Superior Halter award. **Courtesy APHA**

Ima Cover Girl, a 1979 sorrel overo mare by Taurus Jing and out of Barton Jewel, was the 1983 Youth National Champion Trail Horse. That's Farley Pritchard of Macedon, New York, in the saddle. **Photo by Don Shugart**

• Continental Kismet, a 1987 sorrel overo mare out of Continental Jill–Superior Open and Amateur Halter, and 268 halter points.

In the fall of 1992, fate decreed that 22-year-old Taurus Jing should experience one more geographical change. This time, it was to the Cottonwood, California, ranch of Bill and Sylvia Powell–a move that was initially meant to be a retirement.

"We had lived for years in Southern California," Sylvia says. "We knew Ray and Jan Barton, and we knew Taurus Jing. We had bred mares to him and gotten some nice foals. After we moved to Northern California, the Bartons got in touch with us to see if we would be willing to provide Jing with a retirement home. We had more space on our new ranch, so we agreed.

"After we got him settled in, we decided to bred a few of our own mares to him. Then, some of our Paint friends in the area wanted to breed to him. So we used him lightly at stud for several years, until he went sterile between the 1997 and 1998 breeding seasons.

"Even after that, we kept him up and tried to make his last years as comfortable as possible. By the fall of 2001, Jing's general health had begun to deteriorate. We couldn't keep any weight on him and he had become unsteady on his feet. We didn't want him to fall and hurt himself, so, on September 15, we had him put to sleep."

APHA records reveal that Taurus Jing sired 210 registered foals, and of these, 77 performers earned two national championships, three reserve national championships, two world championships, one reserve world championship, three Versatility awards, 18 APHA Championships, 36 Superior event awards, 105 ROMs and 6,000 points in all divisions combined.

Born in the Southeast, shown to prominence in the Midwest and stood at stud in the Far West, Taurus Jing was a well-traveled stallion who got the job done wherever he was.

As one of the first great cropout show horses and sires of his era, he was both a standard-bearer for the present and a harbinger of things to come.

My Ladys Mercedes, a 1985 red roan overo mare by Taurus Jing and out of Sassy Skip, earned a Superior and 98 points at halter.
Courtesy APHA

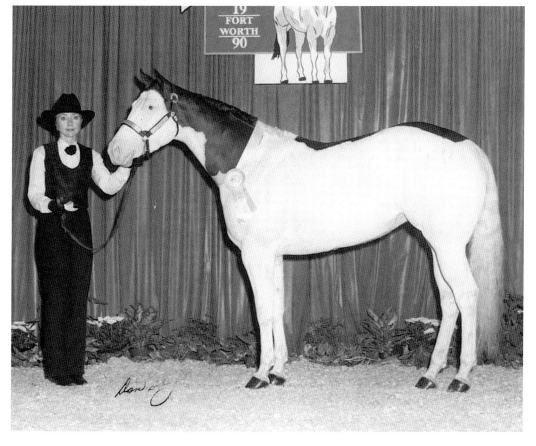

Continental Kismet, a 1987 sorrel overo mare by Taurus Jing and out of Continental Jill, was a Superior Open and Amateur halter horse with 268 points to her credit.
Photo by Don Shugart

15 FLYING FAWAGO
#5495

As the founder of one of Nebraska's first Paint Horse families, this cropout stallion had a profound impact on the breed.

Flying Fawago was a champion show horse and sire in two countries.
Courtesy APHA

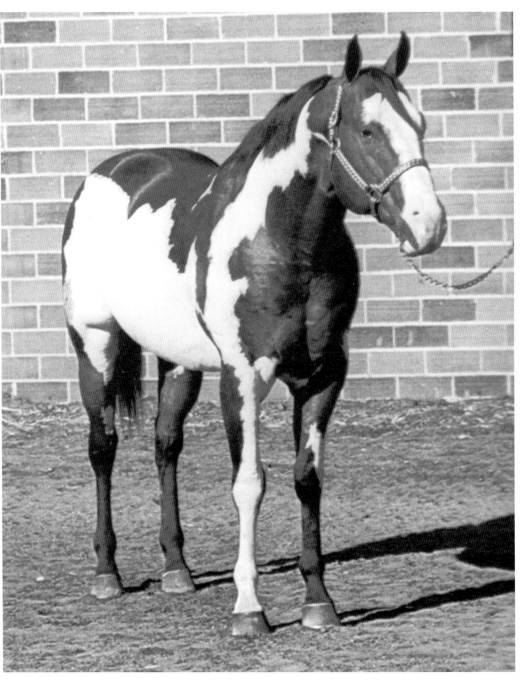

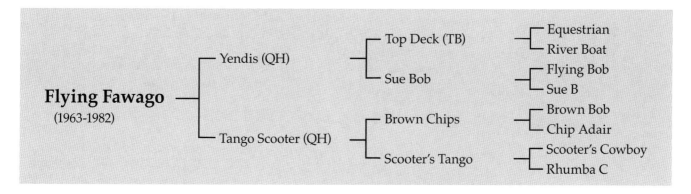

Flying Fawago
(1963-1982)
— Yendis (QH)
— Top Deck (TB)
— Equestrian
— River Boat
— Sue Bob
— Flying Bob
— Sue B
— Tango Scooter (QH)
— Brown Chips
— Brown Bob
— Chip Adair
— Scooter's Tango
— Scooter's Cowboy
— Rhumba C

ONCE THE PAINT Horse movement got its start in the Lone Star State in the early 1960s, it didn't take long for it to spread. By the mid- to late part of that decade, Paints had established footholds throughout the Central and Northern Plains.

In 1967, a loud-colored overo stallion from Nebraska surfaced who would soon become well known throughout the country. His name was Flying Fawago, and he was owned by Donna Loomis of Elkhorn.

A Rare Blend

Flying Fawago, a 1963 bay overo stallion by Yendis (QH) and out of Tango Scooter (QH), was bred by W. E. "Bill" Evans of Scottsdale, Arizona.

Yendis was owned during this time by M. T. Clemans of Florence, Arizona, and Evans had purchased Tango Scooter with a bay Yendis filly at her side and bred back in May of 1961. The following spring, a brown filly was born and Evans decided to take "Tango" back to the court of Yendis for a third and final time.

The result of the "third time's a charm" cross hit the ground on March 3, 1963—a loud-colored bay overo colt who was, for the first four years of his life, relegated to an Arizona back pasture. From a breeding standpoint, the colt was an interesting blend of race and ranch bloodlines.

Yendis was a AAA-rated, stakes winning racehorse by Top Deck (TB) and out of Sue Bob by Flying Bob. Top Deck was, at the time, one of the industry's hottest race sires and Sue Bob was an ROM racehorse in her own right and the dam of three AAA-rated runners.

Tango Scooter, on the other hand, was of pure working horse blood. Sired by Brown Chips and out of Scooter Tango, she was a product of such renowned Texas programs as the King Ranch, JA Ranch and Waggoner Ranch. In addition, she traced to such notable foundation sires as Wimpy P-1, Oklahoma Star P-6 and Waggoner's Rainy Day P-13.

Bill Evans' loud-colored cropout colt, then, was a blend of speed and athleticism that would some day stand him in good stead. But, first, he would have to be discovered.

Which is exactly what happened in the spring of 1967.

One for the Money

By the mid-1960s, Donna Shrader of Elkhorn, Nebraska, was an accomplished "twenty-something" horsewoman. Raised on the family farm, she had grown up showing first in open horse shows and then in AQHA-sanctioned competition.

While still a teenager, Donna had acquired her first Paint Horse. This was Bar-B-Doll, a 1957 sorrel overo mare of unknown breeding. Trained and shown by the young Nebraskan, Bar-B-Doll was APHA's 1967 National Champion Sr. Western Pleasure Horse.

In April of 1967, Donna married an up-and-coming young Nebraska horse trainer named Bob Loomis. On the couple's honeymoon trip to southern Arizona, they happened across a loud-colored Paint stallion in a rural setting.

Donna Loomis, now Donna Brown of Ava, Missouri, recalls the occurrence.

"Back in those days," she says, "there weren't a lot of Paint Horses around. If you ran across one—particularly one that was a good-looking overo—you generally tried to find out what it was.

As captured through the camera lens by renowned photographer Johnny Johnston, who began his career in the Arabian industry, Flying Fawago's headshot (above) and side profile (below) take on a decidedly different air.

Photos by Johnny Johnston

"Bob and I were out driving around in the desert when we spied this Paint Horse up on a hill. We stopped and looked him over, and then checked around until we found out who owned him.

"The man was a small-time breeder, as I recall. He had a few nice mares, and he took them out to be bred to some pretty good studs each year. He was surprised and disappointed when one of his mares foaled this loud-colored Paint cropout colt, so he just hid him out for four years. He never broke him to ride or registered him. He just put him out on pasture.

"To make a long story short," Donna continues, "the man was really wanting to sell the colt, so we bought him right on the spot. And then we went out and bought a trailer to haul him back to Nebraska in.

"I've wondered many times how it was that the man never gelded the colt, but I'm glad he didn't because he turned into a pretty nice horse."

After getting her 4-year-old Paint stallion home, Donna registered him with APHA as Flying Fawago—with "Fawago" being an Anglicized version

of the Spanish fuego, or "fire."

She then went to work making him ready for the show ring.

"Even though 'Fawago' was barely halter broke when I got him," she says, "he was an easy horse to break. He never really gave me any trouble at all. I didn't push him that spring or summer; I just broke him and started getting him ready for pleasure.

"He was a big horse, standing a strong 15-3 hands high and weighing 1,250 pounds. To begin with, he really showed his Thoroughbred breeding. Then, as he matured, he got a lot stouter.

"His head had that 'Top Deck' look; not bad but not real outstanding. He was blessed with a long, slender neck and throatlatch, though, and was well proportioned with big forearms and gaskins. He was just a nice horse all the way around."

Two for the Show

Flying Fawago and Donna made their Paint Horse show debut in late September of 1967. Exhibited at the National Dairy Congress Show in Waterloo, Iowa, Fawago placed fifth in aged stallions and third in senior Western pleasure.

In January of 1968, the pair traveled to Denver, Colorado, to compete at the National Western Stock Show. After placing fourth in aged stallions, Fawago won the senior Western pleasure class. He then came back to place fourth in the all-breed championship Western pleasure stakes.

From Denver, it was on to the Southwestern Fat Stock Show and Exposition in Fort Worth, Texas, where Fawago placed fourth in aged stallions and second in senior Western pleasure.

As the year progressed, the big bay overo began to round out into top show shape. On July 7, 1968, he earned grand champion stallion honors and won the Western pleasure class in Sioux City, Iowa. On September 7, he stood grand ahead of Snip Bar at a Harvester, Missouri, show. The following day, he earned reserve honors behind Snip Bar in Alton, Illinois.

This ad, which appeared in the March-April, 1970 issue of the Paint Horse Journal, shows "Fawago" and owner/trainer Donna Loomis after their winning performance in the sr. western pleasure class.
Courtesy APHA

Exhibited at the 1968 APHA Nationals in Oklahoma City, Oklahoma, Fawago was the co-reserve champion aged stallion and placed fourth in senior Western pleasure. (From a point-tallying standpoint, the 1968 National Show was arguably the most confusing on record. There were no less than 12 co-national champions, and in the aged stallion class alone there were two horses tied for first, two horses tied for second and four horses tied for third.)

Following the Nationals, it was back to the National Dairy Cattle Congress Show in Waterloo, Iowa. This time around, Fawago managed better than he had the year before. Tabbed the grand champion stallion, he also placed first in aged stallions, ahead of J Bar Junior and Apache Norfleet.

As frosting on the cake, the 1968 show season also saw Flying Fawago qualify as an APHA Champion with four grands, one reserve and an ROM in Western pleasure to his credit.

With only limited showing in 1969, Fawago hit the tanbark trail in earnest during the next two years. The highlight of 1970 occurred at the APHA National Show, held August 19–21 in Amarillo, Texas. There, the 7-year-old stallion was named champion aged stallion over a field of 17 that included the likes of Painted Gem, Mr. Blue Eyes, Spunky's Blaise, Joechief Bar and Bear Cat.

Retired at the end of the 1971 show season, Flying Fawago's official APHA record shows him to be the earner of one national championship, one reserve national championship, an APHA Championship, and ROMs in Western pleasure, hunter under saddle and reining. In addition, he earned 37 halter points and 47 performance points: 25 Western pleasure, eight hunter under saddle, eight reining, three barrel racing, two trail and one Western riding.

And, although Fawago had pulled double duty as a breeding stallion throughout his show years, now it was time for him to prove what he could do as a sire.

The Cornhusker Years

Flying Fawago stood in Nebraska for 11 years, from 1968 through 1978. His first foal crop, numbering five, hit the ground in 1969, and from it came a pair of top performers—The Fawago Kid and Fawago Star.

Fawago Star, a 1969 black overo mare by Flying Fawago and out of April's Sunshine (QH), was named as the 1971 Reserve National Champion Jr. English Pleasure Horse.

Photo by George Martin

The following year, Donna Loomis showed "Star" to a pair of national titles at the APHA National Show in Columbus, Ohio.
Photo by George Martin

The Fawago Kid, a 1969 bay overo gelding out of Peggy Warren (QH), was bred by Tom Esse of Butler, Iowa. Sold first to Donna Loomis, he was shown to his APHA Championship. Resold to Kim Coggburn of Pleasant Hill, Missouri, he went on to earn a Youth Versatility award, APHA Youth Championship, and Superiors in youth Western pleasure, showmanship and halter. All told, the versatile gelding earned nine ROMs and 494 points.

Fawago Star, a 1969 black overo mare out of April's Sunshine (QH), was bred by Dean Miller of Hornick, Iowa. Shown by him at the 1971 National Western Stock Show in Denver, Colorado, the Flying Fawago daughter earned grand champion mare honors.

Sold to Lisa Drew of Lincoln, Nebraska, "Star" was shown by Donna Loomis to the National Champion 3-Year-Old Mare and Reserve National Champion Hunter Under Saddle Horse titles at the 1972 APHA National Show in Columbus, Ohio.

Exhibited in youth competition by Lisa Drew, Star was the 1972 National Champion Youth Mare, a Youth APHA Champion, and the earner of Superior awards in youth halter and hunter under saddle.

In 1973, Star was sold and exported to Cuba.

Getting back to the patriarch of the line, Flying Fawago sired no foals during the 1970 season, his second crop hitting the ground in 1971. From it came two more APHA Champions: Yellow Thunder, a 1971 buckskin overo gelding out of Charcoal Pet (QH); and Fawago King, a 1971 sorrel overo stallion out of Yuccas Dream (QH).

Fawago King became his sire's most notable son and will be profiled in the following chapter.

From Flying Fawago's third and fourth foal crops—born in 1972 and 1973—Lewago and Chawago were the top performers.

Lewago, a 1972 blue roan overo gelding out of Blue Roan Time (QH), was bred by Kitty Brown of Abilene, Kansas. Exhibited first by Julie Hull of Keller, Texas, and later by Marci Dringman of Logan, Utah, Lewago

Fawago's Trix, a 1974 sorrel overo mare by Flying Fawago and out of King's Trix, was the 1979 Reserve National Champion Western Riding Horse.
Photo by Don Shugart

earned a Youth Versatility award, two APHA Youth Championships, a Superior youth hunter under saddle award and nine ROMs.

Chawago, 1973 buckskin overo mare out of Charcoal Pet (QH), was bred by Marilyn Drew of Lincoln, Nebraska. Shown in open, amateur and youth competition by a variety of owners, Chawago earned an open APHA Championship, one Amateur Versatility award, two Youth Versatility awards, a APHA Youth Championship, 12 Superior event awards, 31 ROMs and 1,347 points in all divisions combined.

There were several other Flying Fawago performers from the classes of 1972 and 1973. Included among them were:
• Fawago's Peggy, a 1972 sorrel overo mare out of Ace's Pappoose (QH)—APHA Champion.
• Sweet Alice, a 1973 sorrel overo mare out of Ace's Pappoose (QH)—APHA Champion.
• Flying Rocket, a 1973 bay tobiano gelding out of Leo's Flying Paint—Superior Halter and APHA Youth Champion.
Fawago's Trix and Fawago's Barney were their sire's next show ring

superstars.

Fawago's Trix, a 1974 sorrel overo mare out of King's Trix, was bred by Donna Loomis. Transferred to no fewer than a dozen owners over during the next 17 years, "Trix" became her sire's top performer.

Among her top honors were: 1980 National Champion Trail, 1979 Reserve National Champion Western Riding, 1990 Reserve World Champion Western Riding, 1983 National Champion Amateur Hunter Under Saddle, 1983 Reserve National Champion Showmanship at Halter and Western Riding.

In addition, the durable campaigner earned on Amateur Versatility award, two Youth Versatility awards, two APHA Championships, 13 Superior event awards, 26 ROMs and 1,446 points in all divisions combined.

Fawago's Barney, a 1974 sorrel overo gelding out of Ace's Papoose (QH), was bred by Donna Loomis. Sold to Cindy Jensen of Seward, Nebraska, "Barney" became the 1978 Reserve National Champion Trail Horse and the 1979 Reserve National Champion Youth Pole Bending Horse.

In addition, he was the earner of a Youth Versatility award, one Superior Youth Champion award, two APHA Championships, nine Superior event awards, 13 ROMs and 887 points in all divisions combined.

Flying Fawago was, by this time, generally acknowledged as one of the breed's top young all-around sires. Throughout the latter part of the 1970s, he continued to add to his siring record. Among his top performers during this timeframe were:
• Lady Madonna, a 1974 black overo mare out of Dottie Diamond (QH)—APHA Champion.
• Fawago's Freddie, a 1978 chestnut overo gelding out of Cokie Bar (QH)—APHA Champion; Superior Western pleasure, hunter under saddle and trail.
In the summer of 1978, Donna Loomis Brown decided to sell her popular stallion.

"Around this time," she says, "I had the misfortune of losing one of my all-time favorite horses. She was a Quarter

Horse mare named June's Gray Lady, and she died of cornstalk poisoning.

"I had match-raced 'Lady' and run barrels with her, and then she even produced a AAA racehorse for me. Her loss devastated me, and it was while I was still trying to deal with it that some folks from Canada came down and asked me to price Flying Fawago.

"Looking back, I can see that I was probably a little down on everything at the time. But I do remember thinking to myself, 'Well, I'd rather see Fawago leave healthy in a horse trailer than have him die from something like cornstalk poisoning.

"So I priced him and they bought him."

The Calgary Years

APHA records confirm that, on January 5, 1979, Flying Fawago was transferred to the Pioneer Paint Syndicate of Irricana, Alberta, Canada, with Happy and Sharon Tegart of Kathryn, Alberta, the majority syndicate owners. From his Justanother Farm, located 25 miles

northeast of Calgary, Happy Tegart recalls the circumstances surrounding Fawago's move north.

"The Paints were just starting to take hold up here in the late 1970s," he says. "We knew that Flying Fawago was a foundation sire in the States, and we felt he could also be one here in Canada. So we went down and bought him and three of his daughters. Of the three mares, Foxy Fawago was far-and-away the best."

Foxy Fawago, a 1977 bay overo mare out of Dixie Chicaro, was bred by Michael Bennett of Wood River, Nebraska. Sold to the Tegart family in July of 1978, she went on to become one of Alberta's first great show horses, an APHA Champion and earner of three Superior awards, 13 ROMs and 445 points in all divisions combined.

Among Fawago's other top "North Country" performers were:
- Thank Goodness, a 1980 sorrel overo mare out of Debby's Leo Bar (QH)—APHA Champion.
- Fawago's Hoot, a 1981 brown overo gelding out of Sparky Yucca Miss

Hauled to the 1980 National Show at Oklahoma City, Oklahoma, "Trix" was named as the National Champion Trail Horse.
Photo by Don Shugart

Fawago's Barney, a 1974 sorrel overo gelding by Flying Fawago and out of Ace's Papoose (QH), was a top 4-H mount for owner Cindy Jensen of Seward, Nebraska.
Courtesy APHA

Shown in APHA youth and amateur competition, "Barney" and Cindy amassed an impressive array of wins.
Photo by Don Shugart

(QH)—nine ROMs and 234 points in all divisions combined.
- Moonfire Kiara, a 1982 palomino overo mare out of Princess Moonbeam (QH)—APHA Champion.
- Do Yucca Do, a 1982 bay overo mare out of Sparky Yucca Miss (QH)—APHA Champion and Superior Halter.
- Fawago's Legacy, a 1982 bay overo

stallion out of Justanother Goody—ROM Western pleasure, hunter under saddle and hunter hack, and earner of 91 performance points.

The End of an Era

As recalled by his last owner, Flying Fawago's health took a bizarre turn for the worse in the spring and summer of 1982.

"It was during breeding season that we first suspected that something was wrong with Fawago," Happy Tegart says. "He was having trouble maintaining his balance, and when he looked at us, he'd tip his head, like he was trying to relieve some pressure.

"Straightaway, we hauled him down to the Western College of Veterinarian Medicine at Saskatoon, Saskatchewan. They diagnosed him with a brain tumor but weren't able to do anything with it. He passed away in the fall of 1982, when he was 19 years old."

Flying Fawago's 13th and final foal crop hit the ground in 1983. Numbering five, it included the renowned stallion's last point earner, Fawago's Future, a 1983 bay overo stallion out of Justanother Goody and the earner of one amateur halter point.

APHA records verify that Flying Fawago sired 135 registered foals. Of these, 53 performers earned five National Championships, seven Reserve National Championships, one Reserve World Championship, nine Versatility awards, one Superior Youth Championship, 24 APHA Championships, 52 Superior event awards, 184 ROMs and 8,080 points in all divisions combined.

And, according both Donna Brown and Happy Tegart, Flying Fawago should not only be remembered because of his accomplishments as a show horse and sire, but also for another hallmark characteristic—that of being easy to get along with.

"Fawago was the absolute best-mannered stallion that I was ever around," Brown says. "He was easy to train, ride, show and haul. And, around the place, nothing rattled him. And his foals were just like him. I'd break one of them out and ride it for 30 to 60 days, and then sell or lease it to a youth. Those colts were just so gentle and willing that the kids could go on with them and do well."

Tegart adds that the stallion was a big, stout horse.

"I used to rodeo a bit, and then had a small cattle ranch," he says. "I rode Fawago around the ranch a lot, and even though he had a little age on him, he was still a lot of horse.

"My wife, Sharon, and I have stayed in the Paints over the years, but Flying Fawago was our last stud. He was just such an outstanding horse to be around that we didn't think we could ever replace him.

"He had a lot of ability, a lot of 'try,' and he just wanted to be good all of the time."

Blue Max, a 1983 black overo stallion by Blue Mark and out of I'm A Fawago, was an APHA Champion, Superior Halter Horse. Retired to stud, he sired 78 point earners that earned 862 halter and 10,097 performance points.
Photo by G. Willis

16 FAWAGO KING
#18,180

Known as one of the breed's most prolific all-around sires, this Nebraska stallion has kept the Fawago line alive.

Fawago King – the Versatility Sire.   **Photo by Tucker**

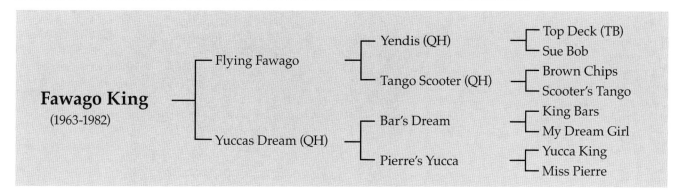

```
                                            ┌── Yendis (QH)          ┌── Top Deck (TB)
                      ┌── Flying Fawago      │                       └── Sue Bob
                      │                      └── Tango Scooter (QH)   ┌── Brown Chips
Fawago King ─────────┤                                               └── Scooter's Tango
(1963-1982)           │                      ┌── Bar's Dream          ┌── King Bars
                      └── Yuccas Dream (QH)  │                       └── My Dream Girl
                                             └── Pierre's Yucca       ┌── Yucca King
                                                                     └── Miss Pierre
```

FLYING FAWAGO, WHOSE life was detailed in the preceding chapter, was a foundation Paint Horse sire in both the United States and Canada. Early on in his breeding career, he sired a son who would go on to become an influential sire in his own right.

That son's name was Fawago King.

Paint Horse Royalty

Fawago King, a 1971 sorrel overo stallion by Flying Fawago and out of Yucca's Dream, was bred by Marilyn Wilber of Peyton, Colorado. As a detailed look at his pedigree reveals, "King" was aptly named.

Flying Fawago was a unique blend of racehorse blood on the top of his pedigree and working blood on the bottom. Yucca's Dream traced once to AQHA Hall of Fame Horse Three Bars (TB) and four times to AQHA Hall of Fame Horse King P-234.

Three Bars remains, 40 years after his death, the most influential sire in Western Horse history. And King stands alone, 50 years after his passing, as the fountainhead of the most potent cutting and reining line of all time.

It was not to either Three Bars or King that Yucca's Dream inherited her primary cropout Paint gene, however. That honor goes to her maternal grandsire, Yucca King, a 1953 black stallion by R. Joking and out of Hobo's Mona. In addition, she was a maternal granddaughter of Yucca King—a black, bald-faced AQHA Champion stallion who made headlines in the early 1960s when he sold for $50,000.

Yucca King was a documented sire of cropout color. What's more, he was also a descendant of the Hobo/Joe Moore family of South Texas

racehorses, which was well known for its ability to produce cropouts.

As for Yucca's Dream, she spent her entire life as a Paint Horse producer. APHA records reveal her to be the dam of nine overo foals from 1971 to 1984. Of these, eight were sired by Paint stallions. The ninth, a 1979 sorrel cropout overo stallion sired by Dino Dell (QH), went on to earn an APHA Championship and Superior Halter award.

Getting back to Fawago King, the first two years of his life were spent in relative obscurity. In March of 1974, as a short 2-year-old, he was sold to H. R. W. and Verna Scott of Plankinton, South Dakota.

The Scotts kept the young Paint for just over two years before selling him to R. D. Robertson of New Brunswick, Nebraska, in May of 1976. Robertson, a Quarter Horse breeder and horse trader, kept the then-5-year-old stallion

After being purchased by Don and Carolyn Croghan of Shuyler, Nebraska, "King" was shown to his APHA Championship.
Courtesy APHA

King's Valentine, shown here with Mindy Dubsky, was one of the top all-around show horses of her era.

Photo by Teri

for only a month before selling him to Don and Carolyn Croghan of Schuyler, Nebraska.

The Croghans were Fawago King's final owners, and together with their children and grandchildren, they created a Paint Horse line that left an indelible mark on the breed.

A Cornhusker Champion

Don Croghan was a third-generation Nebraskan who was born and raised on a small farm near Schuyler. In the early 1970s, he bought his first APHA-registered Paint Horse. This was Skip Sky Hi, a 1969 palomino overo gelding by Skip On and out of Sporty Bell (QH).

Turned over to Don's son and daughter – Mike and Vicki – and granddaughters – Kari Freeman and Courtney Dubsky – "Skippy" earned an APHA Championship and three APHA Youth Championships. More importantly, the versatile gelding put the Croghan clan in Paint Horses to stay.

By the mid-1970s, Don Croghan had put together a band of Paint broodmares and was in need of a

stallion. He was well aware of what Donna Loomis Brown and Flying Fawago were doing in both the show arena and breeding shed, so it was only natural to look to that line for help.

When Fawago King came up for sale in Nebraska, Donna made Croghan aware of the fact, and on June 2, 1976, the Flying Fawago son was installed at the head of the Croghan Paint Horse show and breeding program.

King had been lightly shown prior to this change of ownership. He was taken back to the show ring and, within two months, had acquired the final points necessary for his APHA Championship. APHA records also show that he earned ROMs in Western pleasure and hunter under saddle, and 89 total points: 19 halter, 36 Western pleasure, 21 hunter under saddle, seven Western riding, and two each in reining, barrel racing and pole bending.

This was a modest show record to say the least, but then it was not as an arena performer that Fawago King was destined to make his greatest mark. Instead, he became known as a sire of arena performers.

A Versatile Sire

Fawago King's breeding career actually got underway while he was still owned by the Scott family in South Dakota. APHA records verify that from 1974 through 1976 King sired five foals, with none of them point earners.

After having no foals born in 1977, King's siring record took a decidedly upward turn in 1978 when the stallion's first Nebraska foal crop hit the ground. From it came the line's first legitimate superstar.

King's Valentine, a 1978 red dun overo mare out of Indio's Crosspatch, was bred by Vicki Croghan. Foaled on Valentine's Day, "Valentine" became the Croghan family's first homebred all-around champion. First and foremost, she helped Courtney Dubsky earn honors as the No. 1 Youth in the Nation in 1990.

Then, shown by various members of the family, the mare earned four Versatility awards, two Superior Championships, six APHA

Championships, 24 Superior event awards, 59 ROMs and 3,235 points.

Retired to the broodmare band and bred to the Croghan-owned stallion Fig Newton in 1977, she produced Oliver Newton John the following spring. Shown by the Croghan clan, this double-bred Fawago King grandson earned five Versatility awards, one Superior Championship, five APHA Championships, eight Superior event awards, 81 ROMs and 4,354 points.

Fawago King's second Nebraska foal crop hit the ground in 1979. It numbered six, of which two were performers that earned eight halter and eight performance points.

The next foal crop was destined to meet with a little more success. Numbering nine, it included such top performers as:

• Maris Dream, a 1980 sorrel overo mare out of Dunny's Lisa Rae—1993 Reserve World Champion Youth Western Riding, three Versatility awards, three APHA Championships, 10 Superior event awards, 40 ROMs and 1,516 points.

• Kings Chrome, a 1980 sorrel overo gelding out of Salty's Dusty (QH)—1987 World Champion Youth English Equitation, 1986 and 1987 Reserve World Champion Youth Hunter Under Saddle, one Versatility award, four APHA Championships, nine Superior event awards, 29 ROMs and 1,927 points.

• Kings Bonfire, a 1980 sorrel overo stallion out of Aflame's Blondie— Versatility award, APHA Championship, two Superior event awards, eight ROMs and 332 points.

• Foxy Fawago Pie, a 1980 sorrel overo mare out of Foxy Cutter (QH)—four APHA Championships, two Superior event awards, 15 ROMs and 596 points.

During the next decade—from 1981 through 1990—Fawago King continued his climb up the ladder as one of the breed's top all-around sires. Among his brightest stars during this period were Flashy Fawago Tag, Apple Dumpling, Garth Brooks and Windy Breeze.

Flashy Fawago Tag, a 1982 sorrel overo mare out of Flashy Poco Blaze (QH), was bred by Tim Franklin of Nickerson, Nebraska. Under a variety of owners, she earned four Versatility awards, two Superior Championships, seven APHA Championships, 27 Superior event awards, 52 ROMs and 3,575 points.

Apple Dumpling, a 1982 sorrel overo mare out of Aflame's Blondie (QH), was bred by Donald and Carolyn Croghan. Retained by them, she earned two Versatility awards, two APHA Championships, three Superior event awards, 24 ROMs and 822 points.

Retired to the broodmare band, she produced Scooper Flame, earner of one Versatility award, three APHA Championships, 10 Superior event awards, 35 ROMs and 1,404 points.

Oliver Newton John was a double-bred Fawago King granddaughter who earned more than 4,300 points during her show career. Courtney Dubsky is aboard the versatile performer in this curtain shot.

Photo by Melissa

Flashy Fawago Tag, shown here with Mindy Dubsky in the saddle and Courtney at the head, earned more than 3,500 show ring points.

Photo by Dickson

Garth Brooks, a 1990 sorrel overo gelding out of Salty's Duster (QH), was bred by the Croghans. Sold to Jim and Vicki Pflasterer of Grand Island, Nebraska, he earned two Versatility awards, two APHA Championships, seven Superior event awards, 36 ROMs and 1,432 points.

Windy Breeze, a 1986 black overo mare out of Spartan's Breeze, was also bred by Donald and Carolyn. Shown by the Croghan family, she earned one Versatility award, one APHA Championship, three Superior event awards, 23 ROMs and 819 points.

In addition to those superstars, a host of other Fawago King get proved their worth in the show ring. Included among them were:

- Duster King, a 1981 sorrel overo gelding out of Miss Duster Twist (QH)—1986 Reserve World Champion Amateur Showmanship Horse and earner of two APHA Championships, three Superior event awards, seven ROMs and 427 points.
- Classic King, a 1981 chestnut overo gelding out of Teques Lady 261 (QH)—two APHA Championships, seven ROMs and 256 points.
- Archway, a 1983 sorrel overo gelding out of Tuff Cookie—APHA Champion, four ROMs and 167 points.
- King Frederick, a 1985 bay overo gelding out of I'ma Susie Bar (QH)—two APHA Championships, Superior event awards, 18 ROMs and 510 points.
- Spicey Cookie, a 1989 sorrel overo mare out of Tuff Cookie—one Versatility award, one APHA Championship, one Superior event award, 13 ROMs and 409 points.

As the 1990s dawned, Fawago King entered the last phase of his breeding career. Now in his 20s, he sired 27 foals from 1991 through 1994. Included among these were the stallion's last top performer, King Of The World, and last point earner, Miracle Maker.

King Of The World, a 1993 sorrel overo stallion out of Jodee, was bred by the Croghans. Shown by the family, he earned two APHA Championships, four ROMs and 238 points.

Miracle Maker, a 1994 chestnut overo gelding out of Poppys Memory (QH), was bred by Lois Barrett of Watertown, South Dakota. Sold to Kelli Anderson of Henry, South Dakota, the gelding earned two ROMs and 42 points.

As for Fawago King, the venerable sire passed away of natural causes in the fall of 1993 at the age of 22.

APHA records reveal that he sired 141 registered foals, and of these, 52 performers earned five world championships, seven reserve world championships, 19 Versatility awards, four Superior Youth Championships, 43 APHA Championships, 95 Superior event awards, 377 ROMs and 17,439 points in all divisions combined.

Fawago King had the decided benefit of being owned for most of his life by a highly talented family of horsemen and –women.

Don and Carolyn Crogan, the heads of the family, passed away in

February of 2004 and November of 1995, respectively. Daughter Colleen Croghan Dubsky, who still resides in the Schuyler area, remembers the Fawago King "glory years" with fondness.

"There were five of us children," she recalls, one boy – Mike – and four girls – Donna, myself, Janet and Vicki. By the time you factored in the spouses and the grandchildren, there would be 19 of us that would load up at any given time and head to the shows. And, of these, there were probably 17 that actually showed.

"In recent years, even the great-grandchildren have gotten in the act. Justin Lutjelusche, my grandson, is currently showing in the lead line class at the Paint shows.

"After being a show mom for years to my three kids – Courtney, Mindy and Nathan, I've gotten my amateur can and am doing some all-around showing myself. Just like horses, I think that the gets to be in the human bloodlines as well."

The Line Lives On

Just as Flying Fawago and Donna Loomis Brown formed one of Nebraska's first formidable show and breeding teams, so, too, did Fawago King and the Croghan family advance the Fawago line and keep it alive into the new millennium.

Fig Newton, a 1981 sorrel overo stallion by Fawago King and out of Tuff Cookie, has certainly done his part to add luster to the family name. Bred by Vicki Croghan, he was shown by the family to his APHA Championship. Retired to stud, he eventually replaced his sire as head of the Croghan breeding program.

From a mere 88 foals and 17 performers, Fig Newton sired the earners of more than 12,000 points. In addition to the aforementioned Oliver Newton John, they included:

• Wayne Newton, a 1986 sorrel overo gelding out of Aflame's Blondie (QH)—two Versatility awards, four APHA Championships, seven Superior event awards, 31 ROMs and 1,319 points.

Apple Dumpling and Mindy Dubsky teamed up with lots of support from Colleen Dubsky to earn a Youth APHA Championship on May 26, 1999.
Courtesy the Croghan family

Likewise, Windy Breeze and Nathan Dubsky combined to earn seven Youth ROMs and 178 points during the 1992 show season.
Courtesy the Croghan family

King of the World, shown here with Courtney Dubsky Lutjelusche and Don Croghan, remains a vital part of the family Paint Horse breeding program.

Courtesy the Croghan family

• Izaak Newton, a 1988 chestnut overo gelding out of Foxy Fawago Pie—one Versatility award, five APHA Championships, 10 Superior event awards, 59 ROMs and 1,926 points.
• Sum Red Newton, a 1990 sorrel overo gelding out of Sum Red Cat (QH)—five Versatility awards, two Superior Championships, six APHA Championships, six Superior event awards, 75 ROMs and 3,003 points.
• Figamajic, a 1994 sorrel overo geld-

When the Croghan program was in its heyday, many family members participated in showing. In this group shot they are (from the left) Vicki Pflasterer; Courtney Dubsky; Teresa Croghan; Ed Mullinix; Mike Croghan and son A.J.; Mindy Dubsky; Jani and Carrie Gilson; Missy Freeman and Kari Lowe.

Photo by Teri courtesy Croghan family

ing out of Dusters Sweetrobin—two Versatility awards, four APHA Championships, nine Superior event awards, 22 ROMs and 949 points.

Newtons Top Gun, a 2002 bay overo gelding out of Top Guns Rascal—one Versatility award, two APHA Championships, five Superior event awards, 12 ROMs and 658 points.

And finally, Mike Croghan – Don and Carolyn's only son – remains committed to seeing that the Fawago King line lives one.

Still residing in the Schuyler area, he currently stands two "family" stallions – King Of The World, a 1993 sorrel stallion by Fawago King and out of Jodee; and Obi Wan Keonobe, a 1999 sorrel overo stallion by King Of The World and out of Figs Dot by Fig Newton.

Exhibited by Courtney Dubsky Lutjelusche of Richland, Nebraska, King Of The World earned an APHA Championship, Amateur APHA Championship, 10 ROMs, 33 halter and 205 performance points. Retired to stud, he is the sire of 54 foals. Of these, 10 point earners have tallied 109 halter and 1,623 performance points.

Of these, My Irish World has done the most to live up to the family name. A 1999 sorrel overo gelding by King Of The World and out of My Irish Melody, My Irish World earned a Versatility award, APHA Championship, 12 ROMs, six Superiors, 31 halter and 1,155 performance points.

Again, in keeping with family tradition, he was ridden by three members of the Crogan clan – Courtney Lutjelusche in Amateur, Colleen Dubsky in Novice Amateur and Andrew Crogan in Youth.

Obi Wan Keonobe, like so many of the Fawago King-bred horses that preceded him, also found his way into the show ring. And, in keeping with the long-standing order of things, he was shown to his APHA Championships and Superior Western Pleasure award by family member Mindy Dubsky Kerwin.

Like Flying Fawago before him, Fawago King was known as an athletic horse with an outstanding,

Mindy Dubsky Kerwin showed Obi Wan Keonobe, a double-bred Fawago King descendant, to his APHA Championship in 2003.

Photo by Holman

willing disposition. Paired with the Croghan family, an extensive clan who bred, trained and showed their horses in the full gamut of APHA classes, what you are left with is exactly what the line came to stand for.

Fawago King was, above all else, "The Versatility Sire."

The lifelong partnership between Don and Carolyn Croghan and Fawago King has positioned all three of the participants on several of the APHA All-Time Leading lists. **Courtesy the Croghan family**

17   SNIP BAR

#6389

A cropout from a proven family of color, this versatile athlete went on to enjoy a supreme show and siring career.

AS NOTED IN Chapter 9, APHA inaugurated its Supreme Champion award with considerable fanfare on January 1, 1969. From the outset, the race to become the first Paint Horse to win the prestigious award was a hotly contested one. And, when the dust had settled 15 months later, it was a cropout stallion named Snip Bar who emerged victorious.

A Color-Coded Cropout

Snip Bar, a 1966 sorrel overo stallion by Bar Cliff (QH) and out of Miss Kelly

Snip Bar, the first APHA Supreme Champion.

Photo by Marge Spence

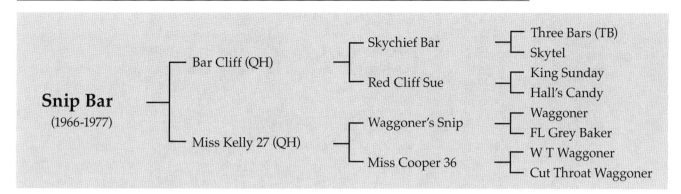

Snip Bar
(1966-1977)

Bar Cliff (QH)
— Skychief Bar
  — Three Bars (TB)
  — Skytel
— Red Cliff Sue
  — King Sunday
  — Hall's Candy

Miss Kelly 27 (QH)
— Waggoner's Snip
  — Waggoner
  — FL Grey Baker
— Miss Cooper 36
  — W T Waggoner
  — Cut Throat Waggoner

27 (QH), was bred by Luther Bolton of Lyons, Kansas. Although the young Paint's excessive white markings were probably something of a surprise to his Quarter Horse breeder, his genetic makeup was such that they could almost have been expected. He was, after all, from two lines that were notorious for "cropping out."

Bar Cliff was a 1962 sorrel stallion by Skychief Bar and out of Red Cliff Sue. An AQHA Champion with 19 halter and 12.5 performance points to his credit, he went on to become a sire of note in two breeds.

On the Quarter Horse side of the street, he sired the earners of one AQHA Championship, 42 ROMs, and 198 halter and 2,465 performance points. On the Paint Horse side, he sired six cropouts, including Snip Bar; Rockabar, 1968 Reserve National Champion Yearling Stallion and 1972 Reserve National Champion Aged Stallion; and Bar's Supreme, 1979 National Champion Pole Bending, Youth Pole Bending and Youth Barrel Race.

Miss Kelly 27, Snip Bar's dam, was a 1957 gray mare by Waggoner's Snip and out of Miss Cooper 36. Bred by Hal Cooper of Fort Supply, Oklahoma, Miss Kelly 27 was the dam of nine Quarter Horse foals, including a performance point earning full brother to Snip Bar.

The Cooper program, one of the earliest and most renowned in western Oklahoma, made liberal use of the blood of the Waggoner Ranch of Vernon, Texas. Among the stallions that headed the program over the years were Red Waggoner by Blackburn, Poco Coop by Poco Bueno, Waggoner's Snip by Waggoner, and Waggoner's 101 by Waggoner's Snip.

The Waggoner's Snip line proved especially prone toward throwing some extra white from time to time. Waggoner's Snip was the sire of the cropout mare Miss Kelly 30, who was out of Snip Bar's maternal granddam, Miss Cooper 37.

In addition, he sired Maybe Sixty Four, an AQHA Champion and the maternal grandsire of cropout great Mr. Winters; and Miss Kelly 13, the maternal granddam to cropout great Coop's Lady Ann. Waggoner's Snip also sired Waggoner 101, who put 14 cropouts into the Paint Horse registry.

Taking both sides of his family tree into consideration then, Snip Bar was absolutely color-coded to be a cropout.

From Promising to Proven

By the time Snip Bar was ready to be weaned, he had come to the attention of pioneer Paint breeder Claude Howard of Sedgwick, Kansas. It didn't take Howard long to figure

Exhibited by Bill Friend of Augusta, Kansas, Snip Bar was the 1968 National Champion 2-Year-Old Stallion.

Photo by Dolcater

Margie Spence ©

At the 1969 World-Wide Paint Review, held inHutchinson, Kansas, Snip Bar earned dual honors– as grand champion stallion and as winner of the reining futurity. Here, Janie Carpenter presents the futurity award to rider Bill James and owner Bill Maher.

Photo by Marge Spence

out that the colt would be a great asset to the recently formed American Paint Horse Association. Armed with that knowledge, he purchased the youngster and registered him on September 16, 1966.

Howard kept the colt for only a few months before selling him in December to Junior Robertson and Jim Smoot. This partnership, which was based in Waurika, Oklahoma, and Gainesville, Texas, had already established a widespread reputation for breeding and showing some of the best Paints in the land. In addition, they made a regular habit of locating and buying top show and breeding prospects.

Snip Bar was acquired by the savvy partners and transferred to their names on December 9, 1966. He was then transported to Smoot's show barn near Gainesville to be made ready for halter competition.

Snip Bar's show ring debut occurred on July 22, 1967. Exhibited at the second annual Texas Paint Horse Club Halter Futurity, in Wichita Falls, Texas, he won his class.

Claude Howard had by this time moved his business from Sedgwick to Gainesville, Texas. There, he had occasion to see Snip Bar on an almost daily basis. After suffering through an apparent case of "seller's remorse," he proceeded to buy the yearling stallion back on August 17, 1967, for what was reputed to be a record-setting price. Shown the following month at the APHA National Show in Oklahoma City, Snip Bar was named the Champion Yearling Stallion.

It was in Oklahoma City that Snip Bar came to the attention of Bill Maher of Augusta, Kansas. Maher was relatively new to the Paint Horse business, but nevertheless he stepped up and purchased the coming 2-year-old national champion on February 22, 1968.

Hauled back to the National Show in Oklahoma City the following September, Snip Bar made it two in a row by garnering the title of National Champion 2-Year-Old Stallion.

The year 1969 was a watershed one for Bill Maher and his Paint show stallion. Turned over during the previous fall and winter to Bill James of Superior, Nebraska, to be trained for performance, Snip Bar proved that he was more than a "one-trick pony."

His performance debut came in January, at the 1969 Fort Worth Stock Show. Ridden by Joy Rose of Gainesville, Texas, Snip Bar placed first in Jr. Western Pleasure. Several weeks later, with Bill James in the saddle, the 3-year-old won the reining at the Houston Fat Stock Show.

Snip Bar's winning ways continued into the summer and fall. By July 5, he had qualified as an APHA Champion. Exhibited in mid-August at the National Show in Kansas City, Missouri, he placed first under all three judges to take the Champion 3-Year-Old Stallion title, and, with Bill James tossing the loops, he took honors as the champion jr. calf roping horse.

All that was left now for the Snip Bar team was to zero in on the only award left to be garnered—the APHA Supreme Championship.

A Supreme Effort

Once again, the tag team of Joy Rose and Bill James was tapped to get the job done. Joy, who currently calls Childress, Texas, home, remembers the campaign well.

"In the mid-1960s," she says, "I was married to Matlock Rose and living in Gainesville, Texas. At the time, Matlock and George Tyler were involved in a partnership and were at the top of their game as far as the Quarter Horse industry was concerned. George was married to Rebecca Lockhart at this time, she had just helped put the American Paint Horse Association together.

"Then Matlock and I were divorced, I was stuck with trying to figure out how I was going to make it on my own with two small daughters.

"Vickie Adams and her parents lived right up the road from me," Joy recalls. "Vickie and I had run barrels together and often hauled together. When her mother and stepfather moved to Louisiana, Vickie lived with me. She was already showing Yellow Mount for Mr. and Mrs. Williamson at this time, and she's the one who first

by George

James returned to the Paint World Wide Review in 1973 to ride Snip Bar to victory in the reining maturity. The Review, by the way, is still being held each fall in Kansas. It is now known as the World Wide Paint Horse Congress.

Photo by George Martin

Snip Bar, shown here with trainer Joy Rose, earned grand champion stallion honors at the 1969 Louisiana State Fair.
Courtesy
Paint Horse Journal

Throughout Snip Bar's performance career, Rose showed the versatile stallion in Western pleasure, English pleasure, trail, barrel racing and pole bending.
Photo by
Marge Spence

In an abbreviated race career that saw him go to the post only two times, Snip Bar was the winner of one contest—a 300-yard event held June 20, 1971, at Eureka Downs in Eureka, Kansas. **Courtesy** *Paint Horse Journal*

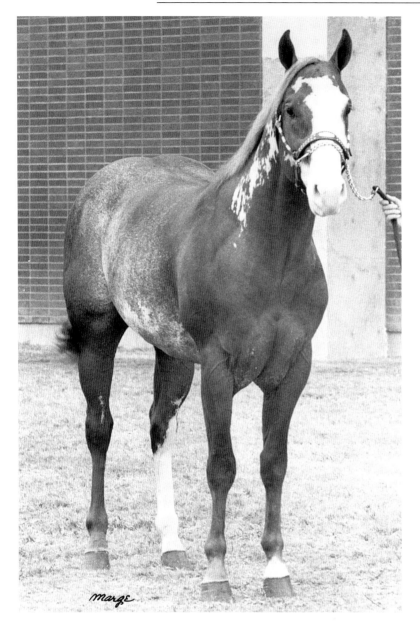

Snip's 7L Bar, a 1971 sorrel overo stallion by Snip Bar and out of Squier's Splash, was an APHA Champion who also earned Superior Halter and Western Pleasure awards.

Photo by Marge Spence

asked me if I would be interested in riding Snip Bar for Bill Maher.

"After I won the Jr. Western Pleasure class with 'Snip' at the 1969 Fort Worth Stock Show, I figured Bill would just take him back home. Instead, he asked me if I would consider showing him. I was scratching to make a living, so I agreed."

Before long, the push to become the first Supreme Champion turned into a two-horse race.

"Snip Bar had been shown quite a bit at halter prior to my working with him," Joy says. "But he hadn't been shown very much in performance. In the beginning, Vickie and I hauled Yellow Mount and Snip to the shows

together. They got so attached to one another that you could ride one and pony the other.

"One time, Vickie took Yellow Mount to Lafayette, Louisiana, a day ahead of when I took Snip. When I got to the show, she was already saddled up and was standing up in the alleyway leading into the arena.

"I rode up to the back of the pack, and Snip kept on squirming his way to the front. I knew what he was doing, so I just gave him his head.

"Finally, he worked his way right up there next to Yellow Mount and gave a low nicker. They were so happy to see each other, and they hadn't been apart but one day."

Before long, Snip Bar and Yellow Mount emerged ahead of the pack in the race to become the breed's first Supreme Champion.

"In June of 1970," Joy recalls, "Snip and Yellow Mount were running neck and neck for the championship. Vickie decided to go to a show in Louisiana, and I took Snip and headed to California.

"On June 5, at Sacramento, we stood reserve grand at halter, but didn't do any good in performance. A couple of days later, at Roseville, we stood grand at halter and won the Western pleasure, barrel racing and pole bending. We headed back home needing only three roping points to finish up.

"Lawton, Oklahoma, was the next weekend, and it was always a big show. I hauled Snip up there, and Bill James drove down from Abilene to show him in the reining and roping.

"Bill won both the jr. reining and calf roping on him, and that was all it took. Snip was the first Supreme Champion of the Paint Horse breed.

"Snip Bar was a smart horse," she continues. "He was easy to haul and easy to show. He had a strong personality, but it was easily managed.

"Bill Maher used to come and get him and take him home to breed mares. Then I'd either go up to get him, or Bill would bring him back and we'd go to the shows. If Snip ever acted up, you could crank on him one time and that's all he ever needed.

"And he was broke. I rode the tar out of Snip and so did Bill James. We used him for everything, and that is what kept him fresh. He liked what he did. He didn't get anything hammered into him until he hated it. He loved trail; he loved those gates.

The final accounting of Snip Bar's show career is an impressive one. APHA records reveal that the colorful cropout earned APHA Supreme Champion #1 and APHA Championship #36. En route to these two awards, he earned a Superior Halter award; ROMs in Western pleasure, reining, pole bending and calf roping; and amassed 68 halter and 98 performance points.

It was now time to see if he could carry his show ring successes over into a new career as a sire.

A Super Sire

Snip Bar had been test-bred to several mares as a 2-year-old. His first foal crop, numbering two, hit the ground in 1970. Both foals–Snip's Julie Bar and Snip's Deano Bar–went on to become APHA point earners.

The stallion's second and third foal crops numbered four and six, respectively, and from them came four show ring superstars: Sunshine Snip, Snip's 7L Bar, Snip's Nettie Bars and Snip's Comet Jr.

Sunshine Snip, a 1971 bay overo gelding by Snip Bar and out of Skip, enjoyed a long and illustrious career in both open and youth competition. As an open horse, he was the 1972 Reserve National Champion, earned an APHA Championship, Superior Western Pleasure award, four ROMs, and 34 halter and 222 performance points. In youth competition, he earned three national championships, one reserve national championship, one Superior award, 15 ROMs, and 63 halter and 729 performance points.

Snip's 7L Bar, a 1971 sorrel overo stallion by Snip Bar and out of Squier's Splash (QH), was the 1972 Reserve National Champion Yearling Stallion. In addition, he earned an APHA Championship, Superior Halter and Western Pleasure awards, four ROMs, and 72 halter and 93 performance points.

Snip's Nettie Bar, a 1973 sorrel overo mare out of Miss Sportie Bar, also enjoyed a two-pronged open and youth show career. In open

Snip's Nettie Bar, a 1973 sorrel overo mare by Snip Bar and out of Miss Sportie Bar, was the earner of three APHA Championships and a Youth Versatility award.
Photo by Rob Hess

Snip's Comet Jr, a 1973 sorrel gelding by Snip Bar and out of Miss Flying Earl, was his sire's top point earner.
Photo by Don Shugart

competition, she was an APHA Champion and the earner of Superior Western Pleasure and Trail awards, four ROMs, and 27 halter and 263

performance points. As a youth mount, she accounted for one national championship, six Superior awards, 12 ROMs, and 83 halter and 1,205 performance points.

Snip's Comet Jr, a 1973 sorrel overo gelding out of Miss Flying Earl, was his sire's top point earning get. In open competition, he was a four-time national champion in halter, Western pleasure and Western riding; a two-time reserve national champion in Western pleasure and Western riding; and the earner of an APHA Championship, two Superior awards, four ROMs, and 215 halter and 369 performance points.

In youth competition, "Jr." earned one national championship, eight reserve national championships, two Versatilities, an APHA Championship, 12 Superior awards, 18 ROMs, and 204 halter and 1,355 performance points.

Getting back to Snip Bar, he continued to sire an impressive array of show ring performers over the next five years. Among them were:

• Snip's Deed Bars, a 1973 black tobiano gelding out of Miss Leo Deeds–Two Superior awards, five ROMs, and 234 performance points.

Bar Star Snip, a 1973 bay tobiano son of Snip Bar, won the 1984 APHA Cutting Maturity.
Photo by Don Shugart

• Bar Star Snip, a 1973 bay tobiano stallion out of Miss Painted Star–1977 Reserve National Champion Cutting; Superior Cutting, and 114 performance points.

• Snip's Miss Kitty, a 1974 sorrel overo mare out of Skippin Kitty (QH)–Three APHA Championships, Youth Versatility, five Superior awards, 12 ROMs, and 163 halter and 529 performance points.

• Snip's Miss Roar, a 1976 sorrel overo mare out of High Walls (QH)–APHA Champion and Superior Halter.

• Snip's Miss Raider, a 1976 sorrel overo mare out of Easter Raider–Four APHA Championships, two Superior awards, three ROMs, and 201 halter and 155 performance points.

• Snip's Kinda Girl, a 1976 sorrel overo mare out of Some Kinda Woman–Open Versatility, Superior All-Around, APHA Champion, four Superior awards, eight ROMs, and 54 halter and 355 performance points.

• Snip Bar Skip, a 1977 black overo gelding out of Barbara Snip (QH)–four ROMs and 106 performance points.

• Revell's Barmaid, a 1977 sorrel overo mare out of May Eddie (QH)–APHA Youth Champion, six ROMs, and 42 halter and 135 performance points.

In mid-June of 1977, the former show champion and promising young sire was sold for the fifth and final time to Earl Jones of Ogden, Utah. Slated to be used as a junior sire on the daughters of Cupid Bar, Snip Bar covered only a handful of mares before succumbing to colic at the age of 11.

APHA records reveal that Snip Bar sired 57 registered foals. Of these, 29 performers earned nine national championships, 14 reserve national championships, five Versatility awards, one Superior All-Around, 18 APHA Championships, 42 Superior event awards, 115 ROMs and 6,468 points in all divisions combined.

Snip Bar lived only half of a normal lifetime. Despite that fact, he managed to secure for himself a permanent spot in Paint Horse history as the breed's first Supreme Champion and an accomplished sire.

Here's Snips Miss Kitty, a 1974 sorrel overo mare by Snip Bar and out of Skippin Kitty (QH). One of her sire's most versatile get, "Kitty" earned three APHA Championships, Youth Versatility award, five Superior awards and 12 ROMs. **Photo by Jill Lender**

Snip's Kinda Girl, a 1976 sorrel overo mare by Snip Bar and out of Some Kinda Woman, earned an Open Versatility, Superior All-Around, APHA Championship, four Superior awards and eight ROMs.

Courtesy APHA

18

AWHE CHIEF
#8643

A performance-bred product of the Lone Star State, this loud-colored stallion impacted several top Paint programs.

Awhe Chief–One of the top performance sires of his era.
Courtesy Marsha McGovney

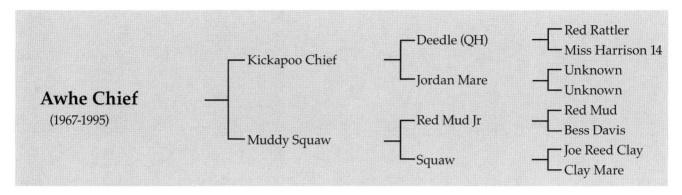

Awhe Chief
(1967-1995)

Kickapoo Chief
- Deedle (QH)
  - Red Rattler
  - Miss Harrison 14
- Jordan Mare
  - Unknown
  - Unknown

Muddy Squaw
- Red Mud Jr
  - Red Mud
  - Bess Davis
- Squaw
  - Joe Reed Clay
  - Clay Mare

AWHE CHIEF WAS bred to be a using horse. Although he was never given much of an opportunity to prove what his own talents were, as a sire he lived up to his genetic heritage by making some noteworthy contributions to a pair of the industry's most storied "on-the-rail" performance programs.

A Blue-Collar Background

Awhe Chief, a 1967 sorrel overo stallion by Kickapoo Chief and out of Muddy Squaw, was bred by Doug Edwards of Ryan, Oklahoma. Edwards was one of the 17 original members of APHA and an extremely active Paint promoter from the get-go.

Like so many of his peers, Edwards scoured the countryside on both sides of the Red River during the mid- to late 1960s, searching for good Paint Horses to buy and register. Kickapoo Chief and Muddy Squaw were brought into the APHA fold in this manner.

Kickapoo Chief, a 1961 sorrel overo stallion by Deedle (QH) and out of a "Jordan Mare," was bred by C.L. Jordan of Bellaire, Texas. Deedle, in turn, was a double-bred Old Sorrel descendant who also traced close up to the famed speed sire Chicaro (TB).

Sold prior to his 2-year-old year to Lee Tom Alls of Aspermont, Texas, "Kickapoo" was registered with the old American Paint Quarter Horse Association and assigned registry number 78. APHA records show that he was transferred into Edwards' ownership on April 4, 1965.

Muddy Squaw, a 1954 sorrel overo mare by Red Mud Jr (QH) and out of Squaw, was bred by Claude Jones of Canadian, Texas. Red Mud Jr was a grandson of Roan Hancock, while Squaw was a granddaughter of Joe Reed P-3.

Awhe Chief's pedigree then, on top and bottom, was packed full with horses that had proven themselves as sires of race, rodeo and arena performance athletes. And while the loud-colored overo stallion's story technically starts on the Ryan, Oklahoma, ranch where he was conceived, it doesn't really begin until he first saw the light of day 750 miles away on the Gregg Reisinger Farm, located on the outskirts of Eldora, Iowa.

Reisinger Roots

Gregg Reisinger grew up in the horse business. K.E. "Kenneth" Reisinger, his father, was one of the most respected cattlemen and livestock auctioneers in the upper Midwest. He also owned and operated the K.E. Reisinger and Sons Livestock Sale Barn in Eldora, and Gregg grew up in it, learning the ins and outs of buying and selling horses of all breeds and types.

Orphaned at birth, "Chief" was nevertheless a good-looking yearling by the time he was registered with APHA.
Courtesy APHA

181

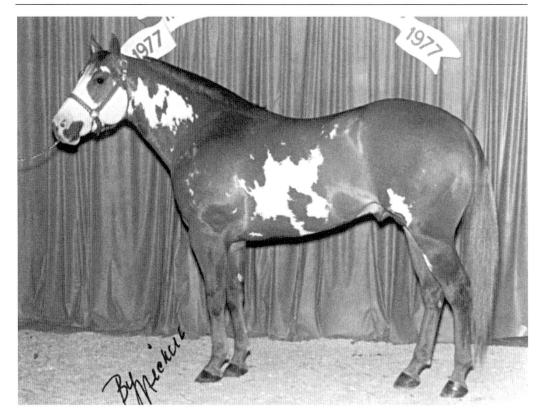

The ill-fated Chief's Norfleet was one of the Awhe Chiefs to make a splash on the national show scene.
Photo by Michelle

By the time Gregg was 13, he was buying and selling on his own. As time went by, he discovered that Paint Horses were a good commodity. They could usually be had for less money than Quarter Horses, and they could often be sold for double and triple their purchase price.

By the mid-1960s, Reisinger had decided that he wanted to launch his own Paint Horse breeding and show program. He registered his first Paint in February of 1965, and within two years had accumulated in the neighborhood of 30 broodmares.

On February 3, 1967, Doug Edwards and a partner held a Paint Horse sale at the Stockyards Sales Arena in Fort Worth, Texas. Reisinger was in attendance and bought a semi-load of horses to ship back to Iowa. Several horses were in the load that would go on to have a positive impact on the breed.

Among the then 23-year-old horseman's purchases at the sale was Apache Norfleet, a 1963 sorrel overo stallion by Sid's 8 (QH) and out of Sandy Calico. In addition to being Reisinger's first Paint breeding stallion, "Apache" was also his first show horse.

"There weren't many Paint shows in Iowa in the late 1960s," he says. "So we had to show Apache in all-breed Western pleasure classes. I had a lady named Judy Adams riding him, and he won just about every class we put him in.

"Looking back, I feel that Apache really did a lot during the late '60s to further the popularity of Paints in this part of the country."

One of the first mares that Reisinger bred to his new stallion was Honera Q, who he had picked up at the Fort Worth sale. In 1968, "Honera" foaled a filly named Awhe Honera.

Reisinger showed Awhe Honera to her APHA Championship, and in 1972 won the National Jr. Reining title in Columbus, Ohio, with her.

Four years after purchasing him, Reisinger sold Apache Norfleet to Larry Sheriff of nearby Sheffield, Iowa. His decision to do so was prompted by several considerations.

"By 1971," Reisinger says, "I had a nice set of Apache Norfleet fillies. I also had a young stallion that was showing signs of being a good breeding horse. So, when Larry, who was just getting into Paints at the time, made me an offer to buy Apache, I could see it was time to let him go."

As it turned out, the transfer of Apache Norfleet from Reisinger to Sheriff was a move that worked out for both men. Apache Norfleet put Larry Sheriff in the Paint Horse business. And Awhe Chief–Gregg Reisinger's young stallion–put him in the Paint pleasure horse business.

The Reisinger Years

To begin with, Awhe Chief came to Iowa inside his dam.

"Muddy Squaw was another one of the mares that I bought at the 1967 Fort Worth Sale," Reisinger says. "She was a nice type of mare for that day and age, and I had high hopes for her as a producer. But she died shortly after foaling that first spring, and we were left with an orphan colt.

"We had an older gentleman named Harm Folkerts working for us at the time. Whenever we were gone to shows or sales, Harm would feed for us morning and night. And, after "Chief" was orphaned, he took care of him and raised him on a bottle.

"Chief was a red roan overo horse that stood 15-1 hands high and weighed 1,200 pounds at maturity. He was a well-balanced horse with a real pretty head.

"We broke him to ride, and I think he would have gone on and made a decent pleasure horse. We only showed him once. The main reason he never got more of a chance as a show horse was because we were showing Apache Norfleet at the time."

APHA records reveal that, shown at a Paint show in Marshalltown, Iowa, on May 2, 1970, Awhe Chief placed third in a class of 10 Western pleasure horses and earned one performance point. Being a performer, then, was not to be Awhe Chief's claim to fame. It was as a sire of performers that the colorful stallion would make his mark.

Installed as a Reisinger Farms herd sire, Chief proceeded to churn out a steady stream of top-notch performers. Chief's Norfleet, Awhe Lucky and Chief's Dun Good were among the first to excel in the show ring.

Chief's Norfleet, a 1973 sorrel overo stallion and out of Awhe Pila by Apache Norfleet, was bred by Reisinger Farms. Sold to Larry Sheriff in May of 1974, he went on to earn honors as the 1974 Reserve National

Awhe Lucky, a 1974 dun overo gelding by Awhe Chief and out of Mamie Dawson (QH), was a top open, amateur and youth mount.

Courtesy APHA

Here's Chief's Dun Good, yet another top Awhe Chief show horse, right after she topped the 1981 APHA National Sale. Bob and Sue Dulin of Bayfield, Colorado, purchased the all-around show mare at the event.

Photo by Don Shugart

Big Mach I, shown here with Lisa Smith, was a Superior Halter Horse and top youth mount.

Courtesy APHA

Sooper Squaw, a 1976 red roan mare by Awhe Chief and out of Lady King, earned a Superior Western Pleasure award.

Photo by Don Shugart

Champion Yearling Stallion, the 1975 Reserve National Champion 2-Year-Old Stallion, and the 1976 Reserve National Champion 3-Year-Old Stallion.

In addition, he earned an APHA Championship, Superior awards in halter and Western pleasure, and 99 halter points and 56 performance points.

Retired to stud, Chief's Norfleet only sired 21 foals before passing away at the age of 4. One of these, however, was Mr. Norfleet, five-time National Champion and APHA All-Time Leading Sire.

Awhe Lucky, a 1974 dun overo gelding By Awhe Chief and out of

Chief's Agent, a 1979 sorrel gelding out of Awhe Pila, was the 1981 National Champion Jr. Western Pleasure Horse. That's breeder/owner Gregg Reisinger on the left.

Photo by Don Shugart

In 1982, Helm Farms of Penalosa, Kansas, acquired "Chief."
Courtesy Marsha McGoveney

Mamie Dawson (QH), was also a top performer. Shown in open, amateur and youth competition, he was the earner of a national championship and a reserve national championship in trail, an APHA Championship, four Superior awards, 13 ROMs, and 69 halter and 1,133 performance points.

Chief's Dun Good, a 1975 dun overo mare by Awhe Chief and out of Mamie Dawson (QH), was one of her sire's most versatile performers. Shown in open competition, she earned a Versatility award, a Superior All-Around award, APHA Championship, two Superior awards, five ROMs, and 51 halter and 121 performance points.

Campaigned in the youth division, she earned two Superior awards, four ROMs, and 41 halter and 144 performance points.

And Awhe Chief sired many more top performers during his "Reisinger Years." Among them were:

• Tuff Chief, a 1972 gelding out of Norfleet's Janie–Superior Western Pleasure, and six halter and 119 performance points.

• Big Mach I, a 1974 sorrel overo gelding out of Gloria Go (QH)–Superior Halter, Youth Versatility, Youth APHA Champion, Youth Superior Halter, Western Horsemanship and Western Pleasure; eight ROMs, and 351 halter and 323 performance points.

• Awhe Miss Bar, a 1974 sorrel mare out of Miss Barbon–Superior Trail and 177 performance points.

• Sooper Squaw, a 1975 red roan overo mare out of Lady King–Superior Western Pleasure, four ROMs, and six halter and 166 performance points.

• Chief's Leah, a 1977 sorrel overo mare out of Awhe Pila–Superior Western Pleasure and 75 performance points.

• Super Tuff I, a 1978 sorrel overo gelding out of Skip Girl–Superior Western Pleasure, Amateur Versatility, Amateur Superior Western Pleasure and Bridle Path Hack, eight ROMs, and one halter and 420 performance points.

• Chief's Secret, a 1979 red roan overo mare out of Panitella (QH)–1984 World Champion Heeling, three ROMs and 70 performance points.

• Chief's Agent, a 1979 sorrel gelding out of Awhe Pila–1981 National Champion Western Pleasure, 1983 National Champion Western Riding, Superior Western Pleasure, two ROMs and 184 performance points.

• Awhe Bobi Jo, a 1979 sorrel overo mare out of Bobi Jo (QH)–APHA Champion, Superior Western Pleasure, eight ROMs, and 32 halter and 296 performance points.

• Chiefs Cheerleader, a 1980 red roan overo mare out of Miss Flirt–APHA Champion, Superior Western Pleasure, two ROMs, and 19 halter and 103 performance points.

• Chiefs Rhapsody, a 1981 sorrel overo gelding out of Miss Flirt–Superior Western Pleasure, one ROM, and 21 halter and 63 performance points.

By the early 1980s, Gregg Reisinger had a pasture full of good Awhe Chief daughters and a young cropout stallion named Teddy's Splash to breed them to. Awhe Chief was not ever put on the market per se, but he was eventually acquired by a second, top-notch pleasure horse program.

The Helm Farm Years

As detailed in Chapter 12, Helm Farms of Penalosa, Kansas, was a 3,200-acre farming and ranching operation that also featured a Paint Horse breeding program headed by Skip's Artist.

By the early 1980s, Marsha McGovney–the heart and soul behind that Paint program–had determined there was room on the farm for a second breeding stallion. In early 1982, a trip was arranged to look at horses in Kansas and Michigan. An impromptu stop was also made in Eldora, Iowa, with the end result being that Awhe Chief was purchased and transferred into the ownership of Helm Farms, Inc. on March 1, 1982.

Marsha remembers the search and the stopover well.

"I remember looking at tons of horses at Gregg's," she says. "We looked at all the up-and-coming show and sale horses, and then we went around the older shed row barns and looked at groups of weanlings and yearlings. I recall that Awhe Chief was the sire of several of the young horses that I liked the best.

"Then we walked back around towards the stall barn and went to a stall built into the side of a short, shed row-type building, and there stood Chief. To make a long story short, we bought him that day, loaded him up the next day and headed back home.

"I also remember that, once we got him home, everyone we met who knew Chief was amazed that we had gotten him away from Gregg. He had apparently never before been offered for sale."

While in Iowa, Awhe Chief had been utilized primarily as a pasture stallion. Despite receiving some sound advice from Gregg Reisinger on how to handle the stallion in a pasture setting,

McGovney initially decided to pursue a different course of action.

"Gregg told us that he turned Chief out with his mares in the spring," she says. "And then he told me that, once Chief was in place with his set of mares, not to add any new mares to the group.

"Well, after we got Chief home, we did turn him into a pasture with a band of mares. Then we bought some more horses and one of the mares was really in heat. She also did not have a baby by her side.

"Chief would come up to the pen where we had her and tease her. So, we turned her out in the pasture with him and his mares. The next morning, Chief and his herd were on the west side of the pasture, and the new mare

HF Chiefs Keepsake, a Helm Farms-bred daughter of Awhe Chief, earned a Superior Western Pleasure award.
Photo by K.C. Montgomery

HF Superchief, a 1986 palomino overo stallion by Awhe Chief and out of Windsand Supremecy (QH), was an APHA Champion with 16 halter and 32 performance points to his credit.
Courtesy APHA

Artistic Merit, a 1989 bay overo stallion by Skip's Artist and out of Awhe Ha, was bred by Helm Farms. Sold to Anthony and Lisa Sinclair of Las Alamos, California, the Awhe Chief grandson earned one reserve world championship in working hunter, a Versatility award, three Superior awards, 12 ROMs, 14 halter and 405 performance points. **Courtesy APHA**

was in the center of the pasture. When we went out to her, she wasn't moving much because Chief had chewed her up pretty good and driven her off. So, from that point on we never added any new mares to his band."

Even though Reisinger had sold Awhe Chief outright, the savvy horse breeder retained five breedings a year to him. And, over the course of the next five years, the stallion continued to sire top performers for both Reisinger Farms and Helm Farms. Among the best of these were:

- HF Chiefs Keepsake, a 1983 red dun overo mare out of HF Skips Dun Lass–Superior Western Pleasure, one ROM and 53 performance points.
- Chiefs Tella, a 1983 sorrel gelding out of Panitella–Superior Western Pleasure, Superior Youth Western Pleasure, 13 ROMs, and 16 halter and 429 performance points.
- HF Chiefs Fancyson, a 1984 sorrel overo gelding out of HF Skips Dun Lass–Youth Versatility, Youth APHA Champion, Superior Youth Western Pleasure and Western Riding, 13 ROMs, and 19 halter and 337 performance points.
- HF Chiefs Caliope, a 1985 sorrel overo mare out of Skip Double–Superior Western Pleasure, Superior Amateur Western Pleasure, two ROMs and 104 performance points.
- HF Chiefs Rhapsody, a 1985 sorrel overo mare out of Miss Lady Ariel (QH)–Superior Western Pleasure, two ROMs and 118 performance points.
- HF Superchief, a 1986 palomino overo stallion out of Windsand Supremecy (QH)–APHA Champion, three ROMs, and 16 halter and 32 performance points.

In the spring of 1987, Helm Farms held a production/reduction sale. Awhe Chief, then 20 years old, was sold to Stephen and Suzanne Sanders of Celina, Texas. In November of 1988, he was sold for a fourth and final time, to Arnie Billmark of Anoka, Minnesota.

Billmark, the stallion's last owner, recalls the circumstances that brought the legendary sire to the Twin Cities region.

"Some friends of ours owned a show gelding by Awhe Chief named HF

Chiefs Whizkid," he says. "They also had some mares that they wanted to breed to Chief, but he was too far away. I had a few broodmares, too, so I just went out and bought the horse.

"Chief was really a nice horse to be around," Billmark continues. "We pasture-bred him, and he was always so easy to get along with in that situation. And his foals were also easy to get along with, easy to break and easy to train."

After leaving Helm Farms, Awhe Chief lived to sire nine more foal crops from 1988 through 1996. Averaging less than three per year, these last siring efforts resulted in four point earners. Chiefs Reatta, a 1991 red dun mare out of HF Skips Dun Lass, was the most accomplished of these. Shown in all four divisions, she earned seven ROMs and 178 performance points.

In the summer of 1995, at the age of 28, the venerable sire suffered a colic attack. After failing to sufficiently respond to treatment, he was humanely euthanized and buried within the confines of his last home.

APHA records attest to the fact that Awhe Chief sired a total of 177 registered foals. Of these, 69 performers earned four national championships, four reserve national championships, four Versatility awards, one Superior All-Around award, 41 Superior event awards, seven APHA Championships, 180 ROMs and 8,107 points in all divisions combined.

As a broodmare sire, Chief's record is even more impressive. On the 1997 Lifetime Leading Dams' Sires Lists, for instance, he appeared on 11 of the 16 individual lists. As the maternal grandsire of performance points earned, he stood second with 4,515 points; in ROMs earned, he was third with 104; and in Superiors earned, he was sixth with 30.

More importantly, however, was the fact that for most of his life Awhe Chief played an integral role in the development of Reisinger Farms and Helm Farms–two of the Paint Horse industry's most storied performance horse programs. Through 2007, these two programs occupy the number 1 and number 2 spots as the Leading All-Time Breeders of performance points earned, ROM earners and Superiors earned.

Both Gregg Reisinger and Marsha McGovney are quick to credit the role Awhe Chief played in their respective climbs to the top of the Paint Horse show world.

Despite having come into this world as an orphan, Awhe Chief enjoyed a full and productive life. His contributions to the Paint Horse breed in general and the Paint pleasure industry in particular, will stand the test of time.

Just Passin Thru, a 1992 bay overo gelding by Pass Perfect and out of Awhe Ha, earned 12 world titles, three Versatility awards, one Superior Championship, two APHA Championships, 29 Superior event awards, 40 ROMs, and 216 halter and 4,658 performance points during his star-studded show career. Christina McGurran, who is in the saddle in this pleasing trail shot, earned more than 2,200 points on the talented gelding.
Photo by Caroline Fyffe

19 BABBY SKIT
#9372

*As the world's first double-registered Paint/Quarter Horse,
this sabino mare foretold things to come.*

*Babby Skit – by hook
or crook – the world's
first AQHA/APHA
double-registered
horse.*

**Photo by
Marge Spence**

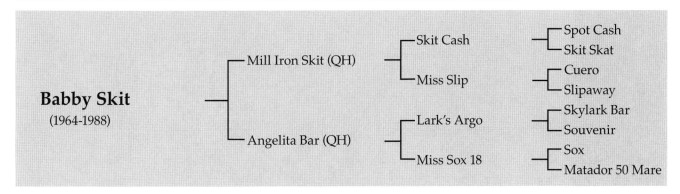

Babby Skit
(1964-1988)

— Mill Iron Skit (QH)
  — Skit Cash
    — Spot Cash
    — Skit Skat
  — Miss Slip
    — Cuero
    — Slipaway
— Angelita Bar (QH)
  — Lark's Argo
    — Skylark Bar
    — Souvenir
  — Miss Sox 18
    — Sox
    — Matador 50 Mare

THE AMERICAN QUARTER Horse Association (AQHA) was formed in 1940 as a "solid-colored" registry. Consequently, otherwise eligible horses with excessive white markings were denied papers.

With the formation of the two Texas-based Paint Horse registries in the early 1960s, however, these "cropout" Quarter Horses were given a place they could call home and reciprocated by contributing much-needed quality to the Paint Horse breed's foundation gene pool.

In April of 2004, AQHA rescinded its so-called "white rule" and began accepting all eligible horses, regardless of their markings. This ushered in the "double-registered" era of horses carrying both AQHA and APHA papers.

While the decision to grant AQHA papers to the cropouts was a controversial one and was years in the making, there was a precedent for it. Some 40 years earlier, a single excessive-white mare wound up being double-registered.

Her name was Babby Skit.

A Radical Roan

Babby Skit was bred by Earl Brown of Adrian, Texas, and foaled on June 16, 1965. Meant to be a Quarter Horse, she was sired by Mill Iron Skit (QH) and out of Angelita Bar (QH).

That Babby Skit was born with excessive white markings on her face, belly and two legs probably came as a surprise to her breeder, but should not have.

To begin with, Mill Iron Skit was a line-bred descendant of Old Fred, the legendary Coke Roberds palomino stallion. In fact, he traced 12 times to that prolific fountainhead of cropout Paint color.

Angelita Bar was from the same Skylark Bar/Skychief Bar family of horses that would put such National Champion cropout Paints as Snip Bar, Rockabar and Bar's Supreme into the APHA registry. And, if that wasn't enough, on the bottom half of her pedigree Angelita Bar also traced back to the Old Fred family through the Matador Ranch-bred stallion Sox.

If, after studying it, the fact that Babby Skit's pedigree was full of horses that were capable of producing Paints might still be in doubt, one need look no farther than the first six horses that appear in it. Of them, four have either sired or produced APHA-registered cropout foals. Given those facts, it should have come as no surprise to anyone who knew anything about how Babby Skit was bred that she came out wearing a little extra chrome.

It was in her genes.

In this rare historical shot, taken in May of 1968, AQHA-registered Babby Skit earns reserve champion mare honors at a Canyon, Texas, Quarter Horse show. As a result, the obviously Paint-marked mares papers were cancelled.
Photo by Dolcater

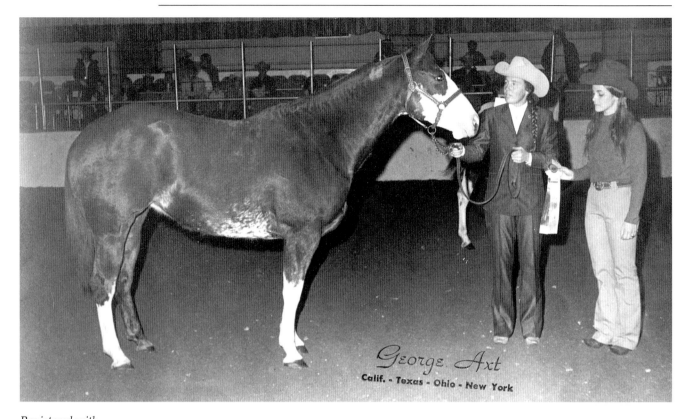

George Axt
Calif. - Texas - Ohio - New York

Registered with APHA, Babby Skit went on to become an APHA Champion show horse. She is shown here with trainer Dorothy Russell after earning reserve champion mare honors at the 1970 Southwestern Exposition and Fat Stock show in Fort Worth.

Photo by George Axt

On Babby Skit's AQHA registration papers, which are dated September 12, 1966, she is described as a "red roan with bald face, white hairs around the right eye and lower lip, white chin, and stockings on both front and right hind legs." As far as it went, the description was accurate. The problem was, it just didn't go quite far enough.

What was not mentioned was that Babby Skit also had a very large belly spot that extended up both her sides. Be that as it may, on April 12, 1968, Roy Plummer of Tucumcari, New Mexico, purchased the then-3-year-old registered Quarter Horse mare from Earl Brown.

Three weeks after acquiring her, Plummer hauled Babby Skit to an AQHA show in Canyon, Texas. Entered in the halter competition there, the colorful mare was named Reserve Grand Champion Mare and earned three halter points.

Whether Plummer took any heat from his fellow competitors for showing what was obviously a Paint mare at a Quarter Horse show is not known. The chances are good that he did though, because immediately after the show he sold Babby Skit to a pair of well-known Paint Horse breeders.

Reclassification Time

By the late 1960s, pioneer Paint breeders Junior Robertson of Waurika, Oklahoma, and Jim Smoot of Gainesville, Texas, had joined forces to establish one of the most successful breeding and showing operations of the day.

As they assembled their broodstock, the partners had put the word out that they were interested in acquiring all the well-bred, well-made cropout Paints they could get their hands on. They were glad to get the loud-colored Babby Skit.

"When Jim and I bought Babby Skit," Junior Robertson says, "she still had her Quarter Horse papers. She was sure enough a Paint though, and I remember her as one of the good ones.

"She might have been a nickel too rough in the head, but she was pretty stout from that point back. She was a deep-hearted mare, with high withers that stretched to the middle of her back. She had a big hip, nice low hocks and a ton of muscle."

As good as Babby Skit might have been, at the time Robertson and Smoot purchased her they already had a barn full of horses just like her. They promptly re-sold her to James Wright of McKinney, Texas. Wright, a dyed-in-the-wool Paint person, did transfer Babby Skit's Quarter Horse papers into his name, but he also went ahead and registered her with APHA on December 12, 1969.

That day marked the end of Babby Skit's Quarter Horse career and the beginning of what would be her far more productive Paint Horse career.

As Good as they Expected

Shortly after purchasing her, Wright turned Babby Skit over to neighbors Ralph and Dorothy Russell to show. The Russells were one of the region's top training teams and also owned and stood Paint Horse legend Painted Lasan (see *More than Color, Vol. 1*). As was to be expected based on her short Quarter Horse show career, she did well.

Babby Skit was shown for the first time as a Paint in January of 1970, at the Southwestern Exposition and Fat Stock Show in Fort Worth. There, she topped a class of 13 aged mares and then came back to stand Reserve Grand Champion Mare, as well.

Following that show and during the next six months, the Russells campaigned Babby Skit at halter throughout Texas and Oklahoma. She proved her Fort Worth win was no fluke by racking up 11 more firsts, seven grand championships, four reserves and 47 open halter points.

Switching to performance events in the late spring of 1970, Babby Skit won her first two outs in Western pleasure. By July 11 of that year, she had accumulated 15 performance points and that was enough to make her APHA Champion #64.

"Babby" was retired shortly thereafter and started on her third career, the one that exerted the greatest influence on the Paint Horse breed. Although she was a good enough individual to win in both Quarter Horse and Paint Horse show ring competition, Babby Skit's true calling turned out to be as a producer.

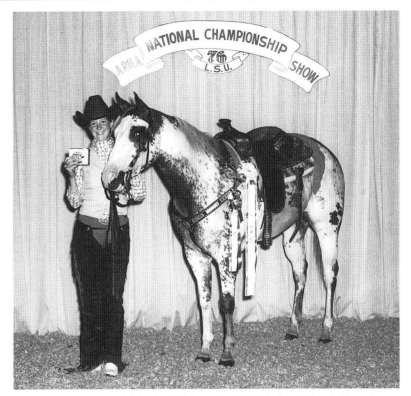

Here's J Bar's Luv and Monica Wark at the 1976 National Youth Show in Baton Rouge, Louisiana. "Luv" and Monica earned championship honors at the show in Jr. Halter Mares and Western Pleasure (14-18).

Photo by Don Shugart

J Bar's Luv also carried Trisha Ryno of Fort Worth, Texas, to a reserve championship in youth western riding at the 1980 National Youth Show in Oklahoma City. **Photo by Don Shugart**

Broodmare Duty

Babby Skit was bred for the first time in 1971, to the Russells' APHA Champion stallion Bueno Bandit. The following spring, she foaled a solid sorrel filly who was registered as Plain Sally, and who would go on to have no show or produce record to speak of.

Babby Skit's next foal, however, was a different story altogether. Bred to Junior Robertson's great foundation sire Mister J. Bar (see *More than Color, Vol. 1*) in 1972, the next year the ex-show mare produced a loud-colored sorrel overo filly who was named J Bar's Luv.

Shown initially in open competition, "Luv" was the 1974 National Champion Yearling Filly. She was also an APHA Champion, earned Superiors in halter and Western pleasure, and an ROM in trail.

As a youth mount shown by Monica Wark, Luv was an eight-time National Champion and Versatility award winner, and the earner of 10 Superiors and 10 ROMs. With youth competitor Trisha Ryno aboard, the colorful mare added a second Youth APHA Championship and a second Versatility award to her record, as well as five more Superiors and 10 more ROMs.

Altogether, the durable campaigner amassed two Versatility awards, three APHA Championships, 17 Superior awards, 19 ROMs and 2,318 points in open and youth competition.

For the next six years, Babby Skit was bred to the red roan sabino C Note's Sawbuck. Sawbuck's Cricket, a 1976 sorrel overo gelding who went on to earn six open and youth halter points, was the first to result from this cross.

Next came Sawbuck's Jubilee, a 1977 sorrel overo mare. Shown in open, youth and amateur competition, she became the second of her dam's produce to achieve show ring star status. All told, the near-white sabino mare earned a Versatility award, eight Superiors, 11 ROMs and 789 halter and performance points in all divisions combined.

Babby Skit's next three foals by "Sawbuck" were Babbyskitsdaughter, a 1978 solid sorrel mare; Jig Saw, a 1979 sorrel overo gelding; and Aruba, a 1980 sorrel overo mare. None of these three compiled APHA show records.

The last foal from the cross, however, did. A 1981 sorrel gelding named Bounty Hunter, he earned 15 amateur performance points.

Sawbuck's Jubilee carried owners Clara Kimbro of Kerrville, Texas, and Robert and Margaret Radloff of Fort Worth, Texas, to a wide array of wins and awards. Kimbro is shown aboard the colorful sabino mare in this curtain shot.

Photo by Don Shugart

Backtracking a little, in February of 1980 Babby Skit was sold once more. This time she went to Rosalis Estes of Lorena, Texas, who owned her for the remainder of the mare's life.

Encore! Encore!

In 1981, Estes decided to take Babby to the court of a new stallion, and the horse she chose was APHA Champion One Hundred Two. This cross resulted in a 1982 sorrel overo stallion named Encore, who wound up being Babby Skit's sole son to be left as a stallion and her only World Champion.

Especially loud-colored, even for one of Babby's foals, Encore was sold by Estes to David Beard of Ore City, Texas, when the colt was 12 months old. Two years later, in March of 1985, Beard sold the then-3-year-old stallion to Jim Eaton of Atlanta, Texas.

Up to this point, Encore had been shown very little. Eaton changed this, and within four months had made him the 1985 APHA World Champion 3-Year-Old Stallion.

Encore, a 1982 sorrel overo stallion by One Hundred Two and out of Babby Skit, was the 19885 APHA World Champion 3-Year-Old Stallion.
Photo by Don Shugart

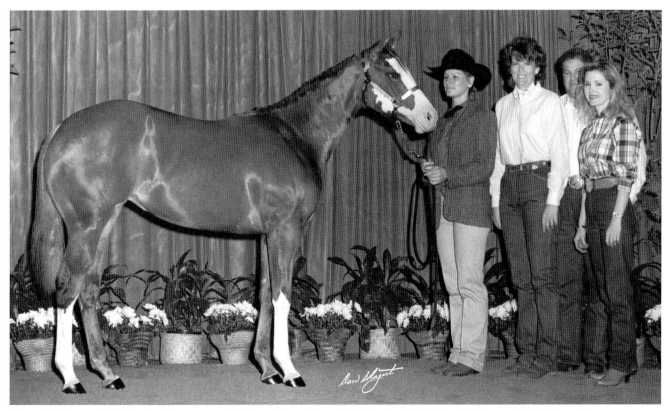

Super Holiday, a 1986 chestnut overo mare by Cross Over Sonny (QH) and out of Babby Skit, earned 67 halter and 22 performance points.
Photo by Don Shugart

195

- Encores Lady, a 1989 sorrel overo mare out of Sure Shot Lady (QH): 1992 World Champion Jr. Western Pleasure, and Superior Halter and Western Pleasure.
- Struttin Encore, a 1991 sorrel overo stallion out of Silent Poise: 1994 Reserve World Champion 2-Year-Old Stallion and Superior Halter.
- Flitten, a 1991 chestnut overo mare out of Bar Babe Flit (QH): Superior Halter.
- Sierra Encore, a 1998 sorrel overo gelding out of Sofonda Te (QH): Superior Trail and Bridle Path Hack; Amateur Versatility award; five Amateur Superior awards and seven Amateur ROMs.
- Cashonencore, a 1998 sorrel overo stallion out of Chinook Cash (QH): 2001 Amateur World Champion 3-Year-Old Stallion and Reserve World Champion 3-Year-Old Stallion, Superior Open and Amateur Halter.

A Hit and a Holiday

Rosalie Estes next bred Babby Skit to the APHA Champion stallion Hit Man. This resulted in Number One Hit, a 1983 chestnut tovero gelding. Shown sparingly at halter as a yearling, he was named grand champion twice and earned five open halter points.

Whereas Babby Skit's first 10 foals were all sired by Paint stallions, her next one was by Cross Over Sonny AQHA. A 1986 chestnut overo mare named Sonny Holiday, she was shown in open, youth and amateur competition, and was the earner of 67 halter and 22 performance points.

Clearly Impressive, a 1987 sorrel overo mare by Eternal Impressive, was Babby Skit's next contribution to the Paint breed. Shown lightly as a weanling, Clearly Impressive was retired to the broodmare band as a 3-year-old. She went on to produce 16 foals, including Clearly A Rose, earner of 91 halter points; Rarely A Rose, earner of 57 halter points; and Super Sonny T, earner of 53 halter points.

For the sire of Babby Skit's next and final foal, Estes chose Zippo Pine Bar AQHA. This cross resulted in Zippo Skit, a 1988 sorrel mare.

Like Plain Sally, Babby Skit's first

Encore, after being retired to stud, has been a major contributor to the Babby Skit story.
Courtesy APHA

Shown sparingly after his win at the World, Encore went on to earn 26 halter points before being retired to stud in 1986. And, like his dam, Encore has proven to be every bit as successful a breeding animal as he was a show horse.

APHA records reveal that, through 2007, Encore sired a total of 332 registered foals. Of these, 89 were performers who earned four world championships, three reserve world championships, one Versatility award, nine APHA Championships, six Superior awards, 135 ROMs and 6,583 points in all divisions combined. Among his top performers are:

- Hug Me Hondo, a 1987 sorrel overo gelding out of Hug Me Clabber: 1994 Amateur World Champion Pole Bending, 1992 Amateur Reserve World Champion Pole Bending, Superior Barrel Racing and Amateur Pole Bending.

Encore's Music, a 1992 red roan overo mare by Encore and out of She Maid Music (QH), was the 1994 World Champion 2-Year-Old Mare. **Photo by Gail Bates**

foal, Zippo Skit was a solid. But in the mare's defense, sandwiched in between these two solids were enough colored, accomplished foals to assure their dam a spot in Paint Horse annals as one of the breed's first great producers.

As an ironic final twist to the colorful mare's story, on December 12, 2005, her AQHA papers were re-issued. This, of course, made her most famous son, Encore, eligible for AQHA papers, and, in April of 2006, he was double-registered as Painted Encore.

Babby Skit—the Quarter Horse turned Paint Horse—was now legally a part of both breeds. And that's not all bad, because no matter how she was registered or under which association's rules she was shown, Babby Skit did well. Likewise, no matter what stallion she was bred to, she produced well.

Simply put, no matter how she was colored or what she was called, she was one of the good ones.

Flitten, shown here with Ernie King, was a Superior Halter Horse with 143 points to her credit. **Photo by Harold Campton**

20 GALLANT GHOST
#21,750

Uniquely marked, this versatile champion made lasting contributions to one of the Northwest's top Paint Horse lines.

Gallant Ghost–"the Ghost with the Most."
Photo by LeRoy Weathers

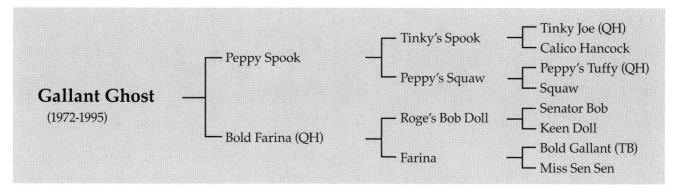

Gallant Ghost
(1972-1995)

- Peppy Spook
  - Tinky's Spook
    - Tinky Joe (QH)
    - Calico Hancock
  - Peppy's Squaw
    - Peppy's Tuffy (QH)
    - Squaw
- Bold Farina (QH)
  - Roge's Bob Doll
    - Senator Bob
    - Keen Doll
  - Farina
    - Bold Gallant (TB)
    - Miss Sen Sen

DR. LYLE AND "Butch" Wonderlich of Twin Falls, Idaho, were two of the far Northwest's earliest and most accomplished Paint Horse pioneers.

As noted in *More than Color, Vol. 1*, the Wonderlichs entered the Paint Horse business in March of 1964.

In the fall of 1965, they acquired a bay tovero weanling named Tinky's Spook who would go on to become one of the breed's cornerstone sires. What's more, he would help shape the Wonderlichs' RoseAcre Farms into one of the country's premier Paint breeding and show establishments.

Cornerstone Color and Class

Tinky's Spook was a grandson of Tinky Poo (QH), one of the Intermountain Region's top foundation sires. A 1949 brown stallion by Wayward Irving and out of Little Peach, Tinky Poo was a AA-AQHA Champion and the sire of 18 ROM racehorses that earned $143,689. On the show horse side, he was the sire of four AQHA Champions, including the legendary Hobby Horse.

The Tinky Poo line was a durable one, and one in which the second and third generations contributed much more than did the first. So it was with the Quarter Horse branch of the family, and so it was with the Paints.

Again, as noted in *More than Color, Vol. 1*, Tinky's Spook was purchased by Lyle and Butch Wonderlich to head their Paint Horse program. This he did in marvelous fashion, becoming the first APHA Champion west of the Rockies and the sire of one APHA Supreme Champion and 14 APHA Champions.

The Wonderlich/Tinky's Spook era came to an end on July 27, 1974, when the Twin Falls couple held the first of

what would be several dispersal sales. Tinky's Spook topped the offering, going to Bud and Betty Crump of Wynnewood, Oklahoma, for what was then a record-setting price of $12,500.

Three of the stallion's daughters–Fancy Fem, Silly Filly and Spook Slippers–were the sale's high-selling mares at $5,400, $5,100 and $4,000, respectively, and J.D. Hooter of Alexandria, Louisiana, was the sale's volume buyer.

Hooter was familiar with the Tinky's Spook horses prior to this, having purchased a son of Tinky's Spook named Peppy Spook in April of 1973 to cross on his Q Ton Eagle daughters.

While the Wonderlichs had advertised their 1974 sale as a dispersal, they retained ownership of several of their best young prospects. Among them was a homebred 2-year-old stallion named Gallant Ghost.

Ghostly Genetics

Gallant Ghost, a 1972 bay tovero stallion, was sired by Peppy Spook and out of Bold Farina (QH). Foaled on RoseAcre Farms on May 1, he was a member of his sire's first Idaho-bred foal crop.

Peppy Spook was a 1969 bay tovero stallion by Tinky's Spook and out of Peppy's Squaw. A versatile performer, he earned four halter and 42 performance points in hunter under saddle, heading, reining, trail, Western pleasure and Western riding.

As a sire, he had 81 registered foals. Of these, nine were point earners that earned 71 halter, 478 performance and 15 reining points. Gallant Ghost was far and away the stallion's top performer, accounting for close to half of the total points.

Peppy Spook, the sire of Gallant Ghost, was a top performer in his own right.

Photo by Marge Spence

Bold Farina (QH) was a 1968 bay mare by Roge's Bob Doll and out of Farina. Roge's Bob Doll, a AAA-rated runner, was a grandson of Flying Bob and Bill Doolin. Farina, a AA-rated sprinter, was a granddaughter of Questionnaire (TB).

In addition to Gallant Ghost, Bold Farina was the dam of two additional APHA-registered foals: Bold Bikini, a 1974 bay tobiano mare by Tinky's Spook–APHA Champion, two ROMs, and 31 halter and 19 performance points; and Bold Banshee, a 1975 bay tobiano gelding by Tinky's Spook–APHA Champion.

Finally, Bold Farina, Farina and Miss Sen Sen–the three mares on the bottom of Gallant Ghost's pedigree–were all speed-bred and all were ROM

race producers. This influx of running blood came into play when it was time for the Wonderlich-bred Paint to show what he was capable of.

Gallant Ghost's name came about in much the same manner as did his famous grandsire's. Although registered by APHA as a tobiano, Tinky's Spook was in reality a tovero, with one blue eye and an obvious set of both tobiano and overo genes.

Gallant Ghost was also registered as a tobiano, but like his sire and grandsire, he manifested obvious overo characteristics.

Viewed from the right, Gallant Ghost looked like a classic tobiano, complete with four white legs, and regularly shaped spots. Viewed from the left, however, he looked like an entirely different horse, with an overo-like white streak going up his left front leg and a white bonnet marking covering the left side of his face. Viewed from the left, there was also an overo marking on his muzzle and an overo-like dark lining around his eye.

The effect of the young Paint's markings was that, viewed from left and right, he looked like two different horses. And, just like his grandsire, he was tagged with the surname "Spook" in deference to his one blue eye. So it was that Gallant Ghost was given his surname in deference to his left-sided, eerie appearance.

A Speedy Start

Gallant Ghost began his performance career on the chariot racing tracks of Idaho and Utah. Raced as an early 2-year-old, he won the Snake River Chariot Racing Association year-end award. He also competed as the only Paint Horse at the All-American Chariot Futurity in Tremont, Utah, finishing fifth overall out of 47 teams of Quarter Horses and Thoroughbreds.

Next up for the speed-bred Paint were a few trips to the straightaway racetracks, at both Idaho pari-mutuel and APHA-approved tracks.

Competing in APHA's fifth National Championship Futurity in August of 1974, he won his 350-yard trial heat in the time of :18.33–the fastest time

Initially trained as a chariot racehorse, "Ghost" acquitted himself well.
Courtesy APHA

recorded during both time trials and the final, and good enough to earn him an 88 speed index. In the finals, the 2-year-old Peppy Spook son "found heavy traffic from his number four hole and finished fourth."

Gallant Ghost made only seven official APHA starts, earning one first, one second, one third and $1,589. He was awarded an 87 speed index and his ROM in racing on July 12, 1974.

Returned to the chariot racing wars in 1976 as a 4-year-old, Gallant Ghost acquitted himself quite well against other teams. The following year, the decision was made to take the fleet competitor off the tracks and make him ready for a show career.

Switched out of harness and into a flat saddle, the Tinky's Spook grandson was a Register of Merit racehorse.
Courtesy APHA

A Supreme Show Record

From the outset, Lyle and Butch Wonderlichs' son Lyle R. handled much of Gallant Ghost's show training and riding. Currently residing with his wife, Kathy, in Nampa, Idaho, the long-time equine reproduction specialist and APHA-approved judge recalls that the big tovero stallion was a rare individual.

" 'Ghost' was a big, bold, 16-hand horse," he says. "After spending several years chariot and flat racing, all he knew when we got him home to stay was to run into the bit.

"Because of that, we never really used a D-ring snaffle bit on him; we began with a hackamore and then graduated to a long-shank snaffle bit. When we jumped him, we used a Pelham bit.

"You have to remember that Ghost was a senior horse by the time we began showing him," he continues. "And that meant it was only one hand on the reins. But he was easy to get a long with and willing to try whatever you asked him to do.

"When we first started hauling him, he'd come off the trailer all drawn up and looking like a racehorse. Eventually, though, he learned to relax and take everything in stride."

In 1977, Gallant Ghost was shown at halter and in on the rail. On June 11th of that year, he earned his ROM in Western pleasure, and an ROM in hunter under saddle followed that on October 23. By January 1, 1978, the big Paint had qualified for a Superior Halter award. Later that year, he added an ROM in Western riding and a Superior award in Western pleasure. On May 30, 1977, "Ghost" was awarded APHA Championship #622.

By 1979, the then 7-year-old stallion had added heading, healing and barrel racing to his show ring repertoire. He added ROMs in these three events to his already impressive resume in May.

Finally, on May 26, 1979, Gallant Ghost and Lyle Wonderlich competed at a three-judge Paint-O-Rama in Filer, Idaho. Shown in heading, heeling, barrel racing and bridle path hack, Ghost earned nine firsts and the final points necessary to qualify for the industry's three top show ring awards: Versatility Award #38, Superior All-Around Champion #16 and APHA Supreme Champion #29.

"Gallant Ghost was a true all-around horse," Lyle Wonderlich says. "He was good at a lot of things. He was a natural lead changer and the type of pleasure horse that would be competitive today.

"When I first started training him as a rope horse, I worried that he'd back into the chute and think he was going to be in a horse race. But he never acted up at all; he just looked at it as something new to learn."

After achieving all that was asked of him in the show ring, Gallant Ghost was retired to stud.

A Supreme Sire

Ghost's first four foal crops, which hit the ground between 1976 and 1979, were born while the stallion was enjoying the height of his success as a show horse. From these initial offerings came some of the line's most accomplished performers, including Ghost Tale and Gallant Hug.

Ghost Tale, a 1976 bay tobiano gelding out of Cristy Copper, was the 1980 Youth World Champion in Western pleasure and Western horsemanship, and the 1986 Youth World Champion in showmanship at halter. In addition, he earned three Versatility awards, four APHA Championships, 15 Superior event awards, 22 ROMs, and 131 halter and 1,670 performance points.

Gallant Hug, a 1976 bay tovero stallion out of Dotty Hug (QH), was a winner as both a race- and show horse. On the tracks, he started 21 races, earning nine firsts, four seconds, four thirds and $7,960. He achieved an 89 speed index, and with 58 points, qualified for a Superior racing award. As a show horse, he earned a Versatility award, APHA Championship, a Superior Hunter Under Saddle award, seven ROMs, and 15 halter and 173 performance points.

Gallant Silhouette was also born during these early years, and more than any other horse from the Tinky's

Ghost Tale, a 1976 bay tobiano gelding by Gallant Ghost and out of Cristy Copper, was a multiple world champion. Here he is at the 1980 National Show with Kelly Lingerfeldt of Riverside, California.
Photo by Don Shugart

Gallant Hug, a 1976 bay tovero stallion by Gallant Ghost and out of Dotty Hug (QH), was the earner of a Superior award on the tracks and a Versatility award in the show ring.
Photo by Skippen

Spook/Gallant Ghost line, this venerable performer most typifies what the RoseAcre Farm Paint Horse breeding program stood for.

"Silhouette," a 1978 bay overo mare, was sired by Gallant Ghost and out of Silly Filly. Both parents were RoseAcre born and bred, and both were APHA Supreme Champions.

Silly Filly was one of the farm's greatest contributions to the breed. A 1970 bay tovero mare by Tinky's Spook and out of Paula Shoe Shine, "Silly" was sold as a yearling to William and Mary Lou Griffin of Spanaway, Washington.

The Griffins showed Silly Filly to multiple honors, as an APHA Champion, Superior Halter Horse and APHA Supreme Champion #20. Repurchased by the Wonderlichs in 1974, Silly Filly produced 13 foals–one by Mighty Tink (QH) and 12 by Gallant Ghost.

Gallant Silhouette, was far and away the most accomplished of the baker's dozen. Shown in open competition, she earned three national or world

APHA Supreme Champion Silly Filly, a Tinky's Spook daughter, was bred 12 times to APHA Supreme Champion Gallant Ghost, a Tinky's Spook grandson.

Photo by Marge Spence

Gallant Silhouette was the most talented performer to come out of the "supreme cross." A multi-talented show mount, "Silhouette" carried youth exhibitor Danielle Brown of Midlothian, Texas, to 10 national and world titles. **Photo by Don Shugart**

titles: 1983 National Champion Sr. Hunter Under Saddle, 1985 World Champion Sr. Western Pleasure and 1985 Reserve World Champion Sr. Western Riding.

Shown in youth competition by Dawn Vest, Danielle Brown and Jana Simons, the talented mare amassed four world championships, three reserve world championships, five national championships and three reserve national championships.

All told, she earned three Versatility awards, four APHA Championships, 21 Superior event awards, 31 ROMs, and 269 halter and 4,348 performance points.

And there were other early Gallant Ghost stars, as well. Among them were:

• Gallant Kim, a 1977 bay tobiano mare out of Kimama Lily (QH)–APHA Champion, Superior BPH, four ROMs, and 19 halter and 217 performance points.

• Gallant Breeze, a 1977 bay tobiano mare out of Miss Westwind (QH–APHA Champion, Superior Western Pleasure, seven ROMs, and 39 halter and 219 performance points.

• Glory Ghost, a 1978 bay tobiano mare out of Nite's Lady Banner–1982 National Champion Pleasure Driving, Open Versatility, Superior Pleasure Driving, seven ROMs, and eight halter and 250 performance points.

• Gallant Tapestry, a 1978 bay tobiano mare out of Jezebel–APHA Champion, Superior Western Pleasure, and 23 halter and 80 performance points.

• Gallant Pirate, a 1978 bay tobiano gelding out of Miss Westwind (QH)–APHA Champion, two ROMs, and 34 halter and 39 performance points.

• Prince Gallant, a 1979 bay overo gelding out of Miss Westwind (QH)–APHA Champion, Superior Bridle Path Hack, two ROMs, and 18 halter and 142 performance points; Youth Versatility, APHA Youth Champion, Superior Youth Bridle Path Hack and Youth English Equitation, six ROMs, and 27 halter and 268 performance points.

Gallant Breeze, a 1977 bay tovero mare by Gallant Ghost and out of Miss Westwind (QH), was the earner of an APHA Championship and a Superior Western Pleasure award.

Photo by Skippen

On August 18, 1979, RoseAcre Farm held its second dispersal sale. By this time, the Wonderlich Paint breeding program was recognized as one of the finest and most progressive in the entire country. As proof of this claim, the event included such headline offerings as Bold Bikini, APHA Champion; Copper Tinky, APHA Champion; Spooka Dot, APHA Champion; Gallant Hug, ROM racehorse; Jag's Leolita, AQHA Champion (open and youth); and Mighty Tink, AQHA Champion.

In addition, top Gallant Ghost champions–past, present and future–were put up for bid. Among them were Ghost Tale, Gallant Kim, Gallant Kiss, Gallant Silhouette, Gallant Breeze, Gallant Pirate.

After the sale was over, the Wonderlich family scaled back its breeding operations. Gallant Ghost and Silly Filly remained in residence at the farm, as did several other well-bred broodmares and young prospects.

Gallant Move, a 1980 bay tovero stallion by Gallant Ghost and out of Ms Move, was the next Wonderlich horse to make Paint Horse national headlines.

Sent to the racetrack under the RoseAcre banner, "Move" had 23 lifetime starts. He earned nine wins, eight seconds, two thirds and $7,586. He also achieved a speed index of 88, and on July 14, 1984, qualified for a Superior Race award.

In August of 1984, Move was sold to Bonnie Christensen of Salt Lake City, Utah. Under her ownership, he earned an APHA Supreme Championship, Versatility award, Superior All-Around award, APHA Championship, Superior Halter award, five ROMs, and 71 halter and 59 performance points.

By the dawn of the 1980s, Gallant Ghost was one of the Northwest region's most popular Paint breeding stallions. And, for the next decade-and-a-half, he continued to turn out a steady stream of champions. Among their number were such top performers as:
- Haunted Princess, a 1980 bay tobiano mare out of Miss Westwind (QH)–APHA Champion; Superior Western Pleasure, three ROMs, and 38 halter and 126 performance points.
- Ima Gallant Lass, a 1981 bay tobiano mare out of Ima Bar–1986 Reserve National Champion Jumping, three ROMs and 64 performance points.
- Pralines N Cream, a 1983 dun tobiano mare out of Jezebe–Superior Western Pleasure, and earner of one halter and 94 performance points.
- Ghostbuster, a 1985 bay tovero gelding out of Artic Spook–Earner of seven ROMs, and seven halter and 200 performance points.
- Gallant Serenade, a 1986 bay tobiano mare out of Arctica–APHA Champion, four ROMs, and 35 halter and 55 performance points.

By the early 1990s, the two RoseAcre stalwarts–Gallant Ghost and Silly Filly–were nearing the end of their productive years.

In 1990, both were sent north to the High River, Alberta, Canada, ranch of long-time family friends Pete and Diane Fraser. Gallant Ghost continued to serve as an active breeding horse until 1995. The following spring, one last foal was born.

Gallant Tapestry, a 1978 bay tobiano mare by Gallant Ghost and out of Jezebel, was likewise an APHA Champion with a Superior in Western Pleasure.

Photo by Skippen

APHA records verify that Gallant Ghost sired 257 registered foals. Of these, 62 performers earned six world championships, four reserve world championships, nine national championships, four reserve national championships, one Supreme Championship, 10 Versatility awards, 18 APHA Championships, 51 Superior event awards, 135 ROMs and 9,441 points in all divisions combined.

Gallant Ghost was part and parcel the product of Lyle and Butch Wonderlichs' RoseAcre Farm Paint Horse breeding program. This storied operation stands alone in terms of its pioneering contributions to the breed–not only the Northwest, but across the entire country, as well.

The big tovero stallion was, in many ways, its crowning achievement.

Gallant Move, a 1980 bay tovero stallion by Gallant Ghost and out of Ms Move, was a RoseAcre Farm-bred all-around performer. **Courtesy APHA**

On January 1, 1992, "Move" became his sire's first get to earn the prestigious APHA Supreme Champion award.

Photo by Rich Reimann

PHOTO INDEX

A U T H O R ' S P R O F I L E

FRANK HOLMES has been penning horse-related feature articles and historical books for more than 40 years. His interests have always been centered on the historical aspects of the western horse breeds, and his broad-based knowledge of the origins of the Quarter Horse, Paint, Appaloosa and Palomino registries have established him as one of the pre-eminent equine historians of all time.

As a former staff writer for *Western Horseman* magazine, Frank co-authored volumes 2 through 7 of the immensely popular Legends book series and authored *The Hank Wiescamp Story*.

As the award-winning Features Editor of *The Paint Horse Journal* he contributed a steady stream of top-notch personality profiles, genetic studies, and historical overviews.

From early 2001 on, Frank has devoted the lion's share of his journalistic efforts to the research and writing of historical books designed to capture the West's rich history and pass it on in a way that both enlightens and entertains. In recent years, he has authored *Wire to Wire - the Walter Merrick Story*, *Spotted Pride - the Appaloosa Heritage Series*, and *King P-234 - Cornerstone of an Industry*.

Now living on a small ranch east of Kiowa, Colorado, he and his wife Loyce, have three sons, Eric, Craig and Morgan.